ROUTLEDGE LIBRARY EDITIONS:
EXCHANGE RATE ECONOMICS

Volume 3

THE IMPACT OF PRICE UNCERTAINTY

THE IMPACT OF PRICE UNCERTAINTY

A Study of Brazilian Exchange Rate Policy

DONALD V. COES

Routledge
Taylor & Francis Group
LONDON AND NEW YORK

First published in 1979 by Garland Publishing, Inc.

This edition first published in 2017
by Routledge
2 Park Square, Milton Park, Abingdon, Oxon OX14 4RN

and by Routledge
605 Third Avenue, New York, NY 10017

Routledge is an imprint of the Taylor & Francis Group, an informa business

British Library Cataloguing in Publication Data
A catalogue record for this book is available from the British Library

ISBN: 978-0-415-79325-4 (Set)
ISBN: 978-1-315-21117-6 (Set) (ebk)
ISBN: 978-1-138-63362-9 (Volume 3) (hbk)
ISBN: 978-1-315-20723-0 (Volume 3) (ebk)

Publisher's Note
The publisher has gone to great lengths to ensure the quality of this reprint but points out that some imperfections in the original copies may be apparent.

Disclaimer
The publisher has made every effort to trace copyright holders and would welcome correspondence from those they have been unable to trace.

The Impact of Price Uncertainty:

A Study of Brazilian Exchange Rate Policy

Donald V. Coes

Garland Publishing, Inc.
New York & London, 1979

Library of Congress Cataloging in Publication Data

Coes, Donald V 1943–
The impact of price uncertainty.

(Outstanding dissertations in economics)
A revision of the author's thesis, Princeton, 1977.
Bibliography: p.
Includes indexes.
1. Foreign exchange problem—Brazil—Mathematical models. 2. Prices—Brazil—Mathematical models. 3. Brazil—Commerce—Mathematical models. I. Title. II. Series.
HG3933.C63 1979 332.4'5'0981 78–75067
ISBN 0–8240–4143–7

All volumes in this series are printed on acid-free, 250-year-life paper.

Printed in the United States of America.

THE IMPACT OF PRICE UNCERTAINTY:
A STUDY OF BRAZILIAN EXCHANGE RATE POLICY

By

Donald Vinton Coes

Originally submitted as a
doctoral dissertation in Economics
to Princeton University
in 1977
and revised for the
Garland Series

Preface

Economists are traditionally accused of hiding their failure to answer a question by inventing another one. More dissertations than many would admit are fruits of such a process, and this book, a revised version of a dissertation submitted to Princeton University in 1977, shares in that tradition. My original intent in beginning research was to conduct an empirical study of changes in effective protection in Brazil, in the context of a general equilibrium model. Aside from a few vestiges which survive in Chapter V, little remains in the book of either effective protection or general equilibrium.

In the course of my research in Brazil it became apparent that the adoption of a crawling peg exchange rate policy in 1968 had had effects on trade which could not be satisfactorily explained by changes in relative prices alone. My intuition, which would probably be shared by economists and non-economists alike, was that less real exchange rate uncertainty after 1968 had favored trade.

Turning to the literature in an attempt to confirm this impression, I was surprised and at times frustrated to find no theoretically coherent account of how greater real price stability would affect trade. Theoretical work centered largely on comparisons of certainty with uncertainty. This was not really the issue, since there was no reason to believe the crawling peg had completely eliminated uncertainty. Equally important, the qualitative comparison of economic behavior under certainty and uncertainty evades the quantitative problem of measuring the level of uncertainty. A theoretically defensible, yet empirically manageable procedure for the measurement of changes in uncertainty is essential if the increasing interest in uncertainty among economists is not to be confined to theoretical analyses of its effects, unaccompanied by empirical testing of the models' predictions.

This book is as a consequence more a theoretical investigation of the effects of changes in price uncertainty and methods for measuring those changes than it is a study of the crawling peg *per se*. Because the question was raised by a specific problem, however, it goes beyond the development of a model of response to changes in uncertainty, proceeding from theory to measurement and finally to application to the Brazilian case.

It is my hope that the book will therefore be of interest to three different groups of readers. For the theorist, the development of a model of firm response to changes in price uncertainty, inspired on one hand by Sandmo's pioneering theory of the firm under uncertainty, and on the other by the seminal characterization by Rothschild and Stiglitz of an increase in risk as a "mean preserving spread" (MPS), unifies and extends a number of earlier results. The graphical approach used in Chapter III to analyze the effects of a MPS is a technique which might be usefully applied to other problems in the economics of uncertainty. Perhaps most interesting from a theoretical point of view, however, is the generalization in Chapter IV of the stochastic dominance criteria for choice among probability distributions and the clarification of the relation of these rules to the moments of a distribution. These results permit uncertainty to be measured in a way more consistent with the expected utility hypothesis, the cornerstone of much of the modern economics of uncertainty, than is possible by identifying increased uncertainty with greater variance.

In an era of substantially greater fluctuations in real exchange rates than occurred before the breakdown of the Bretton Woods system, specialists in international trade and finance have become increasingly interested in the possibility that exchange rate uncertainty might have allocative effects distinct from the effects of the level of the rates themselves. Our model of potential exporter response to changes in the level of real exchange rate uncertainty developed in Chapters II and III provides a theoretical explanation of how these allocative effects might arise. One might still ask if these theoretical effects have any real world importance. The examination of the Brazilian experience in Chapter VI suggests not only that uncertainty matters, but that in some cases it appears to matter more than do relative prices.

Finally, although I do not pretend that this is a book about Brazil, I would hope that Brazilians and other students of its economy find that the empirical results presented in this study contribute in a small way to understanding some of the changes in its economic structure in the past two decades. Brazil's "export model" of growth has been the center of sharp debate, yet even the critics of recent commercial policies have not seriously questioned whether or not these relative price policies were really responsible for the movement to a more open economy in the last decade.

The revisions which I have made in the original dissertation are for the most part concentrated in Chapter IV, and reflect the subsequent discovery of a relation between the stochastic dominance rules and a function of the moments of the probability distributions being compared. The clarification of this relationship permitted the derivation of a series of indices of uncertainty, rather than the single one used in the original dissertation. The regressions whose results are reported in Chapter VI were re-estimated, using the revised indices. In addition, the exchange rate data itself was modified slightly by multiplication by the SDR/US dollar rate, as reported in various issues of the IMF's International Financial Statistics, to reflect the devaluation of the dollar against some of Brazil's other major trading partners' currencies.

The use of the stochastic dominance approach to the measurement of uncertainty rests in part on the assumption of non-normality in the distributions of the random variables of interest. In the original dissertation, non-normality of the random real exchange rate was simply assumed. In this revision the hypothesis of normality was tested formally in several ways and rejected, with the results of these tests presented in Chapter IV.

An alternative to the price uncertainty hypothesis in explaining the increase in the openness of many sectors of the Brazilian economy in the last decade is the possible maturing and consequently greater export orientation of a number of industries. This hypothesis, not examined in the original dissertation, was tested in the revised estimates, and the results are summarized in Chapter VI.

None of these modifications altered the basic conclusions of this study, which might in fact be regarded with a bit more confidence, in view of the efforts made to justify some of the procedures and premises only implicit in the original study. Other revisions have been minor, largely confined to a few changes in wording and the correction of typographical errors.

It is a pleasure to acknowledge the substantial debts I have incurred to many people in the course of this study. Foremost among them are the thanks I owe to William H. Branson, chairman of my dissertation committee, and one of the reasons I am an economist. His faith that my questions would lead somewhere was a self-fulfilling prophecy. To his colleagues at Princeton and fellow members of the committee, Gerard Butters and Mark Gersovitz, I also owe my thanks. The comments of the latter are responsible for my explicit consideration of the assumption of normality, as well as the test of the "maturity effect" in the revised version. Peter Kenen, Polly Allen, and Alan Blinder made many valuable suggestions and comments at earlier stages.

A Fulbright-Hays grant made it possible for me to do research in Brazil in 1974 and 1975. If the final product of that research bears only a faint resemblance to my original proposal, I hope those responsible for the grant will not consider themselves shortchanged. It is impossible to mention all those who helped me in Brazil in one way or another, but I would like especially to thank Werner Baer for his enthusiasm and encouragement, before, during, and after my research in Brazil. Anibal Villela kindly offered the facilities of IPEA, the Planning Ministry's economic research institute, and Dona Fernanda Buarque de Almeida and her staff made my work in the library there both pleasant and productive. Among the IPEA economists, Carlos Von Doellinger, Anna Luiza Ozorio de Almeida, and Wilson Suzigan provided many helpful comments and ideas. Joel Bergsman made a number of useful suggestions both before my departure and in Brazil.

Paul Beckerman, friend and colleague in Princeton, Brazil, and Illinois, deserves thanks for stimulating discussions. The questions and comments of Matthew Canzoneri and Masahiro Okuno made my work more interesting, and to another colleague at Illinois, Richard Kihlstrom, I owe special thanks for encouraging me to push the theoretical arguments in new directions. The Brazilians at Illinois, particularly Paulo de Tarso André, Ernani Hickmann, and Oswaldo Sarmento, were a frequent source of ideas and encouragement.

A grant from the Investors in Business Education at Illinois, administered by Robert Resek, permitted me to spend the summer of 1977 in Brazil and undertake some of the research underlying the revisions. In Brazil John Williamson and Affonso Celso Pastore and his colleagues at the Fundação Centro de Estudos do Comércio Exterior provided a number of welcome comments and specific suggestions.

Finally, instead of the usual uxorial dedication, I would like to thank my dissertation research in Brazil for its most valuable finding, Bulete.

DVC

Rio de Janeiro
February 1979

THE IMPACT OF PRICE UNCERTAINTY:

A STUDY OF BRAZILIAN EXCHANGE RATE POLICY

Table of Contents

List of Tables

List of Figures

CHAPTER I

INTRODUCTION: THE IMPACT OF PRICE UNCERTAINTY A STUDY OF BRAZILIAN EXCHANGE RATE POLICY

Few features of economic life are as uncertain as is the presence of uncertainty itself. Yet this obvious fact has only in the last decade entered the mainstream of economic theory, and the consequences of its recognition have yet to have a significant impact on empirical economics. With the notable exceptions of the theory of games and portfolio theory, there are few areas of economics in which uncertainty is an integral part of the underlying models themselves. Even econometrics, which would hardly exist without uncertainties in observation and measurement, simply adds these stochastic elements to structural relations predicated on complete certainty.

The long and continuing neglect of uncertainty has a number of causes. First, there is a widespread impression that the conclusions of economic theory remain the same in the presence of uncertainty. A growing body of theoretical literature indicates that this assumption is rarely justified.

A related assumption is the view that we may introduce uncertainty into our models by the simple expedient of treating the deterministic variables as the expected values of random variables. A bit of reflection on the fact that few of us would be indifferent to the prospect of a modest income with certainty, or the alternative prospect of equal chances of either great wealth or starvation suggests that this approach is not generally valid.

A more defensible position is the argument that the recognition of uncertainty exacts too high a price, due to the inevitable complexities it introduces into otherwise straightforward arguments. To obtain determinate results while explicitly recognizing uncertainty we must generally make specific assumptions about both the preferences of individuals and the possible outcomes of economic events. If the consequences of recognizing uncertainty are not substantially different from our conclusions when we ignore it, then its neglect is merely a helpful simplification. This position might be summarized as the view that uncertainty may matter, but not much.

A more subtle argument for the omission of uncertainty from economic analysis is the belief that like death and taxes, uncertainty cannot be avoided, but its presence should not distract us from the main lines of our deterministic theorizing. If the level of uncertainty in economic life were as constant as is its presence, one might justify the conclusions of conventional deterministic theory on *ceteris paribus* grounds. But this view ignores the critical question of what might be the effects of more or less uncertainty.

The theory of international trade and finance is no exception to the general pattern of neglect of uncertainty in economics, despite the fact that exposure to trade may introduce a country to new uncertainties it would not face in isolation. Despite a number of recent theoretical contributions to the theory of trade under uncertainty, empirical studies and discussions of policy in international economics still reflect an age of certainty.[1] In the voluminous debate over appropriate exchange rate regimes, for example, the presence of uncertainty is often mentioned, yet no cogent and rigorous argument has been offered explaining why or how exchange rate uncertainties matter.

The recognition of uncertainty in economic life raises three related questions. First, on a theoretical level, how do we define uncertainty and use the concept in a manner that is capable of providing conclusions meaningfully different from those of conventional deterministic theory? Second, how can the level of uncertainty associated with a particular variable of economic interest be measured in a way consistent with our theories? Third, even if we can successfully measure changes in the level of uncertainty and make theoretical predictions about their effects, does actual experience provide any support for the view that uncertainty really matters?

This study is an attempt to answer these three questions. Under the assumption that risk averse firms face a random output price, we develop a theory of the effects of price uncertainty on production and trade. Changes in the level of uncertainty are introduced by a multiplicative spreading of the random output price about an unchanged mean, a concept that is then extended to a more general type of "mean preserving spread" first used by Rothschild and Stiglitz.[2]

A theory of choice under uncertainty is essentially a criterion for choice among distributions. The second stage of our study uses the "mean preserving spread" as a basis for the derivation of a series of rules for ordering distributions. These rules in turn may be used to provide cardinal measures of the level of uncertainty associated with a random variable.

When uncertainty has been explicitly recognized in empirical research in economics, as in portfolio analysis, for example, it has been measured by variance. It is well known, however, that the common use of variance as a measure of riskiness or uncertainty may be inconsistent with the expected utility hypothesis, the cornerstone of much of the modern theory of economic behavior under uncertainty. The recognition of these potential inconsistencies, in addition to being the focus of criticisms of the "mean-variance" approach to choice under uncertainty, may explain the reticence of economists in applying empirically the increasingly rich body of theory dealing with uncertainty.

Our method of ordering distributions and deriving an index of uncertainty from this ordering represents a partial solution to this problem. Under much less restrictive assumptions than those implicit in the mean-variance approach most alternatives can be ordered in a way consistent with the expected utility hypothesis. At the same time we offer some aid and comfort to those of the mean-variance persuasion, showing theoretically why any of these indices will be strongly (and in some cases perfectly) correlated with variance.

Finally, our methods of measuring uncertainty are used to test the predictions of the theory of trade under price uncertainty, in an econometric analysis of the effects of Brazil's adoption of a crawling peg in reducing real exchange rate uncertainty.

In 1968 the Brazilian government adopted an exchange policy of frequent small adjustments in the nominal cruzeiro-dollar rate to offset the differential rates of inflation in Brazil and its major trading partners, thus preventing the real prices of tradable goods from fluctuating as widely as they had previously. Although there is no evidence that this policy was adopted specifically to reduce real price uncertainty in the foreign sector, this was in fact one of its major effects. The Brazilian experience thus provides an interesting opportunity to study the consequences of a reduction in uncertainty on an economy-wide scale.

Beginning in the late sixties, the Brazilian economy entered a period of extremely rapid growth, with the foreign sector growing even more rapidly than did the economy as a whole, making Brazil a more open economy than it had been a decade earlier. Students of this period of rapid growth, or the "Brazilian miracle", as it was grandiosely named by government propagandists, have generally emphasized the role of commercial policy and other relative price incentives in promoting export growth. Although there is no question that these policies played an inportant role in increasing the relative importance of foreign markets in many sectors of the Brazilian economy, they do not in themselves constitute a sufficient or entirely satisfactory explanation of the observed change. Increased relative price incentives to export resulting from changes in commercial policy were highly uneven in their impact, often concentrated in sectors in which Brazil may have few comparative advantages. Despite the dramatic growth of manufactures on Brazil's export list in the last decade, the increase in the relative importance of primary products not traditionally exported is also impressive, despite the fact that these products enjoyed substantially fewer relative price incentives to export than did manufactures.

Traditional deterministic economic theory, with its emphasis on relative prices and on income effects in explaining economic phenomena, ignores the third dimension of economic analysis which uncertainty can add to our understanding. Both the theoretical arguments made in the first part of this study and their application to the analysis of the effects of the Brazilian crawling peg suggest that an awareness of this third dimension is an invaluable addition to economic perspective.

Although the influence of the crawling peg on foreign trade in Brazil has been noted by both scholars and policy makers, they have offered no theoretical explanation of why increased price stability should matter.[3] The apparently innocuous proposition that greater real price stability favors trade is not obvious on closer examination, for a number of reasons. High variability of prices enable a market participant to buy low and sell high. Other markets may permit risks to be shifted to individuals who have no aversion to bearing them. Finally, general risk aversion among individuals is not sufficient for firms, especially large ones, to have the same attitude.

Before outlining briefly the arguments of the succeeding chapters, it is useful to examine the principal premises which underlie this study. Some of these assumptions are explicit and are considered in more detail subsequently; others are only implicit in the succeeding arguments.

Fundamental to our theory of the effects of price uncertainty is the assumption that firms behave as if they were maximizing a concave function of the random variable of interest to them, profits. Although it is common to equate this type of assumption to individual aversion to risk, our formulation of the firm's behavior may be less restrictive, since a number of influences besides risk aversion by owners or managers may make a firm's objective function concave.

A second assumption, which distinguishes our theory from some of the literature on trade and production under uncertainty, is its treatment of price as a primal and not a derivative source of uncertainty. This feature reflects to some extent the partial equilibrium nature of our model. In a general equilibrium context it would be proper to impose explicitly or implicitly market clearing conditons, which would in effect attribute the randomness of a given relative price to some underlying random events, such as changes in technology, weather, supplies of primary factors or natural resources, or changes in preferences.

The insistence of general equilibrium theorists in attributing price uncertainty to a more fundamental cause, however, may not be appropriate in some contexts. In an open economy with money, the authorities may temporarily set a number of prices, most importantly the interest rate and exchange rate, at levels that have little or no relation to market equilibrium conditions. For other participants in these markets it is these fiat prices, which matter for their decision making. In this sense, some of the economic uncertainties affecting Brazil before 1968 were self-inflicted wounds, which could be removed at one stroke by a change in exchange rate policies.

That useful simplification of traditional trade theory, the "small country assumption", provides another justification for treating random prices as fundamental. From the point of view of a small potential exporter facing the international market, it matters little what induces a price change; what matters is that they do change.

A third premise underlying this study is the assumption that price uncertainty must be borne by the producer. This view too is at variance with the spirit of some of the theoretical literature, notably the Arrow-Debreu demonstration that a complete set of contingent claims markets can allocate resources as they would be under certainty.[4] As central as this result is to the general equilibrium theory of uncertainty, no one would maintain that such complete sets of markets really exist. One might argue, however, that even limited forward markets for foreign exchange would permit potential exporters to avoid, or at least lessen exchange risks. With the exception of the currencies of a few major trading nations, however, not even these markets exist. In Brazil a few major exporters may have engaged in a sufficiently large and varied number of transactions to be able to hedge against some exchange risks, but this opportunity was rare, and for the ordinary participant in foreign trade, non-existent.

An interesting related argument is based on the hypothesis that the degree of aversion to risk varies among individuals. In this case one might argue that even though the economic world may be beset with uncertainties, and individuals may be generally averse to risks, uncertainty is of little importance, since risks will be assumed by that part of society, possibly a small minority, most willing to bear them. Thus, even if markets permitting the shifting of risks do not exist, the movement of the least risk averse members of society into those activities where uncertainty is greatest would lessen its overall impact on the economy.

Although this is not an argument that can be accepted or rejected on the basis of casual empiricism, it is clear that it would be most relevant in an economy in which the level of uncertainty attaching to a particular activity was roughly constant. This is unlikely to be the general case; indeed, the very spirit of our inquiry arises from the assumption that the level of uncertainty may change. There is little question that this occurred in the foreign trade sector in Brazil in 1968; the central issue is whether or not this change had real economic effects. The data presented in the empirical part of our study do permit the interpretation that aversion to risk varied by sector, and it would be interesting to know if apparent differences in the degree of response to changes in uncertainty can be explained in this way.

A fourth premise underlying our study is that the degree of flexibility in production is relatively limited. One must live with past mistakes only to the extent that they affect the present; if a new optiaml level of production or sales may be instantly and costlessly chosen with each change in the output price or other random variable of interest, then uncertainty may be irrelevant, even for risk averters. Although it is hardly controversial to assume a certain degree of short run inflexibility in production for most activities in an economy, the assumption becomes more important if output may be stored. High variability of prices may in this case actually be preferred by the producer, since a strategy of selling accumulated output only in periods of high prices would yield greater average profits than would be attainable if the price were constant.

The relevance of this argument to a study like ours is essentially dependent on two factors, the capacity to accumulate inventories, and the ability of the firm to recognize the appropriate times to sell these inventories. Although an adequate treatment of the inventory effect is precluded in our study by the paucity of information on storage capacity and costs in different sectors, it does not appear in practice to have been important. This should not be surprising, since the financing costs of speculative holdings of large quantities of production, particularly of manufactured products, for indeterminate time periods, are even higher in an economy like Brazil's than they would be in an economy with more abundant capital. The ability of firms to forecast opportune sales periods, moreover, was limited, since the variation in the real exchange rate before 1968 can hardly be described as predictably cyclical. The possibility of benefitting from high price variability through an inventory policy, however, cannot be completely discounted,and our data for some primary products at least permits the interpretation that this effect may have been present.

A final assumption underlying this study, and one which is touched upon at several points in the development of our argument, is that the probability distributions of random variables like exchange rates or output prices cannot be adequately represented by the normal distribution. The assumption of normality is probably one of the most abused premises in economics, largely due to the mathematical convenience it offers. Were all variables of economic interest distributed normally, a theoretically satisfactory treatment of uncertainty would be relatively easy, using variance as a measure of risk. There is no reason to assume that the random variables of interest to us are usually distributed normally, however, and one would have little confidence in either theoretical arguments or empirical conclusions which required this assumption. The strength of the Rothschild-Stiglitz "mean preserving spread" concept used in the theoretical model in this study lies precisely in the fact that it does not impose any restriction on the form of the distributions in question. Similarly, the related methods of measurement of uncertainty developed in this study are appropriate for any form of probability distribution.

On an empirical level, however, the ease of analysis and computation provided by the identification of variance with uncertainty, justified by the hypothesis of normality, suggest that we examine the random variable of interest to see if the normality assumption can be used as a simplifying approximation. This was done with the data used in this study; the results reported in Chapter IV lead us to reject strongly the normality hypothesis. Were it possible to maintain the hypothesis, however, one could reasonably argue that the theories and techniques used in a study like ours, while correct, are not really necessary, since mean-variance analysis would give the same answers.

Chapter II analyzes the firm's response to changes in demand uncertainty, using a model developed by Sandmo as a starting point.[5] A new proof of his conjecture that a decrease in uncertainty will increase output is presented and extended to the quantity-setting monopolist as well, a necessary generalization if it is to apply to some sectors of the Brazilian economy.[6] As one of the central questions which this study addresses is the effect of a change in uncertainty on the relative importance of foreign trade, and not simply the level of prodution of an exportable good, the final section of Chapter II is devoted to an analysis of a two market model. It is shown that a ceteris paribus reduction in price uncertainty in one market, such as the export market when exchange rate uncertainty is reduced, will both increase total output and shift sales to that market.

There are a number of limitations to the definition of an increase in uncertainty proposed by Sandmo which is used in Chapter II. Chapter III considers a broader definition, the Rothschild-Stiglitz mean preserving spread, and uses this concept to extend the theory of output determination by the risk-averse firm under price uncertainty beyond the existing literature. The most important result is that under a wide variety of conditons, a Rothschild-Stiglitz increase in uncertainty will decrease the output of the risk-averse firm. Under their broader definition of risk, however, the conclusion of Batra and Ullah that non-increasing absolute risk aversion is sufficient for an increase in uncertainty to decrease output is shown to be incorrect, with a counterexample to this effect presented in Appendix A.[7]

The Rothschild-Stiglitz definition permits us to analyze the effect of increasing price variation when inventories are allowed, a condition which in some cases may qualify earlier theoretical results; this problem is considered in the second section of the chapter. Apparently central to these recent developments in the theory of the firm under price uncertainty is the assumption that it is risk averse, implying the existence of a concave firm utility function. In the last section of Chapter III this assumption is examined; it is argued that a variety of alternative assumptions will yield equivalent results.

The concept of increasing risk requires some operationally useful characterization consistent with the theory of the preceding chapters if their results are to have any more than theoretical significance. Chapter IV is in some ways the most important in this study, since it provides the crucial link between a now relatively rich body of economic theory based on the expected utility hypothesis, of which Chapters II and III are examples, and the data which an uncertain real world offers us. Using the expected utility hypothesis as its starting point, the stochastic dominance method of ordering distributions is derived. It is then shown that this approach provides a series of indices of differences in distributions which may be used as measures of risk or uncertainty. The method is then applied to the real cruzeiro dollar exchange rate to obtain a series of measures of exchange rate uncertainty which are both consistent with the expected utility hypothesis underlying the preceding chapters and econometrically useful, as is shown in succeeding ones.

The central prediction of the theory of price uncertainty developed in Chapters II and III is that a redution in price uncertainty will make an economy more open to trade, independently of any changes in relative prices, under the assumption that firms' attitudes towards profits can be described as risk averse. Relative prices of exportables, however, changed significantly in many sectors of the Brazilian economy in the last decade, providing a potential explanation of many of the observed changes in the past ten years. Any meaningful econometric test of the uncertainty hypothesis must face this fact; Chapter V is devoted to an examination of these relative price changes and the development of a way of testing their effects simultaneously with those induced by changes in the degree of exchange rate uncertainty.

Despite a number of difficult econometric problems which arise in a test of the uncertainty hypothesis, the empirical results of this study presented in Chapter VI tend to agree with the predictions of our theory. They suggest, moreover, that the reduction in exchange rate uncertainty after 1968 was significantly more important in explaining the increase in the relative importance of exports in the Brazilian economy than were changes in relative prices.

Chapter VII concludes briefly with some general observations on the theory of price uncertainty and some of its potential extensions. Our empirical results, which suggest that changes in uncertainty may be at least as important as changes in relative prices in explaining trade and economic structure, imply that this possibility deserves considerably more attention on both a theoretical and a policy level than it has received in the past. In fact, debates over appropriate exchange rate policies or export marketing arrangements, if conducted in the deterministic tradition of international trade theory, may ignore some of the most interesting and important problems raised by the uncertainties of economic life.

FOOTNOTES FOR CHAPTER I

1. Among the recent contributions to the theory of trade under uncertainty are R.N. Batra, Pure Theory of International Trade under Uncertainty, N.Y., Halstead, 1975; M.C. Kemp and N. Liviatan, "Production and Trade Patterns under Uncertainty", Econ. Record, June 1973; W. Mayer, "The Rybczynski, Stolper-Samuelson, and Factor Price Equalization Theorems under Price Uncertainty", Amer. Econ. Rev., Dec. 1976; R.J. Ruffin, "Comparative Advantage under Uncertainty", Jour. Int. Econ., Aug. 1974; and S.J. Turnovsky, "Technological and Price Uncertainty in a Ricardian model of International Trade", Rev. Econ. Stud., April 1974.

2. M. Rothschild and J. Stiglitz, "Increasing Risk I: A Definition", Jour. Econ Theory, Sept. 1970, Vol 2.

3. In one of the most extensive expirical studies of the Brazilian crawling peg to date, E. M. Suplicy, The Effects of Minidevaluations on the Brazilian Economy, unpub. PhD. dissertation, Michigan State University, 1973, has shown a statistically significant difference in export supply and import demand functions estimated before and after the change in exchange policy. He attributes the difference in part to price stability.

4. K.J. Arrow, "The Role of Securities in the Optimal Allocation of Risk Bearing", Rev. Econ. Stud., April 1964; and G. Debreu, Theory of Value, N.Y., Wiley, 1959

5. A. Sandmo, "On the Theory of the Competitive Firm under Price Uncertainty", Amer. Econ. Rev., March 1971.

6. D. Coes, "Firm Output and Changes in Uncertainty", Amer. Econ Rev. March 1977.

7. R. Batra and A. Ullah, "Competitive Firm and the Theory of Input Demand under Price Uncertainty", Jour. Pol. Econ., May/June 1974.

CHAPTER II

EXPORTING AS A DECISION UNDER UNCERTAINTY: THE BASIC MODEL

For potential exporters deciding what level of output to produce and whether to sell it in foreign or domestic markets, the role played by the exchange rate is critical, as has long been recognized by international trade theory. What is often ignored, however, is the fact that if we assume some degree of aversion to risk among potential exporters, their uncertainties about the future course of the exchange rate may be as important determinants of their decisions as are their expectations of the rate itself.

If we recognize that potential exporters are not able to adjust production levels instantly or costlessly in response to changes in relative prices, then the decision to export must be viewed as a form of economic behavior involving risk. This is especially true if the ways of avoiding this risk are limited or non-existent; in Brazil, for example, no futures markets for foreign currencies exist, so that the exporter has no choice but to use the current spot rate or his expectation of its future value in making decisions.

The central purpose of this chapter is to integrate these basic assumptions of risk aversion, uncertainty about future exchange rates, and inability to avoid risk in a systematic way into a model of potential exporter behavior under exchange rate uncertainty, in the expectation that the model will provide testable hypotheses about the effects of changes in exchange rate uncertainty in Brazil in the last decade.

No attempt will be made here to deal with sources of uncertainty other than those induced by exchange policies; the fact that world prices, domestic demands and factor supplies, and technological changes may have been important potential sources of uncertainty is ignored. This *ceteris paribus* simplification might be justified by the fact that unlike exchange rate uncertainty, there appears to be no empirical basis for assuming that the degree of uncertainty attaching to any of these other variables changed significantly in the past decade, and if so, in which direction.

Any model of potential exporter response to exchange rate uncertainty is essentially a form of firm behavior under output price uncertainty. Despite some pioneering work in this area by Mills, McCall, and others, the theory of the firm under uncertainty was for a long time one of the more neglected areas of microeconomic theory. Recent contributions by Sandmo and others, however, have done much to develop this area of economic theory. The model developed in Section 2-1 uses Sandmo's analysis of the purely competitive firm facing an uncertain output price as its starting point, extending the argument to the quantity setting monopolist using the idea of a "random demand curve," a concept introduced by Leland.[1]

Section 2-2 examines a conjecture made by Sandmo that a decrease in uncertainty will increase optimal output, proving it under the assumption of non-increasing absolute risk aversion. It is followed by an examination of the effect of a change in the expectation of price in the model, and the chapter concludes with a generalization of the theory to more than one market.

2-1. The Potential Exporter facing an Uncertain Demand

The recognition of possible risk aversion among firms forces us to abandon the conventional assumption of profit maximizing behavior (or expected profit maximization, if profits are random), which would imply that the firm would be indifferent to the choice between profits of π_1 with certainty, or some linear combination of uncertain profits whose expectation is equal to π_1. A precise definition of the individual or firm's attitude toward risk is only provided by a utility function, which of course could permit profit maximization as a special case, if it is linear.

Following Sandmo, we assume that the firm maximizes the expected utility of profits. The assumption of risk averse behavior implies that the utility function is concave; unlike much early theoretical work concerned with choice involving risk, there is no need to restrict it to a particular form, such as the quadratic. Although Sandmo limited his analysis to the purely competitive firm which treated the distribution of output prices as given and unchanged by the firm's actions, this restriction is not necessary. Instead, we assume that the firm faces a demand curve which inversely relates price and quantity sold in the normal way, but in addition contains an uncertain component u, which we assume to be positively related to quantity and price. Formally, the stochastic demand curve may be expressed as an implicit function

$$f(p, q, u) = 0 \tag{2.1}$$

If the firm sets quantity, as is the only possibility in the competitive case, then 2.1 may be rewritten as

$$p = p\ (q,\ u) \qquad (2.1')$$

where $\partial p/\partial q \leq 0$ and $\partial p/\partial u > 0$. The latter partial derivative reflects the assumption that as expected total revenue increases, the variability of total revenue increases with, a hypothesis which Leland calls the "Principle of Increasing Uncertainty (PIU)."

The firm is assumed to have a subjective frequency distribution for u, so that by setting q, a conditional distribution for p is uniquely determined. Following Leland, we define the certainty demand curve equivalent to the random demand curve as the curve the firm would face if it knew with certainty that the price would equal its expected value for a given q, or

$$p = E\ [p\ (q,u)] = p\ [q,\ u^{o}(q)] = f(q) \qquad (2.2)$$

We can then show that expected marginal revenue, E [MR(q,u)], will equal the marginal revenue which would result from the certainty equivalent demand curve, or

$$\begin{aligned} d\ [q\ f(q)]/\ dg &= f(q) + q\ [d\ f(q)/\ dq] \\ &= E\ [p(q,u)] + q\ [\partial E[p(q,u)]\ /\partial q] \\ &= E\ [p(q,u) + q\ \partial p(q,u)\ /\partial q] \\ &= E\ [MR(q,u)] \end{aligned}$$

Hence there is some function $u^{1}(q)$, given the principle of increasing uncertainty, such that

$$E\ [MR(q,u)] = MR\ [q,\ u^{1}(q)] \qquad (2.3)$$

The firm's problem is then to choose a q which maximizes the expected utility of profits

$$\max_q E\ \{U\ (pq - c(q) - b)\} \tag{2.4}$$

First order conditions for an expected utility maximum are

$$E\ \{U'(\pi)\ [MR(q,u) - MC(q)]\} = 0 \tag{2.5}$$

where MC(q) = dC/dq. Second order conditions require

$$D = E\ \{U''(\pi)\ [MR(q,u) - MC(q)] + \\ + U'(\pi)\ [\partial MR(q,u)/\partial q - dMC(q)/dq]\} < 0 \tag{2.6}$$

From 2.3 we have defined u^1 as the u such that marginal revenue equals its expectation. Consider the case in which $u \geq u^1$. By the assumption of concavity (risk aversion), we have $U'(\pi) \leq U'(\pi^1)$, where π^1 is profits when $u = u^1$. Furthermore, since $\partial p/\partial u \geq 0$, $MR(q,u) \geq MR(q,u^1)$ when $u \geq u^1$. Hence we may write

$$U'(\pi)\ [MR(q,u) - MR(q,u^1)] \leq U'(\pi^1)\ [MR(q,u) - MR(q,u^1)] \tag{2.7}$$

Now consider the case in which $u \leq u^1$. In this case we have $U'(\pi) \geq U'(\pi^1)$ and $MR(q,u) \leq MR(q,u^1)$. With both inequalities reversed, inequality 2.7 holds for $u \leq u^1$ as well. Taking expectations, we have

$$E\ \{U'(\pi)\ [MR(q,u) - MR(q,u^1)]\} \leq U'(\pi^1)\ E[MR(q,u) - MR(q,u^1)] \tag{2.8}$$

since $U'(\pi^1)$ is non-stochastic. But from the definition of the stochastic demand curve and 2.3, it is clear that the expected value term on the right-hand side of the inequality is zero, so that

$$E\ \{U'(\pi)\ [MR(q,u) - MR(q,u^1)]\} \leq 0 \tag{2.9}$$

Noting that $MR(q,u^1) = f(q) + q\partial f(q)/\partial q$, we have

$$E\ \{U'(\pi)\ [MR(q,u) - f(q)]\} - E\ \{U'(\pi)\ q\partial f(q)/\partial q \leq 0$$

Since $E\ \{U'(\pi)\ q\partial f(q)/\partial q\} \leq 0$,

$$E\ \{U'(\pi)\ [MR(q,u) - f(q)]\} \leq 0 \tag{2.10}$$

Rewriting the first order condition 2.5 as

$$E\ \{U'(\pi)\ [MR(q,u)]\} = E\ \{U'(\pi)[MC(q)]\}$$

and subtracting $E\ \{U'(\pi)\ MR(q,u^1)\}$ from each side, we have

$$E\ \{U'(\pi)\ [MR(q,u) - MR(q,u^1)]\} = E\ \{U'(\pi)[MC(q) - MR(q,u^1)]\}$$

But from 2.9, the left-hand side is non-positive, so that

$$E\ \{U'(\pi)\ [MC(q) - MR(q,u^1)]\} \leq 0$$

Since $U'(\pi) \geq 0$ for all q and u, we must have

$$MR(q,u^1) \geq MC(q) \tag{2.11}$$

The economic meaning of 2.11 is clear. Under uncertainty, expected marginal revenue will exceed marginal cost, in contrast to the certainty case, in which 2.11 would become an equality. If marginal costs are increasing, 2.11 implies that firm output in the presence of uncertainty will be less than it is under certainty.

2-2. Firm Output and Changes in the Degree of Uncertainty

The conclusion of the preceding section, that the risk averse firm will produce less facing an uncertain demand than it would under certainty is now a well established theorem of the recent microeconomics of uncertainty. If we recognize that the firm almost always faces some degree of demand uncertainty, then its response to a change in the level of uncertainty is clearly of more empirical interest than is the simple comparison of the certainty and uncertainty case. This is obviously true in an examination of the effects of the crawling peg, since no one would maintain that its adoption eliminated exchange rate uncertainty altogether.

Sandmo advances the intuitively appealing proposition that a marginal increase in uncertainty, which he defines as a "stretching" of the probability distribution of the price around a constant mean, might be expected to decrease optimal output, but concludes that this conjecture cannot be proved. Under the widely accepted hypothesis of non-increasing absolute risk aversion, discussed below, which Sandmo himself uses, the conjecture can be proved categorically, as is shown in this section.

Absolute risk aversion, introduced into economic theory independently by Arrow and Pratt,[2] may be defined as

$$R_a(\pi) = -U''(\pi)/U'(\pi) \tag{2.12}$$

Although $U''(\pi)$ itself might at first appear to provide a natural index of risk aversion, it is not invariant to linear transformations, as is $R_a(\pi)$. Arrow and others have argued that absolute risk aversion is decreasing. This hypothesis has a number of possible economic interpretations. One implication is that as the decision maker becomes wealthier (or as profits, incomes, or returns increase), his risk premium, equal to the extra amount he would pay to receive the expectation of an uncertain prospect rather than face the prospect, would at least not increase. Alternatively, one could interpret the hypothesis to mean that investment in a risky asset is not an inferior activity; put more informally, a wealthy individual would be at least as willing as a poor one to accept a fair bet of a given absolute value. Given the intuitive plausibility of this assumption, as well as its nearly universal acceptance by economic theorists, we shall assume in what follows that

$$R_a'(\pi) = d\,[-U''(\pi)/U'(\pi)]/\,d\pi \leq 0 \qquad (2.13)$$

Let $\bar{\pi}$ refer to the level of profits when $MR(q,u) = MC(q)$. Then if $MR(q,u) \geq MC(q)$, $\pi \geq \bar{\pi}$ and by 2.13, $R_a(\pi) \leq R_a(\pi)$. From 2.12 we then have

$$-U''(\pi)/U'(\pi) \leq R_a(\bar{\pi}) \text{ for } MR(q,u) \geq MC(q) \qquad (2.14)$$

Since $U'(\pi) > 0$ for all q, u, we have

$$-U'(\pi)\ [MR(q,u) - MC(q)] \leq 0 \qquad (2.15)$$

when $MR(q,u) > MC(q)$. Multiplying 2.14 by 2.15, we have

$$U''(\pi)\ [MR(q,u) - MC(q)] \geq -R_a(\bar{\pi})\ U'(\pi)[MR(q,u) - MC(q)] \qquad (2.16)$$

Note that if $MR(q,u) < MC(q)$ then both inequalities 2.14 and 2.15 are reversed, so that 2.16 must hold for all q and u. Taking expectations and noting that $R_a(\bar{\pi})$ is non-stochastic, we have

$$E\{U''(\pi)[MR(q,u) - MC(q)]\} \geq$$

$$- R_a(\bar{\pi})\, E\{U'(\pi)[MR(q,u) - MC(q)]\}$$

But from the first order condition 2.5, the right-hand side is zero, so that

$$E\{U''(\pi)[MR(q,u) - MC(q)]\} \geq 0 \tag{2.17}$$

for all q, u. This result, as shown below, may be used to determine the effect of a marginal change in uncertainty on output, as well as to establish a number of other useful theorems under uncertainty.

Following Sandmo, we shall define a pure increase in uncertainty as a "spreading" or widening of the probability distribution of the random variable about an unchanged mean. For our purposes here, we can define an increase in the uncertainty attaching to the random demand curve as a change in the random element u such that the certainty equivalent demand curve, f(q), is unchanged for any q, while the conditional distribution of p, given any q, is spread, with relatively more weight transferred away from the center toward the tails of the conditional distribution. Letting p^* be the new price, after such a mean-preserving spread has occurred, we can write

$$p^* = \gamma p(q,u) + \theta \tag{2.18}$$

where γ and θ are respectively multiplicative and additive parameters initially equal to unity and to zero. Increasing γ by itself would increase all values of p, thus increasing the expected value of p^*. Hence it is necessary to change the additive parameter, θ, which if changed by itself would simply shift the position of the distribution, in such a way that the mean of the original distribution is unchanged. This would require that $dE\ [\gamma p + \theta] = 0$, or since $E\ [p(q,u)] = f(q)$, $f(q)\ d\gamma + d\theta = 0$, yielding

$$\frac{d\theta}{d\gamma} = -\ f(q) \tag{2.19}$$

Profits after a mean preserving spread are then

$$\pi = (\gamma p + \theta)\ q - c(q) - b \tag{2.20}$$

which when substituted into 2.5 requires us to rewrite the first order condition as

$$\begin{aligned} A = E\ \{U'[(\gamma p + \theta)q - c(q) - b] \cdot \\ [(\gamma p + \theta) + (\partial p/\partial q)q - c'(q)]\} = 0 \end{aligned} \tag{2.21}$$

The first order condition expresses the optimal output, q, as an implicit function of the multiplicative shift parameter, γ. Differentiating A with respect to θ, we have

$$\begin{aligned} \frac{dA}{d\gamma} &= E\ U'(\rho)\ [p + \frac{d\theta}{d\gamma} + q\ \frac{\partial p}{\partial q}] + \\ &+ U''(\pi)\ [pq + \frac{d\theta}{d\gamma}q]\ [\gamma p + \theta) + \frac{\partial p}{\partial q}q - c'(q)]\} \end{aligned}$$

Setting $\gamma = 1$, $\theta = 0$, and using 2.19, we have

$$\begin{aligned} \frac{dA}{d\gamma} &= E\ \{U'(\pi)\ (MR(q,u) - f(q)) + \\ &+ U''(\pi)\ q\ (p - f(q)\ (MR(q,u) - MC(q))\} \end{aligned} \tag{2.22}$$

Using the second order condition 2.6 and the implicit function theorem

$$\frac{dq}{d\gamma} = \frac{-1}{D} E \{U'(\pi) (MR(q,u) - f(q))\} +$$

$$+ q E \{U''(\pi) (p - f(q)) (MR(q,u) - MC(q))\} \quad (2.23)$$

By 2.6, $D < 0$, and by 2.10, $E \{U'(\pi) (MR(q,u) - f(q))\} \leq 0$, so that a sufficient condition for $dq/d\gamma < 0$ is that the second bracketed term in 2.23 be negative.

If actual price equals its expectation, or $p(q,u) = f(q)$, then actual marginal revenue equals its expectation, or $MR(q,u) = MR(q,u^1)$. By 2.1 and 2.3, marginal revenue is monotonic in p, so that

$$MR(q,u) \gtrless MR(q,u^1) \quad \text{iff} \quad p(q,u) \gtrless q(q,u^1) = f(q) \quad (2.24)$$

Hence the second term of 2.23 will have the same sign as the expression

$$\frac{-1}{D} q E \{U''(\pi) [MR(q,u) - MR(q,u^1)] [MR(q,u) - MC(q)]\}$$

which may be expanded to yield

$$\frac{-1}{D} q E \{U''(\pi) [MR(q,u) - MC(q)] \cdot$$

$$\cdot [MR(q,u) - MC(q) + MC(q) - MR(q,u^1)]\}$$

or

$$\frac{-1}{D} q E \{U''(\pi) [MR(q,u) - MC(q)]^2\} +$$

$$\frac{-1}{D} q E \{U''(\pi) [MR(q,u) - MC(q)] [MC(q) - MR(q,u^1)]\}$$

The first term in this expression is unambiguously negative, since $U''(\pi) < 0$ for all q, u. By 2.11, the non-stochastic term $[MC(q) - MR(q,u^1)]$ is non-positive for all q, u. Moving it outside the expected value operator, we have from 2.17 that $E\{U''(\pi)\ [MR(q,u) - MR(q)]\} \geq 0$ under the assumption of non-increasing absolute risk aversion. Hence the second term of 2.23 is unambiguously negative, so that

$$\frac{dq}{d\gamma} < 0 \qquad (2.25)$$

The economic significance of 2.25 is clear. Under the intuitively plausible hypothesis of non-increasing absolute risk aversion, the expected utility maximizing firm will respond to an increase in demand uncertainty by reducing output, where an increase in uncertainty is defined here as a stretching of the conditional probability distribution of p about an unchanged expected value, f(q).

The assumption of non-increasing absolute risk aversion is probably an overly strong sufficient condition for 2.25 to hold. If $R_a'(\pi) = 0$, only one of three negative terms in the expanded form of 2.23 is eliminated, suggesting that for our conclusion to be invalid, not only would absolute risk aversion have to be increasing, but its effect in reversing inequality 2.17 would have to be strong enough to dominate the two other unambiguously non-positive terms in 2.23, neither of whose signs are dependent on the non-increasing absolute aversion hypotheses.

From the definition of Pratt-Arrow absolute risk aversion, it can be seen that $R_a'(\cdot) \leq 0$ requires that the utility function satisfy the inequality

$$(-1/U'(\cdot)^2)\ (U'(\cdot)U'''(\cdot) - (U''(\cdot))^2) \leq 0 \qquad (2.26)$$

The assumption of risk aversion (concavity) requires that $U' > 0$ and $U'' < 0$, so that $U''' > 0$ is necessary, although not sufficient for $R_a' \leq 0$. A number of commonly employed utility functions satisfy this condition; among them are $U(x) = \log x$, $U(x) = x^a$, where $0 < a < 1$, or the constant elasticity function $U(x) = (1/(1-a))\ x^{(1-a)}$. Note, however, that the popular quadratic utility function, $U(x) = ax - bx^2$, cannot possibly show non-increasing risk aversion in any interval for x.

2-3. Output Response to Changes in Expected Prices and in Costs

It was shown in Section 2-2 that the risk averse firm would increase (decrease) its output if the level of uncertainty, defined as a widening of the probability distribution of the output price, decreased (increased). In this section two features of the model of the firm under uncertainty are addressed: first, it is shown that the "normal" positive response of output to an increase in price in the certainty case holds under uncertainty, in which case we replace price by its expectation; and, second, in contrast to the certainty case a decrease in fixed costs, as well as in variable costs, will increase the firm's output.

Using the approach employed to analyze a mean preserving spread in the preceding section, we may define a change in the expected price of output as a shifting of the conditional distribution (given q) of the output price which alters its expected value, while leaving its shape unchanged. We do this by simply adding a constant to each possible price, or in terms of our definition of the post-change output price $p^* = \gamma p + \theta$, Hence we may differentiate the first order condition 2.21 with respect to θ to yield

$$\frac{dA}{d\theta} = E\ \{U'(\pi) + q\ U''(\pi)\ [MR(q,u) - MC(q)]\}$$

in which γ and θ have been set equal to their initial values of unity and zero. By the second order condition 2.6 and the implicit function theorem

$$\frac{dq}{d\theta} = \frac{-1}{D}\ E\ \{U'(\pi)\} - \frac{1}{D}\ q\ E\ \{U''(\pi)\ [MR(q,u) - MC(q)]\} \qquad (2.27)$$

Since $U'(\pi) > 0$ for all q, u, and $D<0$, the first term is clearly positive. Under the hypothesis of non-increasing absolute risk aversion, as was shown in 2.17 in the preceding section, the second expected value term in 2.27 is non-negative for all q, u, so that with the second order condition ($D < 0$), we have

$$\frac{dq}{d\theta} > 0$$

Hence an increase in the expected value of the price of the potential exporter's output will increase the optimal output. The increase in expected price might arise from a number of sources: a change in exchange policy, a shift in the structure of protection, or from changes in the world price of the exportable.

A final problem is the effect of changes in either variable or fixed costs on firm output under uncertainty. Noting that fixed costs (b) are already implicit in the first order condition 2.5, we may rewrite the variable cost function $c = c(q)$ as $c = (q,a)$, where a is some non-stochastic shift parameter such that $\partial c/\partial a > 0$. Marginal costs, MC(q), may now be interpreted as $MC(q) = \partial c/\partial q$, where a is assumed constant. The first order condition then becomes

$$A = E\ \{U'\ [pq - c(q,a) - b]\ [MR(q,u) - MC(q)]\} = 0 \qquad (2.5')$$

Differentiating 2.5' with respect to both the variable cost shift parameter and fixed costs, we have

$$\frac{dA}{da} = E\ \{U''(\pi)\ (-\ \partial c/\partial a)\ [MR(q,u) - MC(q)]\}$$

$$\frac{dA}{db} = E\ \{U''(\pi)\ (-1)\ [MR(q,u) - MC(q)]\}$$

By the second order condition 2.6 and the implicit function theorem, we then have

$$\frac{dq}{da} = \frac{1}{D} \left(\frac{\partial c}{\partial a}\right) E \{U''(\pi) [MR(q,u) - MC(q)]\} \tag{2.29}$$

$$\frac{dq}{db} = \frac{1}{D} E \{U''(\pi) [MR(q,u) - MC(q)]\} \tag{2.30}$$

Once again it is apparent that the signs of these two derivatives depend on the hypothesis of non-increasing absolute risk aversion. If this assumption is accepted, then by 2.17 the expected value term in 2.29 and 2.30 is non-negative, assuring that both dq/da and dq/db are negative.

The second conclusion contrasts with the traditional non-stochastic theory of the firm. Under certainty, changes in fixed costs will have no effect on the output level, which will depend entirely on marginal revenue and cost. Under uncertainty, an increase in fixed costs will reduce the output of the risk averse firm, assuming that absolute risk aversion is non-increasing. This conclusion is of some interest in the Brazilian case, since a number of administrative reforms, as well as trade promotion efforts may be interpreted as policies which in effect lowered fixed costs. Conventional deterministic microeconomic theory would not predict any effect, at least not in the short run, of these policies. The model of the firm under uncertainty, on the other hand, would suggest that these policies might have had some impact or changes in the level of exports from Brazil in the past decade.

2-4. Changes in Uncertainty with Multiple Markets[3]

The argument of the preceding sections rested on the assumption that the firm sold its output in a single market, which in the context of an analysis of exchange rate uncertainty is the export market. It is clearly necessary to inquire if our conclusions remain valid when the firm may sell its output in more than one market, for example the domestic or the export market. In this section we extend the model of the firm under price uncertainty to the multiple market case, showing that under the assumption that the distributions of output prices are independent, an increase (decrease) in the uncertainty of the price of a given market will result *ceteris paribus* in a decrease (increase) in output sold in that market. The effect of this change in price uncertainty on the output sold in the market with no change in its price distribution is indeterminate, as will be seen below. To avoid unnecessary detail, the model developed here considers only the competitive case, although it will be clear that the approach may be extended to the quantity-setting monopolist as well along the lines of preceding sections.

It is interesting to note that under certainty the question of competitive firm behavior in multiple markets is not even conceptually manageable, except in a Kuhn-Tucker inequality-constrained format. This is simply due to the fact that the competitive firm will sell all of its output in the market offering the higher price. Although this feature of the competitive model under certainty is usually ignored by trade theorists, it would logically require that even small changes in relative price differences between export and domestic markets for the same good, such as those induced by changes in the exchange rate or the structure of protection, result in either complete price equalization or complete abandonment of the lower price markets. As this is rarely the observed case, one must appeal to disequilibrium, or to market imperfections if the continued supply to two or more markets with different prices is to be explained under certainty. As will be seen below, this problem does not arise once we admit the possibility of price uncertainty and risk averse behavior.

We assume as usual that the firm maximizes the expected value of a concave function of profits, which are obtained from sales of a single product in two markets. The firm's problem is then to maximize

$$E\,[U(\pi)] = E\,\{U\,[p_1q_1 + p_2q_2 - c(q) - b]\} \tag{2.31}$$

where $q = q_1 + q_2$. We assume that $c'(q) > 0$ and $c''(q) \geq 0$. Each price p_i is distributed randomly, with $E(p_i) = \mu_i$, and $E\,\{(p_i - \mu_i)(p_j - \mu_j)\} = 0$. We do not require that $\mu_i = \mu_j$.

First order conditions necessary for an expected utility maximum are then

$$E_i = E\,\{U'(\pi)(p_i - c'(q)\} = 0 \qquad i = 1,2 \tag{2.32}$$

As $U(\pi)$ is concave, the q_i satisfying the first order conditions 2.32 maximize expected utility. This is equivalent to the following second order conditions

$$E_{ii} = E\,\{U'(\pi)(-c'') + U''(\pi)(p_i - c')^2\} < 0 \qquad i = 1,2 \tag{2.33}$$

$$|E| = E_{ii}E_{jj} - E_{ij}{}^2 > 0 \qquad i,j = 1,2,\ i \neq j \tag{2.34}$$

where $E_{ij} = E\ \{U'(\pi)(-c'') + U''(\pi)(p_i - c')(p_j - c')\}$

Under uncertainty the second order matrix is not singular, as it is in the competitive certainty case, in which all the E_{ij} reduce to $-c''$. Strictly increasing marginal cost ($c'' > 0$), moreover, is not necessary for there to be an expected utility maximum, provided that $U(\pi)$ is strictly concave. We note that a sufficient condition for $|E| > 0$ is the inequality

$$E\ \{U''(\pi)(p_i - c')^2\} < E\ \{U''(\pi)(p_i - c')(p_j - c')\} \qquad i \neq j \qquad (2.35)$$

This inequality, which we use below, may be proved using the first order conditions and the hypothesis of non-increasing absolute risk aversion, under the assumption that p_i and p_j are independent.

We first show that under the assumption of independence of p_i and p_j a condition analogous to 2.9 in the single market case obtains. Letting $\overline{\pi} = \pi|p_j$, $j \neq 1$, when $p_i = \mu_i$, then if $p_i \geq \mu_i$, we have $\pi|p_j \geq \overline{\pi}$, and by the assumption of concavity, $U'(\pi)|p_j < U'(\overline{\pi})$. Multiplying this inequality by $p_i - \mu_i$, we have

$$(U'(\pi)\ |\ p_j)(p_i - \mu_j) \leq U'(\overline{\pi})(p_i - \mu_i)$$

This holds for $p_i < \mu_i$ as well, since both inequalities are reversed. Noting that $U'(\overline{\pi})$ is non-stochastic, taking expectations yields

$$E\ \{U'(\pi)(p_i - \mu_i)\} \leq 0 \qquad (2.36)$$

for all p_i, under the assumption of independence of p_i and p_j.

We next show that $c' \leq \mu_i$, the multiple market equivalent to 2.37. Rewriting the first order conditions and subtracting $E\ \{U'(\pi)\ \mu_i\}$ from each side we have

$$E\{U'(\pi)(p_i - \mu_i)\} = E\{U'(\pi)(c' - \mu_i) \qquad i = 1,2$$

From 2.36 the left-hand side is non-positive, so that $E\{U'(\pi)(c' - \mu_i)\} \leq 0$. Since $U'(\pi) > 0$ for all p_i, we must have

$$c' < \mu_i \qquad \text{for all } p_i, \qquad i = 1,2 \tag{2.37}$$

Inequality 2.37 implies that for all $c'' \geq 0$, optimal output in the presence of uncertainty is less than or equal to output under certainty. This conclusion in turn anticipates the result proved below that an increase in price uncertainty in either market could be expected to reduce overall output, regardless of the allocation of output to either market.

A final inequality necessary for the analysis of the multiple market case is the condition $E\{U''(\pi)(p_i - c')\} \geq 0$, analogous to 2.17 in the single market case. Letting $\overline{\pi} = \pi|p_j$ when $p_i = c'$, $i \neq j$, or profits for any given p_j when p_i equals marginal cost, we then have in the case in which $p_i > c'$ that $\pi > \overline{\pi}$. Under the non-increasing risk aversion hypothesis, this implies that $-U''(\pi)/U'(\pi) \leq R_a(\overline{\pi})$. Multiplying this inequality by $-U'(\pi)(p_i - c')$, which is non-positive for $p_i \geq c'$, we obtain

$$U''(\pi)(p_i - c') \geq - R_a(\overline{\pi})\, U'(\pi)(p_i - c')$$

For $p_i < c'$ this inequality also holds, since both inequalities are reversed. Taking expectations, noting that $-R_a(\overline{\pi})$ is non-stochastic, and using the first order condition, we have

$$E\{U''(\pi)(p_i - c')\} \geq 0 \tag{2.38}$$

We now consider a change in the degree of uncertainty about price in one of the two markets, assuming that the distribution of the other price remains unchanged. In the context of exchange rate uncertainty, this might be a reduction in uncertainty about export prices expressed in local currency terms, with domestic prices also uncertain, but with no change in their frequency distribution. We can follow the multiplicative spread approach used in the preceding section, defining such a spread as a change in the respective multiplicative and additive parameters γ and θ such that the new random price in the ith sector is

$$p_i^* = \gamma p_i + \theta \tag{2.39}$$

subject to $dE(p_i{}^*) = 0$. Since $E(p_i) = \mu_i$, we have $d\gamma\, \mu_i + d\theta = 0$, or

$$\frac{d\theta}{d\gamma} = -\mu_i \qquad i = 1,2 \tag{2.40}$$

Profits after this multiplicative, mean preserving spread are

$$\pi = (\gamma p_i + \theta)\, q_i + p_j q_j - c(q_i + q_j) - b \qquad i,j = 1,2\ (1 \neq j)$$

The revised first order conditions are then

$$E\,\{U'\ [(\gamma p_i + \theta)q_i + p_j q_j - c(q_i + q_j) - b][\gamma p_i + \quad - c']\} = 0$$

and (2.41)

$$E\,\{U'\ [(\gamma p_i + \theta)qi + p_j q_j - c(q_i + q_j) - b](p_j - c')\} = 0$$

Totally differentiating these conditions with respect to the multiplicative shift parameter γ, and q_i and q_j, we have by the implicit function theorem the system

$$\begin{bmatrix} E_{ii} & E_{ij} \\ E_{ij} & E_{jj} \end{bmatrix} \begin{bmatrix} dq_i/d\gamma \\ dq_j/d\gamma \end{bmatrix} = \begin{bmatrix} -E_{i\gamma} \\ -E_{j\gamma} \end{bmatrix} \tag{2.42}$$

where we use 2.40 with $\gamma = 1$ and $\theta = 0$ to obtain

$$E_{i\gamma} = E\,\{U'(\pi)(p_i - \mu_i) + q_i U''(\pi)(p_i - \mu_i)(p_i - c')\}$$

and

$$E_{j\gamma} = E\,\{q_i U''(\pi)(p_i - \mu_j)(p_j - c')\}$$

Expanding the last term of the first expression we have

$$qi\ E\,\{U''(\pi)(p_i - c' + c' - \mu_i)(p_i - c')\}$$

$$= q_i\ E\,\{U''(\pi)(p_i - c')^2\} + q_i(c' - \mu_i)\ E\,\{U'(\pi)(p_i - c')\}$$

A similar expansion of $E_{j\gamma}$ yields

$$E_{j\gamma} = q_i\ E\,\{U''(\pi)(p_i - c')(p_j - c')\} + q_i(c' - \mu_i)\ E\,\{U''(\pi)(p_j - c')\}$$

Subtracting $E_{j\gamma}$ from $E_{i\gamma}$, we obtain

$$\begin{aligned} E_{i\gamma} - E_{j\gamma} = {} & E\,\{U'(\pi)(p_i - \mu_i)\} + q_i\ E\,\{U''(\pi)(p_i - c')^2\} + \\ & + q_i(c' - \mu_i)\ E\,\{U''(\pi)(p_i - c')\} \\ & - q_i\ E\,\{U''(\pi)(p_i - c')(p_j - c')\} \\ & - q_i(c' - \mu_i)\ E\,\{U'(\pi)(p_j - c')\} \end{aligned}$$

From 2.36 the first term in this expression is non-positive, and by 2.35 the sum of the second and fourth terms is non-positive. By an argument similar to that proving 2.38, we may show that $E\ \{U''(\pi)(p_i - p_j)\} > 0$, which with 2.37 requires that the sum of the third and fifth terms be non-positive, permitting us to conclude that $E_{i\gamma} \leq E_{j\gamma}$.

Solving the system 2.42 for $dq_i/d\gamma$ and $dq_j/d\gamma$, we have

$$\frac{dq_i}{d\gamma} = \frac{-1}{E} [E_{i\gamma} E_{jj} - E_{j\gamma} E_{ij}] \qquad (2.43)$$

$$\frac{dq_j}{d\gamma} = \frac{-1}{E} [E_{j\gamma} E_{ii} - E_{i\gamma} E_{ij}] \qquad (2.44)$$

As shown above, $E_{i\gamma} < 0$, and $E_{i\gamma} \leq E_{j\gamma}$. From the second order conditions and 2.35, we have $E_{jj} < 0$, $E_{ii} < 0$, and $E_{jj} < E_{ij} > E_{ii}$; hence the bracketed term in 2.43 is unambiguously positive, which with the second order condition 2.34 proves that $dq_i/d\gamma < 0$. An increase (decrease) in the uncertainty about p_i, defined as a multiplicative spread (narrowing) in its frequency distribution with its mean unchanged, will categorically decrease (increase) the output sold in that market. This effect occurs for two reasons; less output is produced, and sales are shifted to the market in which output price is less uncertain.

The same inequalities and restrictions imply that the bracketed term in 2.44 may be either positive or negative, since $E_{ii} \leq E_{ij}$, but $E_{i\gamma} \leq E_{j\gamma}$. This conclusion reflects the fact that the outcome of an increase in price uncertainty in the other market will have two effects. The first, analogous to the income effect of consumption theory, arises from the fact that the expected-utility maximizing firm will decrease overall output. (This may be seen easily by aggregating the two markets, thus reducing the multiple market model to the model of preceding sections.) The second effect, which works counter to the production effect, is the shift in sales from the ith to the jth market, as the distribution of p_i becomes more uncertain. This effect, analogous to the substitution effect of consumption theory, may be seen clearly in a model which constrains the output to be constant.

The implications of this model for exchange rate uncertainty should be clear. If we consider a change in exchange rate regimes from one characterized by large fluctuations in the real rate to a more stable system like Brazil's crawling peg, we would expect that the firm producing an exportable would both increase its total output and the share of output exported. The quantity of its output marketed domestically, on the other hand, might rise or fall, depending on whether or not the positive production effect outweighed the negative market allocation effect.

FOOTNOTES FOR CHAPTER II

1. Among the first contributions to the theory of the firm under uncertainty were E. Mills, "Uncertainty and Price Theory," Quart. Jour. Econ., Feb. 1959, 116-129, and J. McCall, "Competitive Production for Constant Risk Utility Functions," Rev. Econ. Studies, Oct. 1967, 417-420. McCall's basic results were generalized in A. Sandmo, "On the Theory of the Competitive Firm under Price Uncertainty," Amer. Econ. Rev., March 1971, 65-73. His model was in turn extended to the monopolistic case in H. Leland, "Theory of the Firm facing Uncertain Demand," Amer. Econ. Rev., June 1972, 278-291.

2. See K. Arrow, Aspects of a Theory of Risk Bearing, Helsinki, 1965, and J. Pratt, "Risk Aversion in the Small and in the Large," Econometrica, 1964, 127-136.

3. The argument presented here may be extended to more than two markets; to do so, however, results in no real change in the basic conclusions, simply making the argument more tedious.

CHAPTER III

THE POTENTIAL EXPORTER UNDER UNCERTAINTY: EXTENSIONS OF THE BASIC MODEL

The theory of firm behavior developed in the preceding chapter led to the conclusion that an increase in price uncertainty, defined as a multiplicative spreading of the frequency distribution of the output price, would decrease the optimal level of production. This result, conjectured by Sandmo in his pioneering examination of the firm under uncertainty, was first proved by Batra and Ullah for the special case of the competitive firm whose production is characterized by a "well-behaved" neo-classical two factor production function.[1] As was shown in the preceding chapter, this result holds for a considerably less restrictive assumption; i.e., that marginal cost is non-decreasing. Extension of the model to two markets, moreover, shows that a decrease in uncertainty in either market would be expected to have both a production effect, increasing overall output, and an allocation effect, shifting output to the market in which price has become less uncertain.

Although a model of the firm which explicitly recognizes demand uncertainty is clearly richer and more realistic than the traditional model of deterministic micro-economics, it rests on assumptions which may be considered overly restrictive. The concept of increasing risk used is a multiplicative spreading of the frequency distribution of the random variable, with its expected value held constant. A transformation of this type would increase the variance of the distribution, and as such, represents only a limited advance over analysis of increasing uncertainty which assumes either quadratic utility functions or normal distributions and uses variance alone as a proxy for uncertainty. One can imagine many other types of changes in the distribution of the random variable which we could identify with a change in risk but which could not be produced by the Sandmo-Batra multiplicative spread approach.

A second limitation on several of the conclusions of the preceding chapter is the assumption that the utility function is characterized by non-increasing absolute risk aversion in the Pratt-Arrow sense. Despite the considerable intuitive appeal of this hypothesis and its widespread use among economic theorists concerned with uncertainty, it excludes from our analysis a number of concave utility functions, notably the quadratic. It would consequently be desirable to relax this assumption if possible, extending our conclusions to a larger set of utility functions.

Another problem arises from our assumption that the firm sells its entire output as it is produced. This assumption is valid enough for a firm producing a service, or a commodity which cannot be stored, but the possibility of reserving output during a period of low prices for later sale at a higher price suggests that the firm may benefit from some degree of variation in prices.

Finally, the expected utility hypothesis itself may be more restrictive than is first apparent. Some theorists have interpreted the assumption to mean that all decisions must be made by one individual, due to the well-known difficulties of constructing a group utility function even if individual preferences are known. If correct, this interpretation would appear to be a severe and possibly fatal blow to theories of the firm based on the expected utility hypothesis when extended beyond firms managed by one individual. What this interpretation overlooks, however, is the fact that virtually all the conclusions about the behavior of the firm under uncertainty derive from the assumption that the firm maximizes a concave objective function of uncertain profits. This observation would suggest that we seek sufficient conditions for the firm's behavior to be characterized by the maximization of such a function when more than one decision maker is involved, whether or not we accept the existence of community indifference curves.

This chapter introduces these considerations into the basic theory of the firm under demand uncertainty developed in the preceding chapter. The first two restrictions, the limitation of increases in risk to multiplicative spreads, and the hypothesis of non-increasing absolute risk aversion are shown in Section 3-1 to be overly strong. Sufficient conditions for an increase in price variability to reduce output are derived using a broader concept of increasing risk introduced by Rothschild and Stiglitz. Their definition of increasing risk permits us to consider the effect of inventories in Section 3-2, in which we derive the conditions for an increase in price variability to reduce output even in the presence of inventories. Finally, the form of the firm's objective function is examined in Section 3-3, in which it is shown that a number of simple institutional assumptions are sufficient for the firm's objective function to satisfy the requirements of preceding sections.

3-1. Rothschild-Stiglitz Increasing Risk and Firm Output

If we regard the individual's subjective evaluation of the behavior of a random variable as a probability distribution, then a rather natural way of characterizing a pure increase in the uncertainty attaching to the random variable is to transfer some of the mass of the distribution away from the center towards its tails without altering the expected value of the distribution. The multiplicative-spread approach of the preceding chapter is obviously one example of such a transformation, but one can easily imagine transformations of a probability distribution which can be characterized by increased weight in the tails which cannot be obtained by any type of multiplicative spread. In a seminal contribution to the economics of uncertainty, Rothschild and Stiglitz (RS) have shown the equivalence of the following three propositions:[2]

a) "All risk averters--those with concave utility functions--prefer X to Y."

b) "Y is equal to X plus some noise."

c) "Y has more weight in its tails than X."

In terms of Figure 3.1, the RS propositions would state that distribution f(p) is preferred to g(p) by all risk averse individuals. Note that g(p) in this case is not a multiplicative transformation of f(p), although such a transformation would obviously meet the RS criteria.

More formally, the RS propositions may be stated as

a) $E[U(X)] > E[U(Y)]$ for all concave U

b) There exists a random variable Z such that Y has the same distribution as X + Z, where $E[Z|X] = 0$ for all X.

c') If the points of increase of F and G, the (cumulative) distribution functions of X and Y are confined to the closed interval $[a,b]$, if $H_2(p) = \int_a^p H_1(x)\,dx = \int_a^p G(x)-F(x)\,dx$, then $H_2(p) \geq 0$ for all $p \geq a$ and $H_2(b) = 0$.

It is the third of these three propositions, all of which are stated here without proof, which permits an examination of the effect on firm output of this more broadly defined type of increase in uncertainty. The meaning of proposition c') may be seen more clearly in Figures 3.2 and 3.3. The respective cumulative distributions of $f(p)$ and $g(p)$ are shown in Figure 3.2, with the integral of $H_1(p)$, the difference in the cumulative distributions $G(p)$ and $F(p)$, shown in Figure 3.3.

Consider the competitive firm producing output q with a known cost function $c(q)$, where $c'(q) > 0$ and $c''(q) > 0$. We assume that it sells its entire output concurrently at the uncertain output price p, which is initially distributed as $f(p)$. If the firm maximizes the expected utility of profits, $E\,[U(\pi)]$, and is risk averse, then $U'(\pi) > 0$ and $U''(\pi) < 0$. The expected utility of profits is then

$$E\,[U(\pi)] = \int_a^b U\,[pq - c(q) - c_o]\,dF(p) \tag{3.1}$$

The firm will then choose an optimal q so that

$$\int_a^b U'(\pi)(p - c')\,dF(p) = 0 \tag{3.2}$$

Now assume that $f(p)$ is replaced by a new distribution $g(p)$, which satisfies the RS integral conditions, so that

$$H_2(p) = \int_a^b [G(x) - F(x)]\,dx \geq 0 \qquad \text{for all } p < b \tag{3.3}$$

Figure 3.1

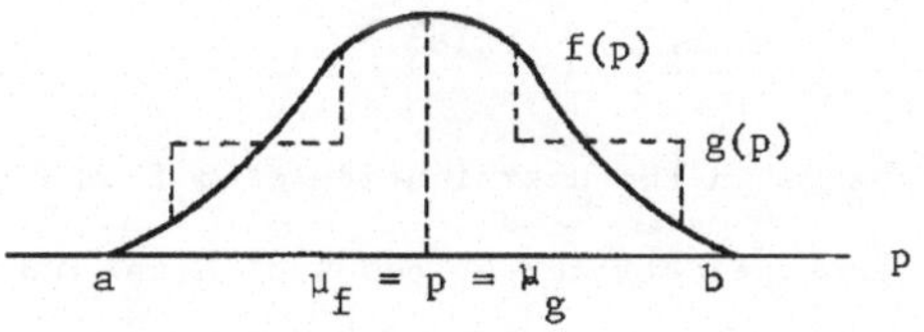

A Mean Preserving Spread in a
Probability Density Function

Figure 3.2

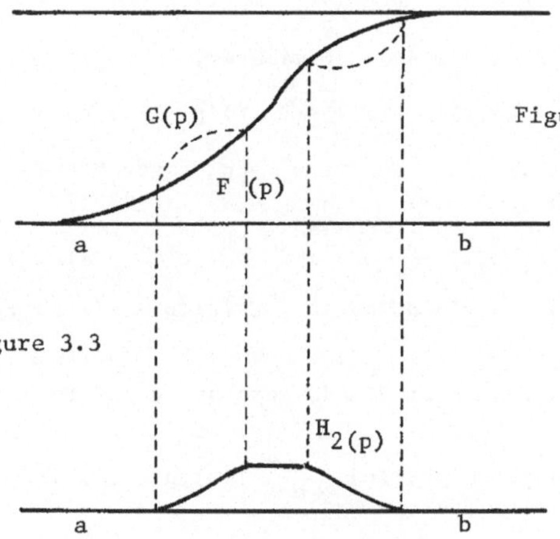

Figure 3.2

Figure 3.3

Figure 3.2 The Cumulative Distributions of a Mean Preserving Spread

Figure 3.3 Integral of the Difference in the Cumulative Distributions

and

$$H_2(b) = H_2(a) = 0 \tag{3.4}$$

After the change in the distribution of p from f(p) to g(p), the firm will maximize expected utility by choosing a new output level, $\hat{q}$, so that

$$\int_a^b U'(\hat{\pi})(p - \hat{c}')\, dG(p) = 0 \tag{3.5}$$

where $\hat{\pi}$ and $\hat{c}'$ are profit and marginal cost for the $\hat{q}$ satisfying 3.5. Suppose first that $\hat{q} \leq q$. Then $p - \hat{c}' \geq p - c'$, since $c'' \geq 0$. If $p > c'$, then $d\pi/dq$ and $d\hat{\pi}/dq$ are non-negative, implying that $\hat{\pi} < \pi$, and by the concavity of $U(\pi)$, $U'(\hat{\pi}) \geq U'(\pi)$. Similarly, if $p < c'$, then $U'(\hat{\pi}) < U'(\pi)$ so that $U'(\pi)(p - c') \leq U'(\hat{\pi})(p - \hat{c}')$ holds for all p. Note that this inequality is true even if $c'' = o$, since $\hat{\pi} < \pi$. Integrating over p, we have

$$\int_a^b U'(\pi)(p - c')\, dG(p) \leq \int_a^b U'(\hat{\pi})(p - \hat{c}')\, dG(p) \tag{3.6}$$

By 3.5, the right-hand side of 3.6 is zero and equal to 3.2, giving

$$\int_a^b U'(\pi)(p - c')\, dG(p) \leq \int_a^b U'(\pi)(p - c')\, dF(p) \tag{3.7}$$

If on the other hand, $\hat{q} > q$, then $p - \hat{c}' \leq p - c'$ and $U'(\hat{\pi}) \leq U'(\pi)$, reversing inequalities 3.6 and 3.7. Hence, using 3.3,

$$\hat{q} \lesseqgtr q \quad \text{as} \quad A = \int_a^b U'(\pi)(p - c')\, dH_1(p) \lesseqgtr 0 \tag{3.8}$$

An increase in uncertainty in the RS sense will consequenty decrease output if $A < 0$. Integrating by parts, we have

$$A = U'(\pi)(p - c')\, H_1(p)\Big|_a^b - \int_a^b H_1(p)\, d[U'(\pi)(p - c')] \tag{3.9}$$

As F(b) = G(b) = 1, and F(a) = G(a) = 0, the first term in 3.9 is zero, yielding

$$A = -\int_a^b H_1(p)\, [U'(\pi) + q(p - c')\, U''(\pi)]\, dp$$

or

$$A = -\int_a^b [U'(\pi) + q(p - c')\, U''(\pi)]\, dH_2(p) \tag{3.10}$$

Denoting by $\phi(p)$ the bracketed term in 3.10, it is evident that the sign of A will be indeterminate unless we can place some restrictions on $\phi(p)$ over the interval [a,b]. Our ability to make categorical statemenys about the effect of changes in risk in an RS sense, in other words, depends crucially on the behavior of the function $\phi(p)$.

If $\phi'(p) < 0$, so that the function is always decreasing over the interval, we may use the second mean value theorem to rewrite 3.10 as

$$A = -\int_a^b \phi(p)\, dH_2(p) = -\phi(a) \int_a^{\bar{p}} dH_2(p) - \phi(b) \int_{\bar{p}}^b dH_2(p)$$

The RS integral conditions 3.3 and 3.4 require that

$$\int_a^{\bar{p}} dH_2(p) = -\int_{\bar{p}}^b dH_2(p) \geq 0$$

yielding

$$A = [\phi(b) - \phi(a)] \int_a^{\bar{p}} dH_2(p) \tag{3.11}$$

As $\phi(b) < \phi(a)$, we must have $A \leq 0$, with strict inequality in all cases except when $\int_a^{\bar{p}} dH_2(p) = 0$. Hence an increase in risk in the RS sense will unambiguously decrease the optimal output of the firm for which $\phi'(p) < 0$ on [a,b].

This conclusion naturally suggests that we seek restrictions on $\phi(p)$ which will guarantee that $\phi'(p) < 0$. Differentiating $\phi(p)$, we have

$$\phi'(p) \quad = \quad q\ [2U''(\pi) + q(p - c')\ U'''(\pi)] \tag{3.12}$$

If $U'''(\pi)$ is small, or zero, as is the case for the quadratic utility function, then $\phi'(p) < 0$, as $U''(\pi) < 0$. It is worthwhile noting that this result cannot be derived using the Sandmo-Batra multiplicative spread approach of the preceding chapter, despite the more limited class of increases in risk considered there.

As noted earlier, theorists have generally accepted the hypothesis that absolute risk aversion, $R_a = -U''(\pi)/U'(\pi)$ is a non-increasing function. As $R_a' = (1/\ U'^2)\ [U''^2 - U'U''']$, this hypothesis is sufficient for $U''' > 0$, raising the possibility that $\phi'(p) > 0$ for $p > c'$. In this case the mean value theorems are inapplicable and a direct proof that $A < 0$ like that used above in the quadratic utility case is not applicable.

It was shown in the preceding chapter that non-increasing absolute risk aversion is sufficient for an increase in risk in a multiplicative sense to reduce output. This conclusion was first proved indirectly by Batra and Ullah, who analyzed the effect of a multiplicative spread in the distribution of the random output price on input demand, which in turn permits a determinate solution for the effect of this type of increase in risk on output. They identify this type of increase in risk, produced by multiplying the distribution of price by some constant γ and then subtracting some constant θ from the transformed distribution so that the expected value is unchanged as a "mean preserving spread." This definition of increasing risk, introduced by Sandmo in his examination of saving behavior under uncertainty, has been characterized elsewhere by Batra as equivalent to an increase in risk in an RS sense. The two definitions are not equivalent, however; multiplicative spreads of the Sandmo-Batra type constitute a proper subset of RS increases in risk. Multiplicative spreads, in fact, are a relatively special type of RS increase, and their application to non-symmetric distributions of a non-negative variable like price may be questioned. If we consider non-multiplicative spreads satisfying the RS conditions, it is not correct to assert as do Batra and Ullah, that non-increasing absolute risk aversion is a sufficient condition for an increase in risk to decrease output. Although their proposition is in general likely to hold, as is argued below, it is not categorically true, and a counterexample is presented in Appendix A.

The concept of relative, rather than absolute risk aversion, may be used to characterize $\phi(p)$. Although less intuitively plausible than is the concept of non-increasing absolute risk aversion, Arrow and others have suggested that relative risk aversion, $R_r(\pi) = -U''(\pi)/U'(\pi)$, is non-decreasing in profits or wealth. Put rather informally, this hypothesis implies that as profits or wealth increase, the individual or firm would not devote a larger proportion of wealth or productive activity to the risky asset or activity. We may use the definition of R_r to rewrite $\phi(p)$ as

$$\phi(p) = U' \{1 + q(p - c')\frac{U''}{U'}\}$$

$$= U' \{1 - \frac{pq - q\,c'}{pq - c(q)} R_r\}$$

If fixed costs are negligible, then $c'(q)\cdot q \geq c(q)$ for all $c'' \geq 0$ cost functions. Hence $\psi = (pq - c'\,q)/\ (pq - c(q)) \leq 1$ and $d\psi/dp > 0$. Differentiating $\phi(p)$, we have

$$\phi'(p) = q\,U'' \{(1 - \psi R_r)\} - U' \{(\frac{d\psi}{dp} R_r + \psi q R_r')\}$$

Hence a sufficient condition for $\phi'(p) < 0$ is that relative risk aversion be equal to or less than unity and non-decreasing. A number of theoretically desirable utility functions have this property; among them are the constant absolute risk aversion function (when the degree of risk aversion is less than or equal to one), $U(\pi) = A - e^{-\gamma\pi}$, $\gamma \leq 1$; the logrithmic utility function, $U(\pi) = \log(\pi)$, and the constant relative risk aversion function, $U(\pi) = \pi^{\alpha}$, $o < \alpha < 1$.

The use of the latter two functions require that we restrict the argument of the utility function to be non-negative. One approach is to assume that the firm maximizes $U(A + \pi)$ where A is some constant greater than or equal to minimum profits. As $\min(\pi) \geq -c(q)$, this formulation avoids the problem raised by fixed costs, since we then have $\psi = (pq - c'\cdot q)\ /\ (A + pq - c(q)) \leq 1$ for all $p > 0$, whether or not we allow fixed costs.

Despite the impossibility of making categorical statements about the effect of an RS type of increase in risk on output, our presumption is that such a change in the price distribution will in fact reduce output in virtually all but a few extreme cases. This conclusion is strengthened by a graphical approach to the problem, which moreover provides considerable insight into the interactions between the form of the utility function and the type of change in risk. Such an approach, moreover, shows why Sandmo, Batra, and others have derived more categorical results with more limited definitions of increases in risk, as well as providing some intuitive understanding of how extreme, perverse cases like that considered in Appendix A may arise.

Figures 3.4a through 3.4f show six members of the class of $\phi(p)$ functions for concave (risk averse) utility functions characterized by $U''' \geq 0$. The dashed line in each figure is $dH_2(p)$, the integrator of 3.10, or alternatively $H_1 dp$, which is simply the difference between the cumulative distributions $G(p)$ and $F(p)$, with p as the integrator. Figure 3.4a represents the quadratic case; as $U''' = 0$, $\phi(p)$ is linear and decreasing over all p. Figure 3.4b represents $\phi(p)$ when $U''' > 0$, but is not sufficiently strong enough for $\phi(p)$ to attain a minimum in the interval [a,b]. When sufficient conditions exist for $\phi'(p) < 0$ for all p, as is the case, for example when $U(\pi) = \log (A + \pi)$ or $U(\pi) - (A + \pi)^{\alpha}$ we have a $\phi(p)$ like that shown in Figure 3.4c.

In all three of these cases the second mean value theorem is applicable, permitting us to conclude that $A < 0$ for any change in risk satisfying the RS conditions, implying that such an increase in uncertainty will always decrease output. In figure 3.4d and 3.4e $\phi(p)$ is not strictly decreasing, eliminating such a straightforward proof that $A < 0$. There is an important difference between the two cases, however. Both may be divided into three regions, I, II, and III, corresponding to intervals in which $\phi(p)$ and $dH_2(p)$ respectively are both positive, positive and

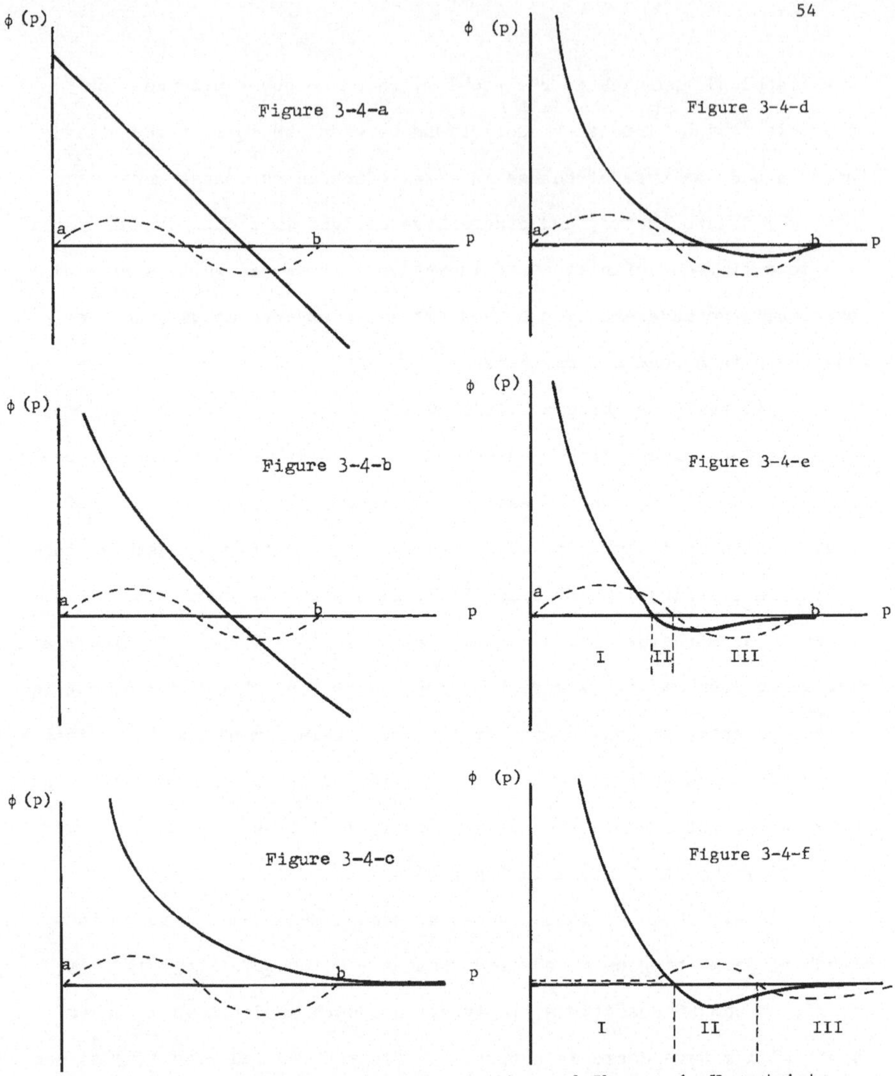

Interactions Between the Utility Function and Changes in Uncertainty

negative, and both negative. As $A = -\int_a^b \phi(p)\, dH_2(p)$, it is clear that regions I and III, which account for most of the value of the integral, will contribute to its negativity, while there will be a positive effect from region II. In Figure 3.4d we may prove that $A < 0$ as follows. As the integral over [a,b] is

$$A = -\int_a^b \phi(p)\, dH_2(p) = -\int_a^{p_2} \phi(p)\, dH_2(p) - \int_{p_2}^b \phi(p)\, dH_2(p)$$

or applying the mean value theorem to the first integral on the RHS,

$$A = -\phi(a) \int_a^{p_o} dH_2(p) - \phi(p_2) \int_{p_o}^{p_2} dH_2(p) - \phi(p)\, dH_2(p)$$

where p_o is some p in the interval $[a,p_2]$. As $\phi(a) > 0$, the RS conditions guarantee the negativity of the first term, while $\phi(p_2) = 0$ eliminate the middle one. As $\phi(p)$ and $dH_2(p)$ are both negative over $[p_2,b]$, we must have $A < 0$.

This particular case provides a graphic confirmation of the theorem first proved by McCall for the constant-risk aversion case and extended by Sandmo to all risk averters that the firm will produce less under uncertainty than it will when facing a certain output price equal to the expected value of the distribution of the uncertain price. If we consider the degenerate distribution f(p), with $f(\mu) = 1$ and $f(p) = 0$ for $p \neq \mu$, then we may produce an RS mean preserving spread by transferring some of the mass of the distribution towards the tails, leaving the mean unchanged. This will yield cumulative distributions like those shown in Figure 3.5a. The difference between these distributions, equal to $H_1(p)$, is shown in Figure 3.5b.

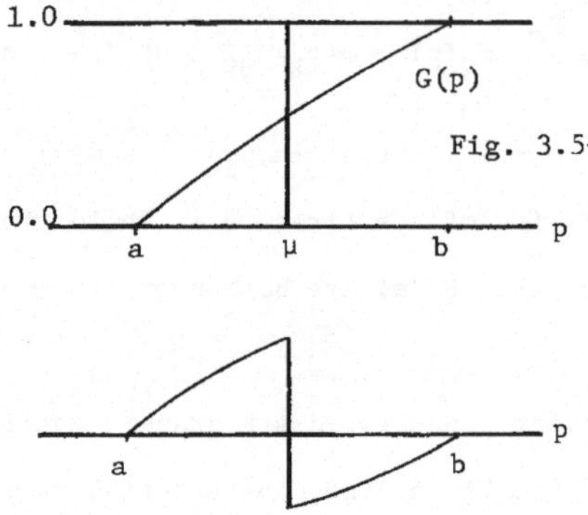

Fig. 3.5-a

Fig. 3.5-b

A Mean Preserving Spread from Certainty

Under certainty, we know that the firm will produce an output such that $c'(q) = \mu$, where μ is the certain output price. Hence $\phi(\mu)$ is strictly positive if the initial situation is one of price certainty, becoming negative only at some $p > \mu$. This is the situation depicted in Figure 3.4d, for which we have shown that $A < 0$. As any type of mean preserving spread away from the degenerate certain "distribution" will satisfy the RS conditions, it is clear that certainty output must exceed output under uncertainty for any risk-averse firm.

Figure 3.4e depicts a situation in which a categorical proof that $A < 0$ along previous lines is not possible. Although it is clear that as drawn $A < 0$ in this case as well, since the small positive effect of the middle region on A is heavily dominated by the negative effect of the other two regions, it suggests how perverse cases might arise.

The examples shown in Figure 3.4a through 3.4e all assume a relatively well-behaved mean-preserving spread, such as that produced by the Sandmo-Batra multiplicative approach. As noted earlier, the RS conditions allow much broader types of changes in the distributions of the random variables, requiring only that the integral of the difference between the cumulative distributions of the riskier and less risky distributions be non-negative. One such change is shown in Figure 3.4f, with the $\phi(p)$ function of Figure 3.4e. It should be noted that such a case is likely to be rare for several reasons. First, as noted above, the restrictions on both the utility function and the cost functions must be strong enough to yield a minimum point for $\phi(p)$ not simply in the interval [a,b], but at a p small enough that $dH_2(p)$ is generally positive. Second, and equally important, the first order conditions severely restrict the interval in which $\phi(p) = 0$. As q is chosen so that $c'(q) \leq \mu$ (with equality under certainty or risk neutrality), either a high degree of risk aversion or initial (pre-spread) uncertainty or both must obtain for c' to be substantially lower than μ. As $\phi(p) > 0$ at c' and $dH_2(p)$ is generally negative for $p > \mu$, $\mu - c'$ must be large enough to include most of the interval in which $dH_2(p) > 0$. Although probably rather remote for these reasons, such a situation is represented by Figure 3.4f, and it is this type of perverse case which provides the counter-example to the Batra-Ullah assertion which is presented in Appendix A.

Although we do not pursue the matter here, the graphical approach used here may be applied to the $U''' < 0$ case as well, with similar results. This case appears to be of little theoretical importance, since it rather implausibly requires absolute risk aversion to be increasing. A second objection is that the interval over which $U(\pi)$ is concave is upper-bounded.

3-2. Inventories and Increasing Price Uncertainty

Our development of the model of the firm under price uncertainty has been essentially static to this point, with no consideration of the impact of past decisions by the firm or the influence of different and possibly more favorable options open to it in the future. The ability to carry output from one period to another forces us to view the firm dynamically, and raises the interesting possibility that increasing price variability could actually benefit the firm which produces output at a steady rate, stockpiling it for sale only in periods when the output price is high.

The general problem of the behavior of the firm with the ability to reserve output in the presence of price uncertainty has been investigated by Zabel; although he does not address the question of the impact of increasing price uncertainty, his basic model lends itself to such an analysis. Zabel examines both the firm under price uncertainty which simply maximizes the expected present value of profits over a given time period and the risk-averse firm which maximizes the expected utility of present value.[3] Despite the fact that the latter case more closely resembles the model we have developed in preceding sections, a specific solution is possible only with a restriction on the utility function which makes it multiplicatively separable by time period. Zabel uses this property of the constant-absolute-risk-aversion utility function $U(PV) = -e^{-\gamma\pi}$ (where inessential constants are omitted) to show that: a) sales reservation will occur at or below a critical price, which is a function of all future discounted utility of profits, b) that the risk averse firm will produce less than the risk-neutral ($\gamma = 0$) firm, given the same price distribution and technology, and c) that increases in risk aversion will <u>ceteris paribus</u> reduce output.

As our principal purpose is to show the possible impact of increasing price variability in the RS sense may have on optimal output when inventories are permitted, we consider the simpler case in which the firm maximizes the expected present value of profits. This is equivalent to assuming that its utility function is linear, so that it is neutral with respect to risk. In line with the RS definition of increasing risk, we assume that p has an upper bound, b.

The firm's problem is then to maximize

$$E\,[PV] = \int_a^b \int_a^b \cdots \int_a^b \pi_1 + \alpha\pi_2 + \ldots + \alpha^{n-1}\pi_n \; dF(p_1)\; dF(p_2) \ldots dF(p_n) \tag{3.12}$$

Profits in any period are then

$$\pi_i = p_i s_i - c(q) - k(q) + inv_{i-1} - s_i \tag{3.13}$$

in which s_i are sales in the ith period and k the cost per unit of output added to inventory in the ith period. The argument of k(•) in 3.13 reflects the fact that sales plus additions to inventory in any period must equal inventory from the preceding period plus output in the current period. We assume k is linear.

The essential feature of the firm's problem in a dynamic context is that it makes its present value-maximizing decisions sequentially; given a price p_i the firm will sell its output q, or carry it to the succeeding period, assuming q has been set at the beginning of the n periods. As the firm's problem is essentially the same for all $n \geq 2$ period situations, we consider here only the two period case, although its generalization is apparent. As a further simplification, we assume no initial inventories.

In the second, final period all output and inventory will be sold at any price if present value is to be maximized, so that $s_2 = q + inv_1$1 Expected present value of profits in the second price is consequently

$$E\ [U(PV_2)] = \alpha_a\int^b p_2(q + inv_1) - c(q)\ dF(p_2)$$

$$= \alpha[\bar{p}\ (q + inv_1) - c(q)] \qquad (3.14)$$

as no inventory storage costs are incurred.

The firm's problem in the first period, given both an output level a and expected profits as shown in 3.14 is to choose s_1 and inv_1 so as to maximize present value for a given p_1, or

$$\max E(PV|p_1) = p_1 s_1 - c(q) - k(q - s_1) + \alpha[p(q + inv_1) - c(q)] \quad (3.15)$$

subject to $s_1 + inv_1 \leq q$. Forming the Lagrangian, we have

$$\frac{\partial \ell}{\partial s_1} = (p + k') - \lambda \leq 0 \quad (3.16a) \qquad s_1 \frac{\partial \ell}{\partial s_1} = 0 \quad (3.16b)$$

$$\frac{\partial \ell}{\partial inv_1} = \alpha\bar{p} - \lambda \leq 0 \quad (3.17a) \qquad inv_1 \frac{\partial \ell}{\partial inv} = 0 \quad (3.17b)$$

$$\frac{\partial \ell}{\partial \lambda} = q - s_1 - inv_1 \geq 0 \quad (3.18a) \qquad \lambda \frac{\partial \ell}{\partial \lambda} = 0 \quad (3.18b)$$

By our assumption of linearity for k(•), the first term in 3.16a is strictly positive, requiring that $\lambda > 0$ for the inequality to hold. Hence 3.18a is a strict equality, so that if $s_1 = 0$, $inv_1 > 0$ or if $inv_1 = 0$, $s_1 > 0$ for all positive outputs. Let $p_1 + k' > \alpha\bar{p}$. Then 3.17a must be a strict inequality, and by 3.17b, $inv_1 = 0$, requiring that all output and existing inventories be sold in that period. If $p_1 + k' < \alpha\bar{p}$, then 3.16a is a strict inequality, requiring that $s_1 = 0$ and $inv_1 = q + inv_o$. The firm's decision rule may be summarized as

$$\left.\begin{array}{l} s_1 = q \\ inv_1 = 0 \end{array}\right\} \quad \text{if} \quad p_1 \geq \alpha\bar{p} - k'$$

$$\left.\begin{array}{l} s_1 = 0 \\ inv_1 = q \end{array}\right\} \quad \text{if} \quad p_1 < \alpha\bar{p} - k' \qquad (3.19)$$

We may then use this rule to find the expected value of the firm's profits in both periods at the beginning of period 1 before either p_1 or p_2 is known.

$$E(PV) = q \left[\int_{\alpha\bar{p}-k'}^{b} p_1 \, dF(p_1) + (\alpha\bar{p} - k') \int_{a}^{\alpha\bar{p}-k'} dF(p_1) \right] + \\ + \alpha\bar{p} \, q - (1 + \alpha) \, c(q) \qquad (3.20)$$

The bracketed term in 3.20 may be interpreted as the expected price received for first-period production; should p_1 fall short of the discounted price in the second period minus storage costs, then the expected price is simply that price, as the firm reserves output. For any higher p_1, the firm will do better selling the output concurrently.

At the beginning of the two-period case, the firm will choose an optimal q maximizing expected present value given the sales strategy derived above. First-order conditions from 3.20 then require that

$$\frac{dE(PV)}{dq} = \left[\int_{\alpha\bar{p}-k'}^{b} p \, dF(p) + (\alpha\bar{p} - k') \int_{a}^{\alpha\bar{p}-k'} dF(p) \right] \\ + \alpha\bar{p} - (1 + \alpha) \, c'(q) = 0 \qquad (3.21)$$

We now consider a mean-preserving change in the distribution of p from f(p) to g(p) of the RS type; that is, one which satisfies the conditions

$$\int_0^b p \, dF(p) = \bar{p} = \int_0^b p \, dG(p) \tag{3.22}$$

and

$$\int_a^y [G(p) - F(p)] \, dp = \int_a^y H_1(p) \, dp = H_2(y) \geq 0 \tag{3.23}$$

for all $y \leq b$.

After the RS transformation, the new first-order condition will be

$$\frac{dE(PV)}{dq} = [\int_{\alpha\bar{p}-k'}^{b} p \, dG(p) + (\alpha\bar{p} + k') \int_a^{\alpha\bar{p}-k'} dG(p)]$$

$$+ \alpha\bar{p} - (1 + \alpha) \, c'(\hat{q}) = 0 \tag{3.21'}$$

Subtracting 3.21 from 3.21' and rearranging, we have

$$\int_{\bar{p}-k'}^{b} p \, dH_1(p) + (\alpha\bar{p} - k') \int_a^{\alpha\bar{p}-k'} dH_1(p) = (1 + \alpha)[c'(\hat{q}) - c'(q)] \tag{3.24}$$

and using 5.22

$$\int_a^{\alpha\bar{p}-k'} (\alpha\bar{p} - k' - p) \, dH_1(p) = (1 + \alpha)[c'(\hat{q}) - c'(q)] \tag{3.24'}$$

Integrating the left-hand side by parts yields

$$(\alpha\bar{p} - k' - p) \, H_1(p) \Big|_a^{\alpha\bar{p}-k'} - \int_a^{\alpha\bar{p}-k'} H_1(p) \, d(\alpha\bar{p} - k' - p)$$

As the first term is zero, we have

$$\int_a^{\alpha\bar{p}-k'} H_1(p)\,dp = (1+\alpha)[c'(\hat{q}) - c'(q)] \qquad (3.25)$$

By 3.23 the left-hand side of 3.25 is positive, requiring $c'(\hat{q}) > c'(q)$. Under the assumption of increasing marginal cost output will therefore increase as a result of an RS transformation in the distribution of output price, provided that inventory costs k' and the discount rate r are sufficiently low so that $\alpha\bar{p} - k' > 0$. Where these factors are high, so that $\alpha p - k' < 0$, then an RS spread in the distribution of p will have no effect on firm output, as the costs of carrying first period output to the next period outweigh the discounted returns.

Although this conclusion provides an interesting qualification of the results of our analysis of the firm under price uncertainty, it rests on several restrictive and possibly unacceptable assumptions. First, we have assumed that the distribution of p is the same in each time period. In a sense this is an extreme form of regressive expectations formation, since it implicitly assumes that if the firm observes price p_i in the ith period lower than its expectation, then it will behave as though its expectation is correct and unchanged by recent events, reserving output for sale at an anticipated higher price. A more satisfactory model might make the firm's expectation of the future price adapt to realized present prices. In such a case it is clear that much, if not all of the potentially positive impact of greater price variability on output would be lost. This argument would appear especially relevant if there are understandable structural and non-random reasons for the price change. In the context of exchange rate uncertainty, a policy of continuing failure to adjust the nominal rate in the presence of inflation suggests that the firm would not regard the real rate in next period as randomly drawn from a distribution unchanged by recent events. A series of temporally correlated low prices would raise the possibility of considerably lower present value resulting from sales reservation than would result from the sale of output as it is produced.

A second criticism arises from the assumption of linearity of storage costs. A more realistic formulation would impose a storage capacity constraint on the system described by 3.15-3.18. In low price periods ($p_1 < \alpha\bar{p} - k'$), this constraint may become operative, implying that we may simultaneously have $s_1 > 0$ and inv_1 = capacity > 0. With such a capacity constraint, the expected present value of profits in the two period case must be rewritten as

$$E(PV) = q \left[\int_{\alpha\bar{p}-k'}^{b} p_1 \, dF(p_1) \right] + cap(\alpha\bar{p} - k') \left[\int_{a}^{\alpha\bar{p}-k'} dF(p_1) \right] + (q - cap) \int_{a}^{\alpha\bar{p}-k'} p_1 \, dF(p_1) + \alpha\bar{p}q - (1 + \alpha) \, c(q) \qquad (3.20')$$

As can be seen from this capacity-constrained version, for low capacity the second term becomes small, reducing the expected value of profits in the limit to

$$E(PV) = q \int_{a}^{b} p_1 \, dF(p_1) + \alpha\bar{p}q - (1 + \alpha) \, c(q)$$

$$= (1 + \alpha) \, (\bar{p}q - c(q))$$

This is simply the model of preceding sections under risk neutrality.

The introduction of risk aversion into the analysis of the firm with storage capacity clearly juxtaposes the output-increasing effect of price variability due to sales reservation possibilities and the output-decreasing effect shown in previous sections. In his examination of the risk-averse firm which may store output, Zabel has shown that for the special case of the firm characterized by the constant-absolute risk aversion utility function $U(\pi) = -e^{-\gamma\pi}$, increases in risk aversion result in a ceteris paribus decrease in output, confirming McCall's earlier results in the one period case. We have shown that even under risk neutrality the output-increasing effects of greater price variability are limited and possibly eliminated by low storage capacity, high marginal storage costs, and high discount rates. As risk aversion increases, these limitations become more severe, since the firm will reserve output in a period of low prices only if the utility-weighted gain from sales at subsequent higher prices is greater than the utility weighted gain from current sales. Since risk aversion is equivalent to declining marginal utility of profits, the critical price at which sales reservation occurs must be higher than in the risk-neutral case. This is equivalent to raising k' or decreasing α, thus moving the firm's behavior toward the no-storage, one-period model of preceding sections, in which an RS increase in price uncertainty resulted in an unambiguous decrease in optimal output.

The presence of inventory possibilities, however, does impose an interesting limitation on the conclusions of preceding sections. Where storage capacity is large, unit storage costs low, and the discount rate low, we cannot a priori rule out the possibility that a firm might increase output as a result of an RS price uncertainty increase, even if its attitude towards its uncertain present value could be described by a risk averse (concave) utility function.

3-3. Alternatives to the Expected Utility Hypothesis

Several recent studies of firm behavior under uncertainty, including those of Sandmo and of Batra and Ullah, have interpreted the expected utility hypothesis to mean that in a short-run sense their conclusions apply only to small firms managed by one individual. Although they do not pursue this restriction further, this view apparently derives from the well known difficulties in constructing aggregate utility functions. In view of the far-reaching implications of risk aversion in the face of demand uncertainty for the theory of the firm and the preponderance of larger firms in which decisions are made by more than one individual, this apparent limitation deserves examination.

The general development of the theory of economic behavior under uncertainty since the original contributions of Pratt and Arrow[4] has been cast largely in terms of utility functions, since a concave utility function is equivalent to risk aversion by the individual. Applications of the approach to the theory of the firm have almost inevitably assumed that the firm has some "utility of profits" function which is concave. It should be noted, however, that all of the conclusions of recent analyses of the firm under uncertainty, including those proved in preceding sections, follow from the concavity of the firm's objective function (or from concavity and the additional restriction that this function has a non-negative third derivative). Viewed in this way, we may ask what conditions are sufficient for the firm to behave in such a way that its objective function exhibits these properties, rather than chase the will'o'wisp of social indifference curves.

One possibility is simply to eliminate any risk preferring behavior among firm owners or managers, requiring that all individual utility functions be either risk-neutral (linear in profits) or risk-averse (concave in profits). Allowing some non-negative weight for each of the n individuals' preferences in the determination of the firm's objective function, we can write this function $\phi(\pi)$ as

$$\phi(\pi) = \sum_{i=1}^{n} b_i\, U_i(a_i\pi) \qquad 0 \leq a_i \leq 1, \quad b_i \geq 0 \tag{3.26}$$

where the a_i represents the ith individual's share of total profits and b_i the weight his preferences receive in the firm's decision. As a positive-weighted linear function of concave functions, it is clear that $\phi(\pi)$ must also be concave. The existence of one risk-averse U_i (with $b_i \neq 0$), moreover, is then sufficient for ϕ to be strictly concave, as may be seen by twice differentiating (3.12).

Although it is intuitively clear that a mixture of risk-averse and risk-neutral firm managers and owners should be sufficient for a firm's objective function to be concave, risk aversion on the part of one or more individuals is not necessary.

Let us assume that the incomes firm owners receive from its profits are taxed at progressively higher rates. A concave (although not strictly concave) firm objective function can then arise in several ways, even if individuals are risk neutral. Suppose that there are $n \geq 2$ risk-neutral individuals each of whom receives a share a_i of the firm's profits, with no other source of income, where $0 \leq a_1 \leq a_2 \leq \ldots \leq a_n \leq 1$. Income is taxed at t_a on amounts between 0 and $\overline{\pi}$ and at t_b thereafter, where $0 < t_a < t_b < 1$. The net income of the firm's owners is then

$$\phi(\pi) = (1 - t_a) \sum_{i=1}^{k} a_i\pi + (1 - t_b) \sum_{i=k+1}^{N} a_i\pi \qquad (3.27)$$

where $a_i\pi < \overline{\pi}$ for individuals $i \leq k$ and $a_i\pi \geq \overline{\pi}$ for individuals $i \geq k+1$. As profits increase, individual k moves into the higher tax bracket, followed by individual k-1 and so on until $a_1\pi \geq \overline{\pi}$. The net income function is thus characterized by $\phi'(\pi)$ decreasing in π, or concavity. If the a_n, a_{n-1} are large, then these higher-shares owners will move into the higher bracket even with small changes in π, while for large π, even $a_1\pi$, $a_2\pi$, etc. exceed $\overline{\pi}$, so that $\phi'(\pi)$ approaches $(1-t_b)$. The objective function thus approximates a declining absolute risk aversion utility function ($\phi''' > 0$), with $\phi'' = 0$ for large π.

A variant of this approach is to permit the a_i to be equal, but to consider income derived from the firm's profit the only source of the individual's income. If the distribution of all other income is continuous, then increases in π will push successive individuals from the t_a bracket into the t_b bracket, yielding an objective function similar to that above.

A second approach, again not requiring individual risk aversion is rather in the spirit of Berle and Means or Williamson, in that it recognizes a difference in the respective objectives of owners and managers.[5] Williamson suggests that the managers will behave as though constrained to earn some minimum profit, but that above that point "discretionary profits" will be spent for larger staff, various managerial emoluments, and other purposes unrelated to owners' interests. The firm's objective function, in this case representing the utility of profits for management, will then be characterized by marginal utility approaching infinity for low profits at or near the minimum level acceptable to shareholders. As discretionary profits increase, their utility would then presumably fall, as the utility of greater staff, more opulent executive suites and other management rewards falls. This effect would be reinforced by any tendency for individual factors, notably labor, to link demands for higher remuneration to increases in the firm's profits. There appears to be some empirical support for this hypothesis, which even alone could give rise to a concave firm objective function.[6]

Still another approach, suggested by the work of Hicks and Scitovsky is to incorporate explicitly leisure into the utility functions of managers or owners.[7] Assuming this function to be linearly homogeneous is then equivalent to the assumption that the firm's objective function is concave in profits, assuming the amount of available leisure time is fixed. It should be noted, moreover, that linear homogeneity is sufficient for the function to exhibit non-increasing absolute risk aversion.

The hypotheses outlined here do not constitute any rigorous model of firm behavior or goals. They are presented instead as justifications for our use in the rest of this study of a concave firm objective function. Whether or not one calls this a utility function is not really the point; our argument is simply that if the firm is assumed to be managed in any sort of purposive, goal-directed manner, the assumption of risk aversion with respect to profits is a robust hypothesis which can rest on a variety of plausible assumptions. These justifications, moreover, hardly limit us to one-owner or manager type firms. There is a strong presumption in most of them, in fact, that risk aversion would actually increase as the number of participants in the firm's decision making process increases.

FOOTNOTES FOR CHAPTER III

1. See Agnar Sandmo, "On the Theory of the Competitive Firm under Price Uncertainty," Amer. Econ. Rev., March 1971, 65-73 and R. Batra and A. Ullah, "Competitive Firm and the Theory of Input Demand under Price Uncertainty," Jour. Pol. Econ., May/June 1974, 537-548. The "well behaved" production function used by Batra and Ullah assumes $Q = F(K,L)$, with $F_i > 0$, $F_{ii} > 0$, $F_{ii}F_{jj} - F_{ij}^2 > 0$, where $i,j = K,L$, $i \neq j$.

2. See M. Rothschild and J. Stiglitz, "Increasing Risk: A Definition," Journal Econ. Theory, Sept. 1970, 2, 225-243.

3. The model of the present-value maximizing firm is developed in E. Zabel, "A Dynamic Model of the Competitive Firm," Int. Econ. Rev., Vol. 8, June 1967, and that of the risk-averse firm in E. Zabel, "Risk and the Competitive Firm," Jour. Econ. Theory, Vol. 3, Sept. 1971, 109-133.

4. J. Pratt, "Risk Aversion in the Small and the Large," Econometrica, 32, 1964, 127-136 and K. Arrow, Aspects of a Theory of Risk Bearing, Helsinki, 1965.

5. A. Berle and G. Means, The Modern Corporation and Private Profits, N.Y., MacMillan, 1933. A more recent version is in O. E. Williamson, "Managerial Discretion and Business Behavior," Amer. Econ. Rev., Vol. 53, No. 5, Dec. 1963, 1032-1057.

6. See, for example, G. L. Perry, Unemployment, Money Wage Rates, and Inflation, Cambridge, MIT Press, 1966.

7. J. R. Hicks, "The Theory of Monopoly," Econometrica, Vol. 3, Jan. 1935, 1-10, and T. Scitovsky, "A Note on Profit Maximization and its Implications," Rev. Econ. Studies, Vol. 11, No. 1, Winter 1943, 57-60.

CHAPTER IV

MEASURING CHANGES IN UNCERTAINTY

It was shown in Chapter III that the concept of increasing risk introduced by Rothschild and Stiglitz permits us to derive a number of comparative statics theorems about the effects of changes in the degree of uncertainty. The concept by itself, however, does not permit any immediate or direct empirical application, despite its theoretical generality. If we limit consideration of changes in uncertainty to multiplicative spreads of the type considered in Chapter II, which are a special case of the Rothschild-Stiglitz class of mean preserving spreads, it might be possible to use variance as a measure of uncertainty, since changes in variance will vary directly with changes in the multiplicative shift parameter γ, in $p^* = \gamma p + \theta$, where p and p* are respectively the random variables before and after the change in uncertainty.

There is no reason to believe, however, that changes in distributions will always, or indeed, often fit within the confines of mathematical convenience. As is now fairly widely recognized by economic theorists, the characterization of uncertainty in terms of variance may be inconsistent with the expected utility hypothesis which underlies the theory developed in the preceding chapters.[1] This is due to the fact that the expected utility maximizing agent may respond to changes in all of the parameters of a distribution, and not simply to changes in the mean and variance. Identification of variance with uncertainty or risk will thus be consistent with the expected utility hypothesis only in the special cases in which either

(1) the distribution is completely characterized by its first two moments, as is the case with the normal, or (2) utility is a function of only the first two moments, as is the case with the quadratic.[2]

The central purpose of this chapter is the development of means of characterizing distributions in an econometrically meaningful and operational way at the level of generality of the Rothschild-Stiglitz definition. It thus provides the crucial link between a developing body of theory dealing with economic behavior under uncertainty, based on the expected utility hypothesis, and our empirical experience, in which uncertainty is ever present, yet rarely examined in a theoretically satisfactory way.

The restrictive assumptions of either normality or quadratic utility are generally viewed as the price which must be paid to obtain any operational and empirically applicable measure of uncertainty. Perhaps the most important message of this chapter is that this price is not necessary. Under the general assumption of concavity, many distributions may be ordered. If we adopt the highly plausible assumption that absolute risk aversion in the Pratt-Arrow sense is non-increasing, then an even larger set of distributions is orderable. Finally, for virtually all commonly used utility functions which exhibit non-increasing absolute risk aversion, an even larger ordering of distributions is possible, as is a corresponding index of uncertainty consistent with the expected utility hypothesis.

The basic approach to the ordering of distributions, using the concepts of first, second, and third degree stochastic dominance, is developed in Section 4.1. This approach is then generalized to nth degree stochastic dominance in Section 4.2. The application of these rules to sets of empirical data is then examined in Section 4.3, and the consistency of the estimators proved in Section 4.4. The stochastic dominance approach to the measurement of uncertainty or risk is justified in part by the presumption of widespread non-normality in the distributions of economic data. For this reason, the application in Section 4.5 of the approach to the data of interest, the real cruzeiro-dollar exchange rate, is preceded by a series of tests of the hypothesis of normality. Despite the rejection of this hypothesis, it is shown that the stochastic dominance rules can effectively identify a marked reduction in real price uncertainty following Brazil's adoption of the crawling peg in 1968.

The stochastic dominance rules provide a partial, or in some cases, complete ordering of distributions in a qualitative sense. They do not provide, however, a quantitative index of uncertainty. This problem is addressed in Section 4.6, in which stochastic dominance based indices of uncertainty are derived. From both a theoretical and an operational point of view, the most important result in this section is the demonstration that these indices may be expressed in terms of the moments of the probability distributions from which the observations are drawn. Section 4.7 applies this method to the real exchange rate data to derive the indices of uncertainty used in the econometric estimates of Chapter VI. Finally, some extensions and limitations of the approach are discussed in Section 4.8. A listing of the FORTRAN-IV program developed to apply the methods presented in this chapter is provided in Appendix B.

4.1 Stochastic Dominance Rules for Choices Involving Risk

The expected utility hypothesis used in the comparative statics analysis in the preceding chapters may also be used to derive explicit criteria for the choice among uncertain alternatives by risk averse individuals. As it is convenient to derive these rules using Stieltjes integrals, we note below several definitions and theorems used in this and subsequent sections:[3]

A) If the functions f(x) and s(x) are defined on the interval (a,b), then a sufficient condition for the existence of the Stieltjes integral $\int_a^b f(x)\,ds(x)$ is that one of the functions s or f is continuous and the other is of bounded variation on (a,b).

B) Stieltjes integration by parts

$$\int_a^b f(x)\,ds(x) = \left| f(x)\,s(x) \right|_a^b - \int_a^b f'(x)\,ds(x)$$

C) Reduction to a Rieman integral

$$\int_a^b f(x)\,ds(x) = \int_a^b f(x)\,s'(x)\,dx$$

D) If $F(x) = \int_a^b f(x)\,ds(x)$ and f is continuous, then $F'(x)$ exists wherever $s'(x)$ exists and is equal to $F'(x) = f(x)\,s'(x)$.

E) If s(x) is a step function defined on (a,b) with a jump, s_k, at x_k and f(x) is continuous, then

$$\int_a^b f(x)\,ds(x) = \sum_{k=1}^{n} f(x_k)\,s_k$$

where $a \leq x_1 \leq x_2 \leq \ldots\ldots x_k \leq \ldots\ldots x_n \leq b$

Let an individual face two uncertain prospects, 1 and 2, whose respective densities are f(x) and g(x). As our argument is conducted using Stieltjes integrals, these densities may be either discrete or continuous. With no loss of economic realism, we assume that the random variable is of bounded variation on the interval [a,b]. The individual is assumed to have a utility function, U(x), which for the moment we simply assume to be concave (risk averse), with $U'(x) > 0$ and $U''(x) < 0$. The expected utility of the first prospect is then

$$E(U)_1 = \int_a^b U(x)\, f(x)\, dx = \int_a^b U(x)\, dF(x) \tag{4.1}$$

with a corresponding definition for $E(U)_2$. Following Hadar and Russells' generalization of the Von-Neumann-Morgenstern expected utility hypothesis,[4] prospect 1 is preferred to 2 if

$$E(U_1) - E(U_2) = \int_a^b U(x)\, [f(x) - g(x)]dx > 0 \tag{4.2}$$

The economic sense of (4.2) is that the individual will prefer the prospect whose distribution attaches greater probabilities to higher values of x. Defining $H_o(x) = f(x) - g(x)$ and $H_k(x) = \int_a^b H_{k-1}(y)\, dy$, for k = 1,...N, we may rewrite the RHS of (4.2) as

$$\int_a^b U(x)\, H_o(x)\, dx = \int_a^b U(x)\, dH_1(x) > 0 \tag{4.2'}$$

Integrating by parts and noting that $H_1(a) = H_1(b) = 0$, we have

$$- \int_a^b U'(x)\, H_1(x)\, dx \tag{4.3}$$

As $U'(x) > 0$, a sufficient condition for 1 to be preferred to 2 is that

$$H_1(x) \leq 0 \quad \text{for all } x, \text{ with } H_1(x) < 0 \text{ for at least one } x. \quad (4.4)$$

This condition, originally stated by Quirk and Saposnik, and termed First Degree Stochastic dominance by Hadar and Russell, requires that the cumulative distributions of 1 and 2 do not intersect.[5] FSD is consequently of limited usefulness, since the distributions of any non-identical pair of uncertain prospects of equal expected value will cross at least once.

As this is precisely the case of most interest in the analysis of risk, and is the basis of the concept of a "mean-preserving spread" in a probability distribution, we assume in what follows that $\mu_1 = \mu_2$. This is equivalent to $H_2(b) = 0$.[6]

Using (B) and (C), we may rewrite (4.3) as

$$- |U'(x)\ H_2(x)|_a^b + \int_a^b U''(x)\ H_2(x)\ dx$$

For distributions of equal means, $H_2(a) = H_2(b) = 0$, and the expression reduces to

$$\int_a^b U''(x)\ H_2(x)\ dx \quad (4.5)$$

By our assumption of risk aversion, $U''(x) < 0$, so that a sufficient condition for 1 to be preferred to 2 is that

$$H_2(x) \leq 0 \quad \text{for all } x, \text{ with strict inequality at least once} \quad (4.6)$$

This condition, termed Second Degree Stochastic Dominance by Hadar and Russell, is identical to the Rothschild and Stiglitz "integral condition", one of their three equivalent characterizations of a mean preserving spread. It should be noted that the rule remains sufficient even when $\mu_1 = \mu_2$.

Although SSD is a considerably more useful and powerful rule than is FSD, it induces only a partial ordering, and for many pairs of distributions, cannot be used to establish preference under the single assumption of risk aversion. If we adopt the generally accepted hypothesis that absolute risk aversion is non-increasing in x, then $U'''(x) > 0$.[7] Restricting admissible concave utility functions by this hypothesis permits the derivation of a more powerful rule, Third Degree Stochastic Dominance (TSD), first shown by Whitmore.[8]

Integrating (4.5) by parts, and noting that $H_3(a) = 0$, we have

$$U''(b)\cdot H_3(b) \quad - \int_a^b U'''(x)\cdot H_3(x)\,dx \qquad (4.7)$$

Hence a sufficient condition for 1 to be preferred to 2 by any individual whose absolute aversion to risk is non-increasing is

$$H_3(x) \leq 0 \quad \text{for all x, with strict inequality at least once} \qquad (4.8)$$

If we add the restriction that $H_2(b) \leq 0$, the rule may be extended to cases in which $\mu_1 = \mu_2$. As SSD is sufficient, but not necessary for TSD, it is clear that the latter rule orders a larger set of uncertain prospects, increasing its potential usefulness.

4.2. Generalized Stochastic Dominance

In the preceding section it was shown that the hypothesis of non-increasing absolute risk aversion permits the derivation of a rule for choice under uncertainty which is more powerful than that derived simply by assuming risk aversion. The hypothesis is hardly objectionable, indeed, assuming the contrary leads to conclusions at variance with both intuition and observation.[9]

Although it might appear that nothing more can be said about preferences under uncertainty without placing additional explicit and probably unacceptable restrictions on the form of the utility function, this conclusion may be unduly pessimistic. In this section we consider the possibility of more powerful orderings than the TSD criterion, based on a characteristic of a wide class of utility functions which exhibit non-increasing absolute risk aversion.

In his seminal article introducing the concept of absolute risk aversion, Pratt derived a large family of utility functions which are strictly decreasingly risk averse for $x > 0$, and noted that except for this family, utility functions for which absolute risk aversion is decreasing are difficult to find. Among the members of this class of transcendental functions are such convenient and widely used forms as $U(x) = (x + d)^q$, where $d > 0$, $0 < q < 1$, and $U(x) = \log(x + d)$, where $d > 0$, as well as less common ones, such as $U(x) = \arctan(ax + b)$, or $U(x) = [1 + (ax + b)^{-2}]^{-\frac{1}{2}}$, where $a > 0$, $b > 1$. If the multiple argument Cobb-Douglas and CES functions, often employed as utility functions, are reduced to a single argument by holding the other argument constant, they may be seen to be members of this class as well.

Although it does not appear easy to prove a general theorem to this effect, an important characteristic of this class of decreasingly risk averse utility funccions is that their higher order derivatives alternate in sign. This feature permits the derivation of stochastic dominance rules up to an arbitrary degree, following the approach of the preceding section. Continuing the integration by parts of (4.7), and using the fact that $H_k(a) = 0$, $k = 1,\ldots N$, we may derive the general Nth degree expression for the difference in expected utilities

$$E(U)_1 - E(U)_2 = \sum_{k=1}^{N} (-1)^k \cdot U_k(b) \cdot H_{k+1}(b) + (-1)^{n+1} \int_a^b U_{n+1}(x) \cdot H_{n+1}(x)\, dx \qquad (4.9)$$

where U_k is the kth derivative of the utility function. Use of the alternating sign characteristic of the derivatives of the functions discussed above then permits us to derive the nth degree stochastic dominance rule for Prospect 1 to be preferred to 2:

$H_{n+1}(x) \leq 0$ for all x in a,b with strict inequality at least once, and

$$H_k(b) \leq 0, \qquad k = 1,\ldots.. N \qquad (4.10)$$

As may be seen by repeated integration by parts of the second term on the RHS of (4.9), this residual integral tends to zero as N increases. Hence for suitably large N, the first part of the Nth degree stochastic dominance rule given in (4.10) may be ignored, requiring only the evaluation of the series of integrals $H_k(b)$. If these integrals do not vary in sign, one prospect would be preferred to the other by all individuals whose preferences can be characterized by the family of utility functions discussed above.

The application of higher degree stochastic dominance rules presents a number of problems, some of which are considered in succeeding sections. It is clear, however, that in principle they offer an attractive way of reducing our ignorance about choice under uncertainty. As successively higher degree rules are imposed, the area of ignorance is correspondingly reduced, until all pairs of distributions are either ordered, or shown to be definitively non-orderable, so that no higher order rule is necessary.

4.3 Empirical Application of the Stochastic Dominance Rules

The derivation of the stochastic dominance rules in terms of Stieltjes integrals facilitates their application to sets of discrete observations, which we assume to be drawn from the two distributions we wish to compare. Let us assume we have samples of m and n independent observations from distributions 1 and 2 respectively, with $\mu_1 = \mu_2$. By the assumption of independence, $\text{prob}(X_{1,i}) = 1/m$ and $\text{prob}(X_{2,j}) = 1/n$, where $i = 1,\ldots m$ and $j = 1,\ldots n$. Let X_h, $h = 1,\ldots p$ ($= m+n$) be the set of pooled observations, arranged in ascending order over the interval $[a,b]$, where a,b are respectively the minimum and maximum of the pooled set. Hence for any X_h in $[a,b]$, $X_{1,i} \leq X_h < X_{1,i+1}$ and $X_{2,j} \leq X_h < X_{2,j+1}$, the respective empirical cumulative distributions are $F_m(X_h) = i/m$ and $G_n(X_h) = j/n$. Letting $H_{1,m,n}(X_h) = F_m(X_h) - G_n(X_h)$, it can be seen that $H_{1,m,n}(X_h)$ is a step function of bounded variation on $[a,b]$.[10]

Defining $H_{2,m,n}(X)$ as the integral of $H_{=,m,n}(y)$, y in $[a,b]$, evaluated from a to X, it can be seen that $H_{2,m,n}(X)$ is then a piecewise linear function, defined on $[a,b]$, with its value at X_h, $h = 1,..p$ given by

$$H_{2,m,n}(X_h) = \sum_{k=2}^{h} H_{1,m,n}(X_k)\,(X_k - X_{k-1}) \tag{4.11}$$

since $H_{2,m,n}(X_1) = H_{2,m,n}(a) = 0$. The piecewise linearity of $H_{2,m,n}(X)$ guarantees that maxima and minima will occur only at points on $[a,b]$ where $H_{1,m,n}(X_h) = 0$, corresponding to a proper subset of the m+n sample observations. This fact permits a simple test of the SSD rule, using (4.11). If $H_{2,m,n}(X_h) < 0$ for all h = 1,...p, with strict inequality for at least one h, then the condition is satisfied for the samples drawn. If each sample is representative of the underlying distribution from which it is drawn, we conclude that any risk averter would prefer Prospect 1 to 2. No further restriction on the form of the utility function is necessary; since SSD is sufficient for TSD, it is clear that the latter condition is also satisfied.

As many pairs of samples may yield a value of $H_{2,m,n}(X_h)$ which varies in sign over [a,b], the SSD test given by (4.11) may be inconclusive. The hypothesis of non-increasing absolute risk aversion, as noted above, permits the ranking of some of these distributions by the TSD criterion.

Defining $H_{3,m,n}(X)$ as the integral of $H_{2,m,n}(y)$, evaluated between a and X, it can be seen that $H_{3,m,n}(X)$ is a piecewise quadratic function. Interior maxima or minima, which exist if and only if the SSD criterion (4.11) is failed, will occur at points X' where $H_{2,m,n}(X')$ = 0. This fact allows testing of the TSD condition to be limited to the set X'. At these points, we have

$$H_{3,m,n}(X') = \frac{1}{2}\{\sum_{k=2}^{r} [H_{2,m,n}(X_k) + H_{2,m,n}(X_{k-1})] \cdot (X_k - X_{k-1}) - [H_{2,m,n}(X_r))^2/(H_{2,m,n}(X_r) - H_{2,m,n}(X_{r-1}))] (X_r - X_{r-1}) \} \qquad (4.12)$$

If $H_{3,m,n}(X') \leq 0$ for all X', with strict inequality for at least one X', then the TSD condition is satisfied. On the basis of the samples drawn, we conclude that any individual whose utility function is characterized by non-increasing absolute risk aversion would prefer Prospect 1 to 2.

If the TSD rule is in turn failed, we may apply successively higher rules, following the approach discussed above. A number of points involved in the application of higher degree rules in practice deserve some attention. As the Fourth Degree Stochastic Dominance rule (4SD) is based on a piecewise cubic, derived by integrating the TSD quadratic, maxima or minima will occur at points on $[a,b]$ where the quadratic is zero. In this particular case, this raises no great difficulties, as the roots of each quadratic segment are easily computed. If successively higher rules are applied, however, the problem of determining the roots of the corresponding piecewise polynomial may become computationally burdensome.

This problem is to some extent alleviated by two factors. First, the number of interior maxima or minima of the kth degree piecewise polynomial cannot exceed the number of roots of the k-1 th degree piecewise polynomial, and in fact only exist if the k-1 th rule is not satisfied. Second, for k-degree rules where $k > 3$, we may apply the second part of the general rule (4.10), prior to evaluation of $H_k(x)$. If for any $H_i(b)$, $i \leq k$, $H_i(b)$ and $H_i(X_2)$ have opposite signs, then no ranking of any degree is possible, terminating our search.

4.4. Consistency of the H-estimators

One of the principal advantages of the Rothschild-Stiglitz and Hadar-Russell characterizations of increasing risk is their distribution free nature. While this feature prevents the derivation of small sample properties of the H-estimators in the absence of specific assumptions about the probability distributions from which the samples are drawn, we can show that these estimators converge in probability to the respective SSD and TSD integrals for any two distributions as the sample sizes increase. In this section we present a proof of this proposition, which is a direct consequence of the Glivenko-Cantelli theorem.[11]

Theorem: Let $X_{1,i}$, $i = 1,..m$ and $X_{2,j}$, $j = 1,...n$ be samples of m and n independent observations, distributed respectively as F(x) and G(x). Then for any $\varepsilon > 0$,

$$\lim_{\substack{m \to \infty \\ n \to \infty}} \text{Prob} \{ |H_{2,m,n}(x) - H_2(x)| < \varepsilon \} = 1 \tag{4.12}$$

Proof: Define the empirical distribution $F_m(x) = (1/m) \sum_{i=m}^{m} \emptyset(X_i)$, where $\emptyset(X_i) = 0$ if $X_i \geq x$ and $\emptyset(X_i) = 1$ if $X_i < x$. By the Glivenko-Cantelli theorem, Prob $\{\lim_{m\to\infty} \sup |F_m(x) - F(x)| = 0 \} = 1$ for all x in $[a,b]$. Thus for almost every sample, $F_m(x)$ converges uniformly on $[a,b]$ to F(x).[12] (This theorem, the basis of the Kolmorgorov-Smirnov statistics, in effect states that the probability of a maximum discrepancy between the sample distribution and the population distribution greater than some $\varepsilon > 0$ can be made arbitrarily small for all x by increasing the sample size.) By an identical argument, we may show the almost uniform convergence of $G_n(x)$ to G(x) on $[a,b]$.

As $H_{1,m,n}(x) = F_m(x) - G_n(x)$, there exists some N, dependent only on $\varepsilon > 0$, such that $m > N$, $n > N$, implies $H_1(x) - \varepsilon < H_{1,m,n}(x) < H_1(x) + \varepsilon$ for almost any sample. Hence $H_{1,m,n}(x)$ is almost uniformly convergent to $H_1(x)$ as $m,n \to \infty$. Since $H_{1,m,n}(x)$ is of bounded variation on $[a,b]$, it is integrable.

By definition, $H_{2,m,n}(x) = \int_a^x H_{1,m,n}(t)\,dt$. Applying the uniform convergence theorem, $H_{2,m,n}(x)$ converges almost uniformly to $H_2(x)$ on $[a,b]$.[13] As almost uniform convergence implies convergence in probability, $\operatorname{plim} H_{2,m,n}(x) = H_2(x)$, so that $H_{2,m,n}(x)$ is a consistent estimator of $H_2(x)$.

The extension of the argument to show the almost uniform convergence of $H_{3,m,n}(x)$ to $H_3(x)$ is obvious, since $H_{2,m,n}(x)$ is integrable and almost uniformly convergent. More generally, we may show that $H_{k,m,n}(x)$ is almost uniformly convergent to $H_k(x)$, where k is any positive integer.

4.5 Application of the SD rules to the real cruzeiro-dollar rate

Were all random variables in the economic world distributed normally, as many of our models and econometric procedures implicitly assume, variance would be a completely adequate measure of uncertainty or risk, and the procedures developed in preceding sections not necessary. As our presumption of widespread non-normality is as yet unsupported in this study by any empirical evidence, we address this issue before continuing with the application of the stochastic dominance approach to the variable of central interest in this study, the real cruzeiro-dollar exchange rate.

The real exchange rate, as we have defined it in this study, is simply the nominal rate corrected for inflation in the two countries, or

$$r_t = \frac{nr_t \quad USPI_t}{BPI_t} \tag{4.13}$$

where nr_t is the nominal rate and the $USPI_t$ and BPI_t the respective US and Brazilian wholesale price indices. As monthly data is available for all three variables, a monthly series was constructed for r_t. For most of the 1957-74 period, the real cruzeiro dollar rate is a reasonable reflection of the cruzeiro price for Brazil of the currency of the rest of the world. As the dollar depreciated against the currencies of several currencies of several of Brazil's other major trading partners in the early 1970's, however, the cruzeiro was effectively devalued by more than definition (4.13) would indicate. For this reason the real rate r_t was multiplied by the US$/SDR rate in an attempt to capture some of the added movement in real rates in the early seventies. We may consequently rewrite (4.13) as

$$r_t = \frac{nr_t \; USPI_t \; SDR_t}{BPI_t} \qquad (4.13')$$

The approach usually adopted in this study was to treat each year's twelve monthly observations as a sample from that year's distribution of the real exchange rate. This division of the entire set of observations is to some extent arbitrary, and one could with some justification use samples of other sizes, depending on the periods of interest. The principal reason for choosing a yearly division is its compatibility with other sets of data, among them relative prices, and export and production data, available only on an annual basis. Although larger samples increase the probability that our estimates will be close to the true difference between the two distributions, as was proved in the preceding section, they reduce the number of degrees of freedom available for hypothesis testing with a finite data set. This may be a problem of considerable practical importance, as will be seen in Chapter VI.

In the preliminary examination of the data for normality, three different procedures were used. First, the mean, variance, skewness, and kurtosis were computed for the entire set of 216 monthly observations for the 1957-74 period. If the data were all drawn from a single normal distribution, we would expect the estimate of the skewness to be close to zero, and that of kurtosis to close to three. The results of this type of calculation, however, are only suggestive for two reasons. First, the data might come from a group of normal distributions whose parameters varied over the period ; indeed the hypothesis that the distribution of the real exchange rate altered during the period is the basis of our study. Second, the data might come from some transformation of the normal, such as the log normal, which by an appropriate transformation would permit the application of the mean variance approach to study the effects of uncertainty. For this reason, the statistics were also calculated for three transformations of the variable: natural log, first differences, and logged first differences. In addition, the period was divided into six subperiods of three years each in an attempt to see if the first variable, the real exchange rate, could be approximated by a normal distribution for shorter periods. The results are shown below in Table 4.1.

Table 4.1 Estimates of the Parameters of the Distribution of Real Exchange Rates

Variable and period		Mean	Variance	Skewness	Kurtosis
r_t	1957-74	2.616	.239	1.357	5.012
$\ln r_t$	1957-74	.946	.030	.820	3.714
Δr_t	1957-74	.005	.052	-.528	18.643
$\ln(\frac{r_t}{r_{t-1}})$	1957-74	.002	.005	.500	14.408
r_t	1957-59	2.741	.325	.073	2.485
r_t	1960-62	2.947	.252	1.457	4.016
r_t	1963-65	2.987	.281	.930	2.978

Table 4.1 (continued)

Variable and period		Mean	Variance	Skewness	Kurtosis
r_t	1966-68	2.274	.025	-.429	2.371
r_t	1969-71	2.225	.005	.866	2.602
r_t	1972-74	2.518	.024	-.068	1.411

Although the results shown in the table are only suggestive, they offer little support for the hypothesis of normality during the period. This hypothesis was more formally tested by using two different methods, the Kolmogorov-Smirnov test and the Shapiro-Wilk test.

As the power of the former test is low for small samples, it was only applied to the data set as a whole, and not used for individual years or for three year periods. A two-sided test of the hypothesis was made, using the sample mean and variance to specify the parameters of the hypothesized normal. For 216 observations (or 215 for first differences and logged first differences), the critical maximum distances of the empirical cumulative distribution from the hypothesized normal distribution at the 90, 95, and 99 percent levels are respectively .083, .093, and .111.

Table 4.2 Kolmogorov-Smirnov Test of the Normality Hypothesis

Variable	Distance	Probability
r_t	.1313	.0012
$\ln r_t$	.0918	.0524
Δr_t	.1922	.0001
$\ln (r_t/r_{t-1})$	.1463	.0002

As can be seen from the table, the normal hypothesis can be rejected at a high level of significance for all but the log normal transformation. Even in this case, we can reject the hypothesis at close to the 95 percent level.

To test the hypothesis of normality on a yearly basis, the Shapiro-Wilk test was used. This test, a form of analysis of variance, is generally more powerful than other tests of normality, particularly for small samples. For details of the method and tabulation of the critical values, the reader is referred to Shapiro and Wilk.[14] To accept the hypothesis of normality at the 90 percent level or higher, the computed W statistic would have to exceed .973 for N = 12, while to reject normality at the 90 percent level or higher, W would have to be less than .883. Intermediate values are inconclusive for the significance level chosen.

Table 4.3 Shapiro-Wilk Test for Normality of the Real Exchange Rate by Year

Year	W	Year	W
1957	.921	1966	.918
1958	.963	1967	.941
1959	.932	1968	.960
1960	.925	1969	.929
1961	.956	1970	.944
1962	.821	1971	.827
1963	.949	1972	.817
1964	.826	1973	.868
1965	.947	1974	.883

Note that in no case can the hypothesis of normality be accepted at the 90 percent level. A number of years, however, appear to have been decidedly non-normal, particularly in the early 1960's. Application of the test to ln r_t, Δr_t, and $\ln(r_t/r_{t-1})$ yielded similar results with no year permitting acceptance of the hypothesis of normality. Despite the inconclusiveness of the test for a number of years, it is probably the best suited for our purposes of all three approaches used to examine the hypothesis of normality. The results argue strongly for methods which do not assume normality, which from an empirical viewpoint, is perhaps the greatest virtue of the stochastic dominance approach.

The methods developed in preceding sections were used to write a computer program to perform the stochastic dominance tests on each pair of years between 1957 and 1974. A listing of the program, which also computes some stochastic dominance based indices of uncertainty discussed subsequently, is provided in Appendix B. Table 4.4 shows the results of the ordinal SSD test. A plus sign indicates preference for the row distribution over the column distribution by the SSD criterion. Analogously, a minus sign represents a case in which the column year dominates the row year, while a zero indicates that a ranking on the basis of SSD is impossible. Note that of a total of 153 comparisons, 24 ties occurred.

Table 4.5 shows the analogous results for the TSD test. As noted earlier, even in this case, not all distributions may be ranked; nevertheless, the number of nonrankable pairs is reduced from 24 to 19 using this more powerful rule. Examining either table, we can see clearly the effect of the crawling peg policy in reducing exchange rate uncertainty. All of the years after 1968 dominate or at least tie earlier years,

Table 4.4. Second Degree Stochastic Dominance Matrix for the Real Cruzeiro Dollar Rate

	1957	1958	1959	1960	1961	1962	1963	1964	1965	1966	1967	1968	1969	1970	1971	1972	1973	1974
1957	*	+	-	-	-	+	+	+	-	-	0	-	-	-	-	-	-	-
1958		*	-	-	-	+	0	0	-	-	-	-	-	-	-	-	-	-
1959			*	0	-	+	+	+	-	-	0	-	-	-	-	-	-	-
1960				*	0	+	+	+	-	0	0	-	-	-	-	-	-	-
1961					*	+	+	+	-	0	0	-	-	-	-	-	-	-
1962						*	0	0	-	-	-	-	-	-	-	-	-	-
1963							*	0	-	-	-	-	-	-	-	-	-	-
1964								*	-	-	-	-	-	-	-	-	-	-
1965									*	+	0	0	-	-	-	-	0	-
1966										*	0	0	-	-	-	-	0	-
1967											*	-	-	-	-	-	-	-
1968												*	-	-	-	-	0	0
1969													*	-	-	-	-	+
1970														*	0	-	-	+
1971															*	0	+	+
1972																*	+	+
1973																	*	0

Table 4.5. Third Degree Stochastic Dominance Matrix for the Real Cruzeiro Dollar Rate

	1957	1958	1959	1960	1961	1962	1963	1964	1965	1966	1967	1968	1969	1970	1971	1972	1973	1974
1957	*	+	-	-	-	+	+	+	-	-	0	-	-	-	-	-	-	-
1958		*	-	-	-	+	0	0	-	-	-	-	-	-	-	-	-	-
1959			*	-	-	+	+	+	-	-	0	-	-	-	-	-	-	-
1960				*	0	+	+	+	-	0	0	-	-	-	-	-	-	-
1961					*	+	+	+	-	0	0	-	-	-	-	-	-	-
1962						*	-	-	-	-	-	-	-	-	-	-	-	-
1963							*	0	-	-	-	-	-	-	-	-	-	-
1964								*	-	-	-	-	-	-	-	-	-	-
1965									*	+	+	0	-	-	-	-	0	-
1966										*	0	0	-	-	-	-	0	-
1967											*	-	-	-	-	-	-	-
1968												*	-	-	-	-	0	0
1969													*	-	-	-	-	-
1970														*	-	-	-	+
1971															*	0	+	+
1972																*	+	+
1973																	*	0

strictly dominating the whole 1957-74 period. The early 1960's were the period of greatest uncertainty, and the end of the period, 1972-74, shows a slight increase in uncertainty compared to immediately preceding years.

An extension of the basic stochastic dominance approach suggested by the generalization of the rule was also tried. Following the argument of Section 4.2, a fourth degree rule was used to attempt to eliminate some of the cases of nonrankability which occur even with the TSD rule. Its use eliminated two ties, showing that 1958 dominates 1963, and that 1966 dominates 1961. The relatively small gain may reflect the reduction of the tied cases to a "hard core" which would presumably be nonrankable by any degree rule.

4.6 Indices of uncertainty

The stochastic dominance rules derived in Sections 4.1 and 4.2 permit us to make qualitative statements about preferences for given distributions. They do not, however, provide *per se* a quantitative measure or index of uncertainty. As some type of measure of this type is indispensable for econometric studies of uncertainty, it is worthwhile to derive such an index, even at the possible cost of some loss of generality.

For this purpose it is useful to introduce the degenerate distribution $c(x) = c_o$, in which all of the mass of the distribution is concentrated at a single value, equal to c_o. With zero variance and higher moments, this "distribution" is a natural definition of complete certainty, and in the measurement of uncertainty might be thought of as playing a role analogous to absolute zero in the measurement of temperature. If we then apply the stochastic dominance rules to this distribution and one of non-zero variance with an expectation equal to c_o, it is clear that the degenerate distribution would be preferred by any risk averter. Evaluation of the SSD integral ($H_2(x)$) from point a would then yield a positive number for any x in $[a,b]$. If we were then to apply a mean preserving spread to the uncertain distribution, this positive number would increase.

An apparently natural cardinal measure of uncertainty would therefore appear to be the value of $H_2(x)$, where $H_o(x) = f(x) - c(x)$. There is a serious difficulty, however, with this approach. The choice of the upper limit for the integral, with the exception of point b, is arbitrary, and the statistic derived will not be sufficient, in the sense that it sacrifices some of the information available in the sample. If evaluated at b, however, $H_2(b)$ is zero, for any pair of distributions of equal means, so that it is useless as a measure of uncertainty.

The approach, however, does suggest a viable method. Consider the set of SSD orderable distributions, each of which could be derived by a sequence of mean preserving spreads about the certain "distribution", as Rothschild and Stiglitz have shown. By definition, any distribution which is preferred to another in the SSD sense will have $H_2(x) \leq 0$ for all x. Hence the less preferred distribution must have a larger SSD integral relative to the certain distribution than does the preferred distribution, whose SSD integral relative to c(x) is also positive, but smaller. The integral of $H_2(x)$ for this distribution and the certain distribution will thus be monotonically increasing over the interval [a,b], always exceeding the corresponding non-negative integral for the preferred distribution. These statements become more obvious if represented graphically. Figure 4.1.a shows uniform densities f(x) and g(x), equal in expectation to each other and to the degenerate density concentrated at c_o. The difference between F(x) and C(x), the cumulative distribution of c(x), is represented in 4.1.b by the solid line, while the dashed line represents the corresponding difference between G(x) and C(x), which we may denote respectively by $H_1(x; f,c)$ and $H_1(x; g,c)$, where the latter two arguments refer to the distributions being compared.

STOCHASTIC DOMINANCE INTEGRALS

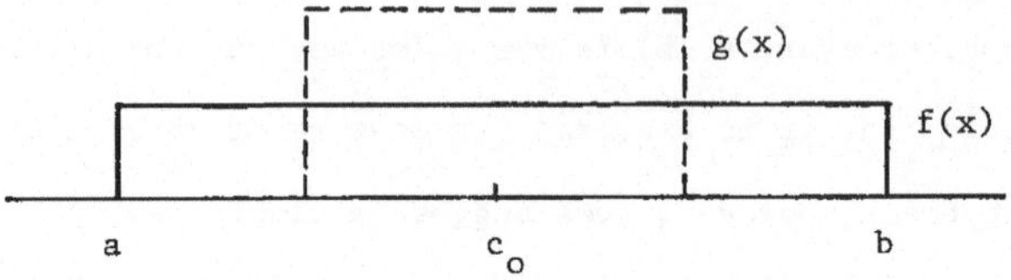

Figure 4.1.a

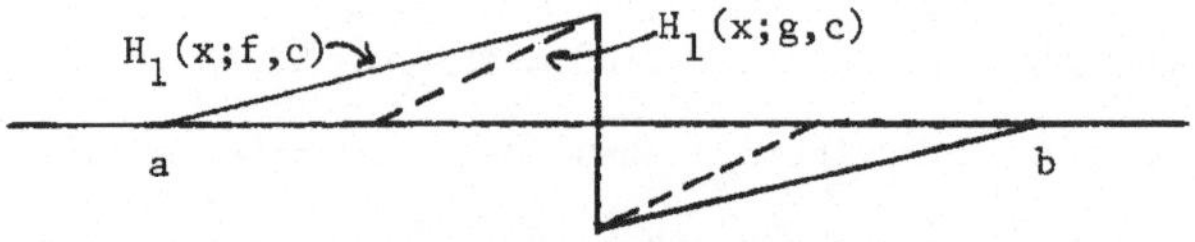

Figure 4.1.b

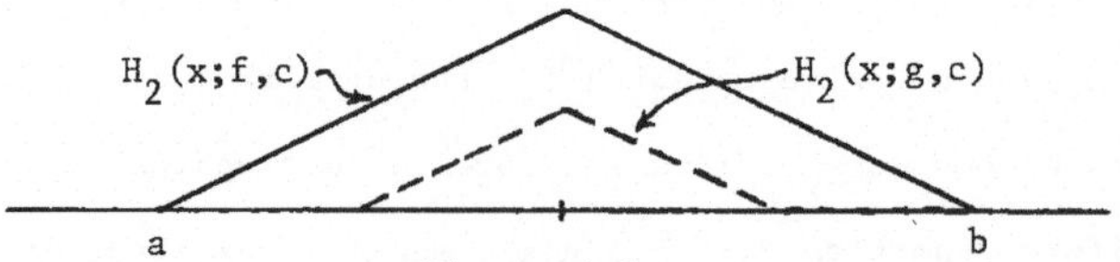

Figure 4.1.c

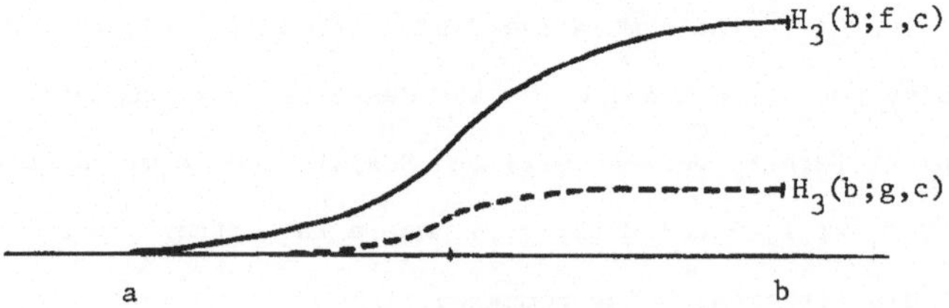

Figure 4.1.d

The SSD integrals, or $H_2(x; f,c)$ and $H_2(x; g,c)$, are shown in Figure 4.1.c. Note that $H_2(b)$ is zero for both integrals, despite f(x) being superior to g(x) by SSD. Integrating these integrals, however, yields the two monotonically increasing functions represented in Figure 4.1.d.

Evaluated to any point $p \geq b$, each of these integrals is simply the value of the TSD integral, $H_3(b; f,c)$ or $H_3(b; g,c)$. Hence for the set of SSD orderable distributions, $H_3(b; i,c)$ correctly orders the distributions, where i indexes the set of distributions and b is the maximum value attained by x for any of the distributions in the set.

Expanding the set of distributions considered to the TSD orderable set, we can see by an identical argument that $H_4(b; j,c)$ correctly orders this set, whose members we denote by the index j. Generalizing the method, we may show that for the set of distributions orderable by a k-degree stochastic dominance rule, $H_{k+1}(b; i,c)$ provides the appropriate index of uncertainty. For economy of notation, we shall in subsequent sections suppress the latter two arguments of $H_{k+1}(b; i,c)$, except where otherwise ambiguous.

For sets of distributions orderable by a k-degree stochastic dominance rule, we have thus reduced the problem of measurement of uncertainty to the evaluation of $H_{k+1}(b)$. There are two apparent difficulties with this approach. First, not all sets of distributions are orderable, even by an arbitrarily high degree rule. Second, from a practical point of view, the evaluation of these multiple integrals would appear to be computationally infeasible. It is to this latter problem which we now turn, returning to the former in Section 4.7.

By definition, $H_k(b) = \int_a^b H_{k-1}(x)\,dx$. Integrating by parts, we may write

$$H_k(b) = \left| H_{k-1}(x)\cdot x \right|_a^b - \int_a^b x\cdot dH_{k-1}(x)$$

$$= H_{k-1}(b)\cdot b - \int_a^b H_{k-2}(x)\cdot d(\tfrac{x^2}{2})$$

where we use the fact that $H_k(a) = 0$ for $k = 1,\ldots n$. Again integrating by parts, we have

$$H_k(b) = H_{k-1}(b)\cdot b - \left| H_{k-2}(x)\cdot\tfrac{x^2}{2} \right|_a^b + \tfrac{1}{2}\int_a^b x^2\cdot dH_{k-2}(x)$$

$$= H_{k-1}(b)\cdot b - \tfrac{b^2}{2} H_{k-2}(b) + \tfrac{1}{2}\int_a^b H_{k-3}(x)\cdot d(\tfrac{x^3}{3})$$

Repeated integration by parts leads to the general expression

$$H_k(b) = \sum_{i=1}^{k-1} (-1)^{i+1} \frac{b^i}{i!} H_{k-i}(b) + (-1)^{k+1}\cdot\frac{1}{(k-1)!} \int_a^b x^{k-1}\cdot dH_1(x)$$

As $dH_1(x) = H_o(x)\,dx = (f(x) - g(x))\,dx$, where $f(x)$ may be any distribution, including the degenerate one, $c(x) = c_o$, the last term is a function of the difference between the (k-1) st moments of the two distributions. Hence any $H_k(b)$ is a function of lower order k-degree integrals and the difference between the (k-1) st raw moments of the two distributions.

Noting that $H_1(b) = 0$ and $H_2(b) = -(\mu'_f - \mu'_g)$, we may successively substitute for the $H_{k-1}(b)$ terms in the above equation, expressing it completely in terms of differences in the moments of the two distributions. Collecting terms, this expression becomes

$$H_k(b) = \sum_{i=1}^{k-1} \frac{(-b)^{k-i-1}}{i!\ (k-i-1)!}(\mu'_{i_f} - \mu'_{i_g}) \tag{4.14}$$

where $0! = 1$. Hence any stochastic dominance integral evaluated over the whole interval $[a,b]$ may be expressed as a function of the differences in the moments of the two distributions. Note that this conclusion is independent of a number of assumptions made earlier; we do not impose any conditions on the utility function, nor require the means or the other moments of the two distributions to be equal.

If the means of the two distributions are set equal to zero, then the first term is eliminated and $H_k(b)$ becomes a function of the differences in variance and higher central moments about the mean. If in addition we impose the restriction employed earlier, that the derivatives of the utility function alternate in sign, and substitute (4.14) into the general expression for the difference in expected utilities (4.9), we see that the nth degree rules imply a preference for distributions with higher odd central moments and lower even central moments. In other words, the individual whose preferences are characterized by the transcendental functions discussed in Section 4.2 would prefer distributions with higher means, lower variances, higher (positive) skewness, lower kurtosis, and so forth. This conclusion means that the answers given by mean variance analysis may sometimes be wrong, as Rothschild and Stiglitz have argued, but only to the extent that differences in the higher central moments dominate the effects of differences in lower ones. Examination of (4.14) shows that these higher order moment differences receive steadily decreasing weight, requiring them to be substantial (or alternatively, requiring that differences in variance be small), to reverse the conclusions drawn from an analysis only of means and variances.

4.7 Indices of Exchange Rate Uncertainty

The application of the stochastic dominance rules to the real cruzeiro dollar exchange rate data discussed in Section 4.5 showed that most of the years in the 1957-74 period could be ordered in a way consistent with the expected utility hypothesis. Using the SSD rule, about 85 percent of the 153 pairs of distributions are orderable; by TSD, 88 percent, with a small gain to 89 percent if 4SD is used. Under the assumption that our data form sets completely orderable by the stochastic dominance rules, it was shown in the preceding section that cardinal measures of uncertainty which preserve these orderings are possible.

These theoretical results are of little help, from an empirical point of view, if we insist on applying them only to completely orderable sets, since the "real world" is unlikely to be so kind. The alternative approach, and the one followed in this study, is to use the $H_k(b)$ indices with partially orderable sets, forewarned by the qualitative results of the application of the stochastic rules that in a few cases we may be imposing a spurious ordering on a nonrankable pair of distributions.

Before turning to the estimates of $H_k(b)$ for the real exchange rate, it is worthwhile examining the consequences of calculating these indices for a set of data which is only partially orderable. First, it should be noted that even the weakest of the rules permit us to order more than 80 percent of the years, which might provide some justification for application of the $H_k(b)$ indices.

A stronger argument can be made if we examine the indices corresponding to lower degree stochastic dominance rules. Assuming, as we have earlier, that the second "distribution" is the certainty case, and that the distributions have been standardized to have a mean of zero, we may use 4.14 to determine the $H_k(b)$ indices corresponding to their respective orderings. For second through fifth degree stochastic dominance, we have

$$H_3(b) = \frac{1}{2}\mu_2 \qquad (4.14.a)$$

$$H_4(b) = \frac{b}{2}\mu_2 - \frac{1}{6}\mu_3 \qquad (4.14.b)$$

$$H_5(b) = \frac{b^2}{4}\mu_2 - \frac{b}{6}\mu_3 + \frac{1}{24}\mu_4 \qquad (4.14.c)$$

$$H_6(b) = \frac{b^3}{12}\mu_2 - \frac{b^2}{12}\mu_3 + \frac{b}{24}\mu_4 - \frac{1}{120}\mu_5 \qquad (4.14.d)$$

where the μ_i are the ith moments about the mean of the distribution. The $H_3(b)$ index, appropriate for an SSD orderable set, is seen to be simply a function of the variance. As such, it represents no advance over mean-variance analysis, despite the rather different path we have travelled to derive it. If a pair of distributions are SSD orderable, however, then they are necessarily orderable by TSD and any higher rule. This implies that the $H_k(b)$, $k > 3$, indices are also appropriate for the SSD orderable set, and in addition will be the correct indices for their respective (k-1) st order rules, as well as all lower order rules.

Consider the $H_5(b)$ index for example. For the exchange rate data we can state categorically that it orders correctly nearly ninety percent of the pairs. In the remaining cases, we cannot make such a categorical statement, but as is clear from $H_5(b)$, $H_6(b)$, or any higher level indices we may derive using (4.14), moments greater than μ_4 would have to be extremely large to dominate the effects of the first three in (4.14.c), due to the higher weights the lower moments in the $H_k(b)$ indices receive.

The $H_k(b)$ indices were estimated for the exchange rate data using equations 4.14.a. - 4.14.d. As the raw data was standardized by subtracting from each observation the sample mean, higher level sample moments of the form $N^{-1}(\sum_{i=1}^{N}(X_i - \overline{X})^k)$ are biased estimators of the true population moments. The unbiased estimators of the second through fifth sample moments were derived by taking the expectation of the unadjusted sample moments. These unbiased estimators were then substituted into 4.14.a - 4.14.d. The largest observation in the group of observations of mean zero, 1.2198, was used as the value of b, although any value for b greater than this would also be consistent with the approach developed here

The estimated indices are shown in Table 4.6. As $H_3(b)$ is simply half the sample variance, and the other $H_k(b)$ indices are heavily weighted by the variance, they are highly correlated. Rankings of the distributions using the indices are unchanged between $H_3(b)$ and $H_4(b)$, with a single change from $H_4(b)$ to $H_5(b)$ and from $H_5(b)$ to $H_6(b)$. Referring back to Tables 4.4 and 4.5, it can be seen that these changes in ranking by the indices, for 1963 and 1964 and for 1958 and 1964, correspond to years nonrankable by any of the three rules applied.

Table 4.6 Estimates of Exchange Rate Uncertainty

Year	$H_3(b)$	$H_4(b)$	$H_5(b)$	$H_6(b)$
1957	.0393	.0469	.0284	.0116
1958	.0880	.1011	.0613	.0259
1959	.0216	.0260	.0157	.0064
1960	.0155	.0191	.0118	.0049
1961	.0170	.0203	.0123	.0050
1962	.2337	.2700	.1638	.0693
1963	.1052	.1170	.0694	.0288
1964	.1281	.1246	.0672	.0256
1965	.0094	.0114	.0070	.0029
1966	.0169	.0202	.0122	.0049
1967	.0118	.0149	.0095	.0040
1968	.0062	.0077	.0048	.0020
1969	.0022	.0027	.0017	.0007
1970	.0007	.0008	.0005	.0002
1971	.0005	.0006	.0003	.0001
1972	.0003	.0004	.0003	.0001
1973	.0044	.0056	.0036	.0015
1974	.0061	.0076	.0047	.0020

Note: Apparent ties due to rounding.

4.8 Limitations and Extensions of the Stochastic Dominance Method

Perhaps the most obvious criticism that can be made of the stochastic dominance approach to ordering distributions is that it is a qualitative ordering, complete only under rather favorable circumstances. In most cases, including that of Section 4.5, a number of nonrankable pairs of distributions remain. If we then attempt to derive a quantitative measure of uncertainty, we run the risk of making spurious and possibly invalid choices.

This is, of course, the fundamental theoretical objection to the use of variance as a measure of uncertainty. It was shown in Section 4.6, however, that the use of higher order indices than $H_3(b)$ removes a large part of the threat of invalid orderings posed by the use of variance alone. As the higher order indices corresponding to higher degree stochastic dominance rules are used, higher order central moments affect the choice of distributions, reducing substantially the likelihood that omitted moments would reverse the choice.

From this point of view, the stochastic dominance rules, in particular the lower order ones, can be seen to be an extraordinarily cautious way of choosing distributions, which is of course the price we pay such categorical generality. Nonrankability under these rules can arise if a single value of an otherwise preferable distribution is less than the lowest value of another distribution. This situation appears to explain a large number of the ties in the analysis of the exchange rate data; 1966, for example, would generally have been preferred to many of the years with which it is tied, were it not for the low real exchange rate prevailing in January of that year, prior to a substantial devaluation.

One might view this sensitivity of the rules to a few extremely low values as their very strength. What the rules are telling us in such cases is that there are concave, and possibly non-increasingly risk averse utility functions which could be used to justify the choice of either distribution. This is surely a useful piece of information even if it is not definitive.

Alternatively, we might selectively eliminate "suspect" low observations from our sample. Unless we know a great deal more about the data than is usually the case, however, this is likely to be an arbitrary and perilous procedure, especially for hypothesis testing. Extremely low values of a random variable that is an argument in a concave utility function, moreover, are in a sense what risk aversion is all about. Their elimination from a sample for the sake of complete orderability is probably not worth the price for this reason alone.

The stochastic dominance method developed in this chapter leaves a number of other unanswered questions. While we have shown that the estimators are consistent, their behavior in small samples is an open question. The method is distribution free, and to learn more about their small sample properties we would of course have to make specific assumptions about the distributions from which the samples are drawn. Monte Carlo and other simulation methods might provide partial answers to these questions.

The application of the stochastic dominance method to distributions of real exchange rates, or to other relative prices raises some other questions. One of them is the appropriate measure of central tendency. Flemming, Turnovsky, and Kemp have argued that the geometric, and not the arithmetic mean is the proper location measure for the analysis of mean preserving spreads in relative price distributions.[15] Standardization of a group of distributions about the same geometric mean would require the division of each observation by the geometric mean, rather than subtraction, and the resulting standardized samples would then have geometric means of one, rather than zero. An alternative would be to apply the stochastic dominance method to the log of the distribution of relative prices.

A study of the distributions of exchange rates for a number of major trading currencies by Westerfield concluded that these distributions were not adequately represented by the normal distribution, but were better approximated by other, more "fat-tailed" members of the class of stable Paretian distributions, to which the normal itself belongs.[16] Her conclusions would appear to constitute an excellent argument for the use of a distribution free method like the stochastic dominance approach. This conclusion must be qualified however, by the fact that the stable Paretian family includes distributions like the Cauchy, whose mean and higher moments do not exist. Indices like the $H_k(b)$ estimators, which are functions of sample moments, may then be rather unstable, particularly in small samples.[17]

Another question which our use of the stochastic domiance approach opens up is raised by its application to time series data like the real exchange rate. While an adequate answer to this question lies far beyond the scope of this study, the question is obviously an important one. The exchange rate data were treated as if they were a set of independent samples. In reality, as we have noted earlier, the division of these monthly observations into groups of twelve is a decision more forced on us by the availability of the other data relevant to our study, and not for any intrinsic theoretical reason. One can easily develop simple dynamic models generating monthly time series which if sampled in annual groups might show a high degree of orderability under the stochastic dominance rules, yet if sampled for a different length period might be nearly unorderable. In experiments with different length samples for the exchange rate data, however, this did not appear to be a serious problem, and our conclusions about the reduction in uncertainty in 1968 are robust to such variations.

FOOTNOTES FOR CHAPTER IV

1. See for example G. Hanoch and H. Levy, "The Efficiency Ana-Analysis of Choice Involving Risk", Rev. Econ. Studies, Vol. 36, July 1969

2. This is shown by M. Richter, "Cardinal Utility, Portfolio Selection, and Taxation", Rev. Econ. Studies, Vol. 27, June 1960

3. For proofs see T. Apostol, Mathematical Analysis, Reading, Mass., Addison Wesley, 1957

4. J. Hadar and W. Russell, "Rules for Ordering Uncertain Prospects", Amer. Econ. Review, March 1969

5. The original statement of FSD is found in J. Quirk and R. Saposnik, "Admissibility and Measurable Utility Functions", Rev. Econ. Studies, Vol. 29, 1962

6. Proof: $H_2(b) = \int_a^b H_1(x)\,dx = |H_1(x)\cdot x|_a^b - \int_a^b x\cdot dH_1(x)$
$= F(b) - G(b) - F(a) + G(a) - \int_a^b x\,|f(x) - g(x)|\,dx =$
$-\mu_f + \mu_g = 0$

7. $R'(x) = d\,[-U''(x)/U'(x)]/dx \leq 0$ implies inter alia that the absolute amount of wealth devoted to a risky asset would at least not decrease with an increase in wealth. As $R'(x)$ equals $[(U''(x))^2 - U'(x)U'''(x)]\,/\,[U'(x)]^2$, and $U'(x) > 0$ and $U''(x) < 0$, this hypothesis is sufficient, but not necessary for $U'''(x) > 0$.

8. TSD was demonstrated by G. Whitmore, "Third Degree Stochastic Dominance", Amer. Econ. Review, June 1970

9. See note 7 above. Studies of portfolio behavior among Brazilian investors show clearly an increase in the absolute amount of wealth allocated to riskier assets with increasing wealth, consistent with the non-increasing risk aversion hypothesis. See J.L. Melo, Perfil do Investidor no Mercado de Açoes, Rio de Janeiro, IBMEC, 1976

10. In the event of tied observations ($X_i = X_j$ or $X_i = X_{i+1}$), $p < m+n$, with the jump in $H_{1,m,n}(X_h) = 1/m + 1/n$ or $2/m$ respectively.

11. See E. Lukacs, Stochastic Convergence, Second ed., New York, Academic Press, 1975, for proof, and W. Feller, An Introduction to Probability Theory and its Applications, Vol. II, New York, J. Wiley, 1966

12. The sequence $\sup |F_m(x) - F(x)|$ is almost uniformly convergent (and hence convergent in probability), but not convergent in the analytic sense that there is some M for which $m > M$ necessarily implies $\sup |F_m(x) - F(x)| < \varepsilon$. See Lukacs, op. cit., Ch. 2

13. For proof, see Apostol, op cit. p. 399

14. S. Shapiro and M. Wilk, "An Analysis of Variance Test for Normality (Complete Samples)", Biometrica, Dec. 1965

15. J. Flemming, S. Turnovsky, and M. Kemp, "On the Choice of Numeraire and Certainty Price in General Equilibrium Models of Price Uncertainty", Rev. Econ. Studies, Vol. 44, Oct. 1977

16. J.M. Westerfield, "An Examination of Foreign Exchange Risk under Fixed and Floating Exchange Rate Regimes", Jour. Int. Econ., Vol. 7, May 1977

17. The data studied by Westerfield, in contrast to the Brazilian real exchange rate data in a number of years, was approximately symmetric in distribution, justifying her characterization of the distributions as members of the stable Paretian family, which are symmetric. As a distribution free method, the stochastic dominance approach does not require us to assume a given distribution.

CHAPTER V

RELATIVE PRICE INCENTIVES TO EXPORT: BRAZILIAN COMMERCIAL AND EXCHANGE POLICIES AND THEIR EFFECTS

The central argument of this study is that changes in price uncertainty per se may have important effects on trade and economic structure independently of changes in relative prices. This argument rests on the theory of the risk averse firm's response to changes in price uncertainty developed in preceding chapters; the succeeding chapter is devoted to an econometric test of this hypothesis using data from Brazil over the past two decades. Had the adoption of the crawling peg and the consequent reduction in exchange rate uncertainty been the only important change in Brazilian international economic policy in this period, the results of these tests of the uncertainty hypothesis might be sufficient to complete our argument. Commercial policy, however, also changed significantly during this period, creating what even an orthodox, deterministic theory of trade would predict to be strong incentives to relatively greater exports from some sectors. Any consideration of the role of reduced uncertainty in Brazilian foreign trade must consequently avoid attributing to it an increase in the relative importance of exports which in fact may have been due to the changes in relative prices induced by commercial policy. As a necessary prelude to the econometric testing of the uncertainty hypothesis, this chapter examines the major relative price incentives to greater exports created by Brazilian commercial and exchange policies in the last decade and a half. After a brief summary of the history and operation of the major commercial policies, defined here to include indirect export subsidies and tax rebates, as well as direct tariffs and subsidies, the potential export incentives created by import liberalization are examined. The relative price effect of the crawling peg itself is then considered, and the chapter concludes with an explanation of the method used to quantify the combined effects of different commercial policies and exchange policy on relative prices for use in the econometric tests of the effects of changes in both relative prices and exchange rate uncertainty in the next chapter. The discussion here is not intended to be either theoretically complete or historically definitive; for a theoretical treatment of the commercial policies examined here, the reader is referred to Bhagwati, Corden, and Kemp, while actual Brazilian commercial policies have been discussed in detail by Bergsman, Tyler, Von Doellinger et al., and Savasini et al.[1]

5-1. Major Commercial and Exchange Policies before 1964

The single most striking characteristic of Brazilian economic history up to World War II is the economy's almost complete dependence on the export of a few primary products. Although a small industrial sector began to develop in this century, encouraged at times by import substitution resulting from balance of payments difficulties, there was no conscious political decision in the pre-war period to industrialize.

As a result of considerable pessimism in the immediate post-war period about the future rate of growth of demand for Brazil's traditional exports, the idea took root that future development should be oriented toward the internal market, making the Brazilian economy less vulnerable to adverse trends in its foreign trade. Domestic production of importables, it was argued, should be protected if necessary by high tariffs, which in the past had been viewed principally as a source of public revenue. From June 1947 to January 1953 this policy was implemented through a system of import licenses, which were granted according to the presumed necessity of the importable good and its domestic availability. The exchange rate was fixed at Cr$ 18.7 per dollar, which with prices increasing considerably more rapidly in Brazil than in its major trading partners, resulted in a steady decline in exports during the period. By 1952 only a few products in which Brazil had a commanding comparative advantage could be profitably exported, with coffee alone accounting for about three quarters of the value of total exports. Although the disincentive to export was slightly alleviated after 1949, when some exporters of less traditional exports were allowed to sell their foreign exchange receipts directly to importers of non-essential goods, in effect establishing a quase-free market, this period was in general one of stagnation and even decline in non-traditional and manufactured exports.

In 1953, following a sharp drop in exports at the end of the Korean war and increasing difficulties in managing the exchange licensing system, a multiple exchange rate was adopted.[2] Exports were sold at the official rate plus a premium, which varied by product, while foreign exchange for imports was auctioned by categories. In general capital goods and some intermediate imports were favored by the lowest rates, with the highest rates applied to finished consumer goods. Tourism and a number of capital account transactions were allowed to operate in a free market. The system was further modified in 1955, when four categories of exports were established, with higher rates allowed for those in which Brazil's comparative advantage was assumed to be lower, and lower rates for coffee, cacau, and several other traditional exports. Exchange premia, or bonuses paid in addition to the official rate, were varied from time to time, and products were occasionally reclassified, adding to the uncertainty about the profitability of particular exports.

The arbitrary nature of the system, as well as the adjustments required by continuing inflation, made it increasingly unwieldy and unpopular. In September 1957, the import regime was replaced by two import categories, the first comprised of essential goods not available domestically, and the second other importables. An ad valorem tariff was adopted, which despite a number of modifications in specific rates remained generally the same until 1967. A number of exports were transferred to the free market, and in December 1959, all products except coffee, cacau, and a few minor items were allowed to be sold at the free rate. The policy appears to have had a positive effect on exports, especially of manufactures, which rose substantially during this period, despite fairly sharp fluctuations in the real exchange rate.

The early sixties were initially marked by a continuation of the movement toward a free and unified exchange rate. In March 1961, imports were authorized at the free rate, with subsidies continuing at reduced levels for several essential imports, including wheat and petroleum. In May coffee exports were allowed at the free market rate, subject to an export tax. During this period the cruzeiro was effectively devalued in real terms, as the free market dollar rate increased more rapidly than inflation. This trend may be seen in Table 1 of Appendix C, which shows the monthly exchange rate adjusted for inflation in Brazil and in the U.S.

The movement toward a free, unified rate was arrested by the economic and social unrest of the 1962-64 period. As the government lost control of the general price level, restrictions were again placed on a number of imports, with subsidies for some essentials, and premia allowed for a few exports. The exchange rate, which officially continued to be characterized as "free," was increasingly subject to government intervention, and adjustment in the rate fell behind inflation, which in early 1964 was approaching an annual rate of 100 percent. The erratic nature of exchange rate policy is evident in Table C-1; it was in this period that exchange rate uncertainty was greatest, even in comparison with the 1964-1968 period of high rates of inflation with infrequent adjustments in the exchange rate.

One of the important features of Brazilian commercial policy before 1964 was the application of domestic excise and other indirect taxes to the foreign trade sector, in addition to those taxes specific to imports and exports. Until 1960, exports were subject to state and federal sales taxes, as were inputs used in their production. In some cases exports crossing state lines were even subject to the taxes of several states. Although significant changes in this situation were not made until after 1964, there was some recognition of the disincentives to export created by the tax system. The tariff reform of 1957 had in principle allowed tariff exemptions for imports used as inputs in the production of an export. This provision of the law was not implemented until 1961, and it appears to have been insignificant before June 1964, when the law was revised.[3]

5-2. Commercial Policy Incentives after 1964

Among the most pressing problems facing the new government installed by the military in April 1964, was the balance of payments deficit. In the two years preceding the coup it had widened substantially, as the net capital inflow, which traditionally helped to finance a current account deficit, declined and actually became negative in 1963. The new regime's economic policy makers, moreover, led by the Minister of Planning, Roberto Campos, considered the possibilities for further import substitution to be virtually exhausted, and viewed the high levels of protection required by import substitution as one of the many inefficiencies whose reduction was one of the principal economic goals of the new regime. Increased exports were a logical response in this context, and substantial reforms in Brazil's commercial policy were underway within a few months after the coup.

The first important change was a revision of the "drawback" provisions of the 1957 tariff law. Although the law had allowed exporters an exemption from duties paid on imported inputs, this provision was only implemented in 1961, and apparently had little effect, due in part to administrative difficulties involved in obtaining the exemption. With the revision of the law in June 1964, the provision created a significant incentive, particularly in industries with a high import content. The drawback as applied in Brazil, however, was used only for imports which went directly into an export; the imports which might be used indirectly, and which for a number of sectors were considerably greater than imports used directly, were not exempted.

The actual impact of the drawback provision is difficult to estimate with any degree of accuracy. The Interministerial Price Council (CIP) input-output table prepared for 1971 estimated the import content for manufacturing at 5.6 percent, ranging from zero in traditional sectors like tobacco to about 13.5 in chemicals. Indirect requirements were considerably greater, double or even triple the direct requirements. Imports for which the exemption was granted totalled US$ 42.8 million in 1970, while manufactured exports were US$ 197.8 million, yielding an import coefficient for exported manufactures of over 21 percent and suggesting that the drawback provisions may actually have made Brazilian manufactured exports more import intensive than manufactures as a whole.[4]

Several of the most important export incentives in the post-1964 period involved excise or sales taxes. Manufactured products sold in Brazil are subject to two excise or sales taxes, the federal Imposto sôbre Produtos Industrializados (IPI), and the state Imposto de Circulação de Mercadorias (ICM). Both these taxes are in effect value-added taxes, since they allow deductions for taxes paid on intermediate inputs. A firm's purchase of an input includes the tax, which is then deducted from the tax owed by the firm when it sells the finished product.[5]

In November 1964, Decree Law 4502 exempted exports of manufactured products from payment of the IPI, with the effective implementation of the law beginning in August 1965. As Tyler and others have noted, the structure of production and the incidence of the tax tend to make the incentive greater for exports whose production involves a number of intermediate inputs. This bias towards highly processed products arises from the fact that the exporter receives the normal credit for taxes charged on earlier stages of production, but does not pay the IPI on the export. The exemption in effect favors the exporter at the expense of firms producing the intermediate input, since the whole IPI paid in different producing sectors at earlier stages of production is rebated to the exporter.

A related export incentive was created in February 1967, when Article 24 of the Brazilian constitution exempted exports from payment of the state ICM or value added tax. This provision was applicable only to the sales, with exporters continuing to pay the ICM on their purchased inputs, in contrast to the IPI rebate export incentive. As a result, the impact of this incentive did not vary among sectors as did the IPI incentive. Since the ICM is imposed at the state level, there is some variation among states, but in all of the major industrial states (including São Paulo, Rio de Janeiro, Minas Gerais and Rio Grande do Sul) from which come the majority of Brazil's exports subject to the tax, the rate in recent years has been 16.5 percent of the factory price.

Another incentive was provided in 1967 with the implementation of an income tax exemption, originally legislated in 1965. The measure allowed a firm to deduct from its total corporate income tax liability an amount corresponding to the percentage of its total production which was exported, in effect allowing the firm to sell in international markets at lower prices while maintaining the same after tax profits. Associated with the main exemption were several minor income tax incentives, including the allowance of deductions for promotional costs and other expenses specific to exporting.

Any attempt to measure the incentive effect of the income tax exemptions is necessarily an approximation, as profits as a percentage of sales are not known with any precision, and presumably vary among activities, due among other reasons to imperfect capital markets. Some estimates, however, have been made and are discussed in Section 5-4. Tyler has argued that the presence of a number of other income tax exemptions designed to stimulate regional or sectoral development in effect diminish the impact of the exemption as an export incentive, since income earned on domestic sales is taxed at considerably less than the nominal rate; such considerations make estimates of the effect of this incentive on output price even more imprecise than they would otherwise be.

The export incentives discussed to this point were essentially exemptions from taxes which had been imposed on exports before 1964, and as such are little different from practices in the European Common Market and in some other countries. Actual export subsidies, however, have also been used as part of Brazil's recent commercial policy. Beginning in July 1968, exports received a further incentive based on the IPI, in addition to the actual rebate of this tax discussed above. Exporters were allowed a tax credit, to be charged against their total tax liability, of up to 50 percent of the IPI which would have been charged if the export had been sold domestically, up to a limiting IPI rate of 10 percent. In July 1969, this incentive was further increased, with the firm allowed a 100 percent credit rather than the 50 percent allowed earlier. In addition, the maximum applicable IPI rate was raised from 10 to 15 percent, and for some products, such as textiles, firms were allowed the tax credit of 15 percent even though actual IPI rates for the particular product are lower.

In 1971 a similar export incentive based on the ICM was created. Justified by the argument that the ICM paid on earlier stages of production of goods eventually exported lowered their international price competitiveness, the measure provided a direct subsidy to offset this assumed cost. Unlike the ICM exemption instituted in 1967, the 1971 credit or subsidy varied among sectors in its effect, as the indirect cost added by the ICM varied by sectors. In general, the credit closely paralleled the IPI credit, with sectors having a smaller value added in relation to purchased inputs enjoying higher rates. As the base to which the credit was applied was defined as the FOB export price minus imported inputs, and the rate was based on the IPI rate for the same product, the credit was generally slightly less than the IPI credit for the same sector.

5-3. The Potential Export Incentive Effects of Import Liberalization

Although the tax exemptions, credits, and other incentives discussed in the preceding section were the most obvious and direct measures designed to increase exports, changes in Brazilian commercial policy after 1964 were not limited to the export side of the trade balance. Convinced that import substitution was responsible for many of the inefficiencies of the economy, the new regime's policy makers viewed tariff reform as one of their principal goals once the immediate problems of stabilization were solved.

In March 1967, the tariff schedule was substantially revised, with cuts in nominal protection ranging from 20 to 50 percent of initial tariffs in the majority of sectors. Estimates of the corresponding reduction in effective protection made by Bergsman and others indicated a drop in the average level of effective protection from 181 to 76 percent.

The full extent of the 1967 import liberalization was relatively short-lived. Imports increased sharply in late 1967 and 1968, due not only to the tariff reduction, but also to the increase in the rate of growth of the Brazilian economy in 1968. This trend, as well as pressure from sectors which lost protection with the 1967 reductions led to a partial reversal of the liberalization in December 1968, when tariffs on a number of products were raised, restoring protection in several sectors to levels comparable to those prevailing before 1967, according to estimates made by Bergsman.[6] Despite this partial reversal, however, protection of Brazilian industry was generally less after 1968 than it had been before the initial reductions in 1967.

In terms of conventional trade theory, an import liberalization of this type would not only make an economy more open in an import sense, but would provide an incentive to exports as well. Despite the limitations inherent in a two-sector model, this can be seen clearly in the common general equilibrium model depicted in Figure 5.1. Initial tariffs result in production of X_1 of the exportable and M_1 of the importable good, represented by point P_1. Consumption of the two goods is represented by C_1, with trade corresponding to the triangle C_1AP_1.

Partial import liberalization, by bringing internal relative prices closer to world prices, moves the production point to P_2, consumption to C_2, and expands the trade triangle to C_2BP_2. Exports as a percentage of national product, measured in terms of either good, have ambiguously increased.

Most contemporary studies of trade liberalization, including Bergsman's analysis of the structure of protection in Brazil, are in essence refinements of this basic model. Even though commercial policies may be directed primarily at imports, they are assumed to have an accompanying effect on exports. The high level of protection encourages domestic production of importables, transferring resources from the export sector. On the consumption side, the higher relative price of the importable encourages more domestic consumption of the exportable, further reducing exports.

Although formally correct, this model rests on several implicit assumptions which may limit its applicability to the Brazilian experience. First, it assumes full employment, substitutability, and domestic mobility of the factors of production. Hence a higher level of domestic

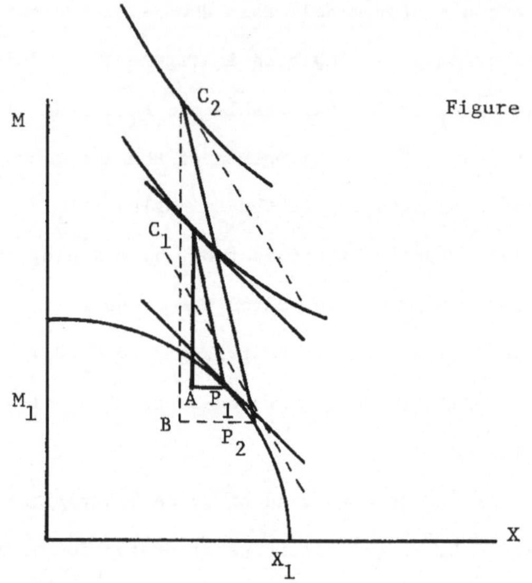

Figure 5.1

The Conventional Model of Trade Liberalization

production of the importable necessarily requires less production of the exportable. It is not clear that this assumption is entirely appropriate for Brazil, since the principal resource common to both sectors is unskilled labor, with the other factors of production often specific to particular sectors. As labor in Brazil has rarely been fully employed, an increase in importable production does not necessarily imply an offsetting reduction in the production of exportables.

Second, as a consequence of the barter nature of trade in the model, it is implicitly assumed that trade is balanced at world prices, or equivalently, that there is no capital account in the balance of payments. The "exchange rate" within the country is then simply the world terms of trade modified by the tariff. An imposition or increase in the tariff is equivalent to appreciation of the exchange rate, thus reducing the competitiveness of the export sector in world markets.

Had Brazil been subject to some kind of balanced trade requirement this assumption might be appropriate; in fact, the large capital inflows of recent years suggest that it is invalid. In terms of the model, import liberalization in Brazil would have resulted in a deterioration of the current account, requiring an appropriate devaluation of the cruzeiro to maintain balance of payments equilibrium; Bergsman's estimates of the sectoral levels of protection, in fact, assume that this adjustment would actually take place. In reality, massive capital inflows in the late 1960s more than financed any trade deficit resulting from import liberalization, consequently eliminating any incentive effect it might have had on exports. As a result the real cruzeiro dollar exchange rate actually appreciated slightly between 1967 and 1973.

If we relax the rather restrictive assumption of only two tradable goods, the resource allocation effects of import liberalization become even more complex, and the conclusion that the production of the exportable will increase rests on even more tenuous grounds. Even under the assumption of full employment of primary factors and balanced trade, there is no longer any necessary relation between the change in the degree of protection received by a sector and its output response, as is the case with two tradable goods. If factor intensities and the partial elasticities of substitution between primary factors vary among sectors then it is entirely possible that the price of the output of sector 1 may increase relative to 2, with production in 1 decreasing and in 2 increasing.

These apparently perverse responses of output to changes in protection have been noted by Corden and others, and constitute an important limitation to the usefulness of changes in measured rates of effective protection as a guide to changes in production. It should be noted, moreover, that such possibilities may arise even assuming, as does Corden, that intermediate inputs are used in fixed proportion to output.[7] Although the problem may at first appear to be merely of theoretical interest, it in fact has some relevance to Brazilian experience in the last decade. The relation between the change in the relative degree of incentives to export received by different Brazilian industrial sectors appears to bear little relation to the response of exports by sector, with some industries absorbing a high level of subsidies and other incentives without a marked response. Assymetries in substitution among primary factors in different sectors might explain some of the weak relation between export incentives and actual export response. Other causes may include assymetries in substitution among produced or intermediate inputs, a problem which has been examined by Ramaswami and Srinivasan and others.[8]

5-4. Export Incentives and Economic Openness

It was suggested in the preceding section that assymetries in substitution among either primary factors or produced inputs could weaken the relation between a given export incentive and the actual export response of that sector. Another hypothesis for such a relation is briefly examined in this section, since it appears to offer a simple alternative explanation of the apparent absence of any strong relation between Brazilian export incentives for industrial products and actual export response.

As was noted earlier, the majority of incentives to export created by the Brazilian government favored highly processed, industrialized products, since both IPI and ICM exemptions, as well as the subsidies added later, applied primarily to manufactures. Agricultural exports, and exports of primary products in general were virtually ignored by Brazilian commercial policy, since the IPI and ICM were generally not applicable to products in these categories. Of the principal incentives discussed in section 5-2, only the income tax exemption was not biased towards industrial exports.

Although the identification of sectors in which Brazil has a comparative advantage is still an open question and subject to considerable debate, both Brazilian and foreign economists have generally assumed it is strongest in the agricultural and primary product areas and weakest in high technology, capital-intensive industrial sectors, at least in the short run. If Brazil's tradable goods were to be divided into two broad categories, imports could generally be characterized as industrial, with the exception of several items such as petroleum, while exports could be considered as basically agricultural or otherwise related to the primary sector. Viewed in this context, Brazilian commercial policy has in part been directed at encouraging the export of potential importables, while goods which under free trade might be exported in fact have received considerably less encouragement.

Since each of the two broad categories of tradable goods, primary products and manufactures, include both exportables and importables, the effects of these export promotion policies do not lend themselves to the type of general equilibrium approach used in the preceding section to analyze the export incentive effects of trade liberalization. A simple partial equilibrium analysis, however, can provide considerable insight into these policies, despite the inherent limitations of this approach. Figures 5.2a and 5.2b represent two markets, the former for a good which under free trade would be an importable and the latter for a good which would be exported under free trade. We assume that initially a tariff (t) is imposed on the importable, sufficiently high that domestic demand is entirely supplied by domestic production, represented by the quantity Q_a^o in Figure 5.2a. No initial trade intervention is assumed in the market for the exportable, in which production is Q_b^o and exports X_b^o in Figure 5.2b.

Assume now that a small incentive to exports is created in the form of a subsidy of r percent of the domestic sales price. In Figure 5.2b this would simply be added to P_b^o, raising both the domestic price and the price received by exporters to P_b^2, consequently increasing the export coefficient from X_b^o/Q_b^o to X_b^2/Q_b^2.

In the tariff ridden market, however, the export subsidy is calculated on the basis of the domestic price, P_a^1, but for the producer is

Fig. 5-2-a

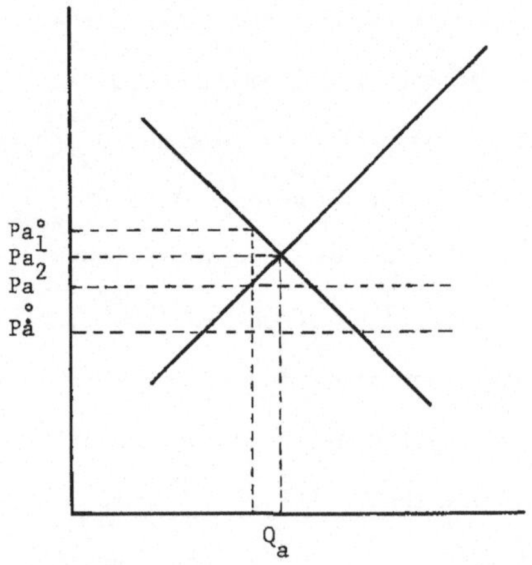

Fig. 5-2-b

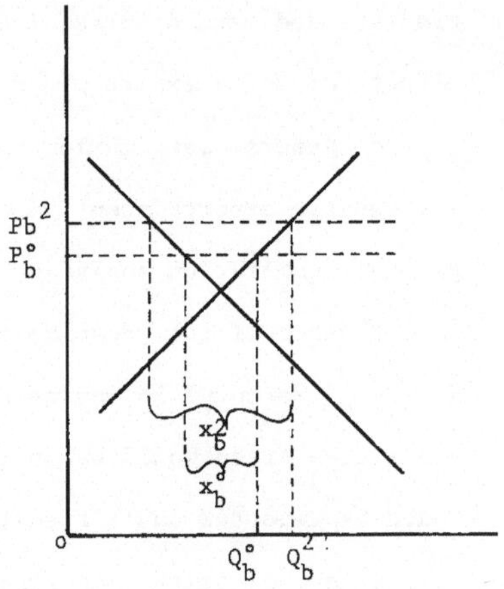

Differential Effects of an Export Subsidy

added to the international price, P_a^o, yielding an effective price for exports of P_a^2. As drawn in Figure 5.2a, even this higher price is insufficient to cover the costs of production, so that no exports actually occur, with the export coefficients remaining at zero.

The basic argument here is simply that in an initially tariff ridden situation like that of Brazil in the mid-sixties, and to a lesser extent, even now, the creation of export subsidies like those examined here without regard to international comparative advantage may produce little or no export response if the initial divergence between domestic and international prices is relatively large. As there was no particular guide or rationale for the choice of sectors which received the greatest incentives in Brazil after 1964, there is no reason to expect a close relation between the degree of subsidy and the response of exports. The actual incentive system, moreover, because it is primarily based on the federal and state value added taxes, tended to provide a greater degree of subsidy to those products which earlier had received a high level of protection and which would presumably be imported under free trade.

Some indirect empirical support for this explanation comes from several recent Brazilian studies of the domestic resource costs of a dollar of foreign exchange earned by exports from different sectors. One study, by Mendonça de Barros et al., found that the 1971 domestic costs of earning a dollar of export receipts varied from about two cruzeiros for products like oranges and peanuts to over ten cruzeiros for radios and typewriters. They concluded that a large part of this variation could be explained by the application of the export incentive to sectors in which

Brazil had no comparative advantage. Similar results have been noted by Von Doellinger and by Bergsman.[9]

5-5. The Relative Price Effect of the Crawling Peg

The adoption of a crawling peg by Brazil in August 1968 has been treated in other chapters of this study as a policy whose principal effect was to reduce uncertainty. Although the effect of a reduction in uncertainty is our principal theoretical concern, it should be noted that the adoption of the crawling peg could have a significant impact on the expected value of the exchange rate, independently of any effect it had on the degree of uncertainty attached to it. For this reason, studies like that of Suplicy, which used a Chow test to show a statistically significant change in the parameters of export functions estimated before and after the adoption of the crawling peg, are not sufficient in themselves to permit the acceptance of our hypothesized relation between the reduction in exchange rate uncertainty and an increase in the relative importance of exports.

As the potential effect of the crawling peg on the expected value of the exchange rate is analogous to commercial policy in that it also alters the relative price of tradable goods, it is appropriate to extend our examination of relative price incentives to export to include the deterministic aspects of the crawling peg. We may alternatively assume that a) the magnitude and timing of exchange rate changes, as well as the future course of internal prices is known, or b) that the firm is risk neutral, rather than risk averse. Either assumption would permit us to ignore temporarily the effect of uncertainty discussed in preceding chapters.

In its most simple form, we may assume that the potential exporter uses purely domestic inputs to produce a single output, all of which is exported as it is produced. Both the prices of the required inputs in local currency and the world price of the output are known, at least over the period during which the firm fixes its level of production. In an inflationary context, we may interpret this assumption to mean that the time path of domestic costs is known even if local currency costs are not fixed. We assume, moreover, that even if the firm recognizes that its decision may have an impact on the market price of its output, it sets the quantity produced rather than the price at which it is sold, as of course must be the case for the purely competitive firm.

At any time t, the firm's net earnings are given by

$$\pi_t = r_t p_t q - c_t(q) - b_t \tag{5.1}$$

where r, p, c, and b are respectively the exchange rate, the foreign price, and the domestic variable and fixed costs. We assume that marginal costs are increasing, at least in the short run with which we are concerned here.

If the exchange rate and all goods and factor prices were constant, first order conditions would reduce to the familiar requirement that output be chosen so as to equate marginal costs and marginal revenue. Alternatively, if prices and the exchange rate were variable, but the output level could be instantly and costlessly adjusted to a new optimum, the same condition would hold at each moment.

Once we allow the exchange rate to vary, however, while fixing the output level over some finite time period, it is apparent that optimizing behavior will not necessarily equate marginal cost and revenue at each moment. Expectations, or in the certainty case assumed in this section, knowledge of the future course of the exchange rate will determine an optimum output level.

If total domestic costs are increasing at a constant rate s, the firm's net earning at any moment t are

$$\pi_t = p\ q\ r_t - (c(q) + b)e^{st} \qquad (5.2)$$

where s is the rate of change in the domestic price level. We assume that the exchange rate is given by a step function, representing an exchange policy of regular, fixed percentage devaluations. This process might be regarded as a rough approximation of a crawling peg regime like Brazil's after 1968. The exchange rate at the moment t is then simply

$$r_t = r_o\ (1 + d)^i \qquad (5.3)$$

in which i is the largest integer less than t/m, where m is the fixed time period between devaluations. If there are n evenly spaced devaluations of the same percentage over the firm's production period, so that n = T/m, where T is the end date,[10] we may substitute 5.3 into 5.2, expressing net earnings at time t as the difference between a step revenue and a continuous cost function or

$$\pi_t = p\ q\ r_o\ (1 + d)^{i(t)} - (c\ (q) + b)\ e^{st} \qquad (5.4)$$

Integrating 5.4 over the time of the production period yields

$$_o\int^t \pi_t = p\ q\ [r_o m \sum_{i=0}^{n} (1 + d)^{i-1}] - (c(q) + b)\frac{(e^{s^T} - 1)}{s} \qquad (5.4)$$

Using 5.3 and the identity n = T/m, the mean exchange rate, $\bar{r}$, may be written as

$$\bar{r} = \frac{r_o + r_1 + \ldots + r_{n-1}}{n} = \frac{mr_o}{T} \sum_{i=0}^{m-1} (1 + d)^i \tag{5.5}$$

Substituting 5.5 into 5.4, we then have

$$_o\int^T \pi_t = p \cdot q \cdot T \cdot \bar{r} - (c(q) + b) \frac{(e^{s^T} - 1)}{s} \tag{5.4'}$$

first and second order conditions for a profit maximum are then

$$MR \; T \; \bar{r} - c'(q) \frac{(e^{s^T} - 1)}{s} = 0 \tag{5.6}$$

and

$$D = \frac{dMR}{dq} T \; r - c''(q) \frac{(e^{s^T} - 1)}{s} < 0 \tag{5.7}$$

The first order condition thus defines the optimal output level as an implicit function of the percentage size of each devaluation, d, and the length of the time period between devaluations, m, so that differentiating 5.6 with respect to d and m, we have

$$\frac{dq}{dd} = \frac{-1}{D} MR \frac{\partial r}{\partial d} \tag{5.8}$$

$$\frac{dq}{dm} = \frac{-1}{D} MR \frac{\partial r}{\partial m} \tag{5.9}$$

For all $d \geq 0$ and $n = T/m \geq 1$, it can be shown that $\partial\bar{r}/\partial d > 0$ and $\partial\bar{r}/\partial m < 0$. Equation 5.8 simply makes explicit the fact that as the average percentage devaluation increases, _ceteris paribus_, the average exchange rate prevailing over the firm's production period is higher, thus raising net earnings and hence optimal output. Analogously, as the time elapsed between devaluations increases, other things being equal, the average rate is lowered, decreasing optimum output.

Perhaps less obvious is the fact that $\bar{r}$ is higher in an exchange rate regime with frequent devaluations even when the percentage devaluation is proportionately lower. This point may be made clear by comparing two regimes over the period $0 < t < T$, both of which devalue from r_o to the same r_T, so that initial and final rates are identical. Letting the time between devaluations be k times as great in the lower frequency regime, so that $m_2 = k\, m_1$, with $k > 1$, we have

$$(1 + d_2)^{T/km_1} = (1 + d_1)^{T/m_1}$$

$$\ln\,(1 + d_2) = k \ln\,(1 + d_1)$$

$$d_2 = (1 + d_1)^k - 1$$

By the definition of r, we then have

$$\bar{r}_2 = \frac{r_o\, km_1\, \{[1 + (1 + d_1)^k - 1]^{T/km_1} - 1\}}{Td_2}$$

$$= \frac{r_o\, k\, m_1\, [(1 + d_1)^{Tm_1} - 1]}{T\, [(1 + d_1)^k - 1]}$$

Hence the ratio of the higher frequency regime's average rate to that of the lower one is then

$$\frac{\bar{r}_1}{\bar{r}_2} = \frac{[(1 + d_1)^k - 1]}{k\, d_1} > 1 \quad \text{for all } k > 1 \qquad (5.10)$$

If we view the adoption of the crawling peg policy as a move from a low to a high frequency regime, then inequality 5.10 suggests that the policy could have an incentive effect on exports even if end-of-period real exchange rates were to remain unchanged. From the point of view of hypothesis testing, this possibility requires that we use average exchange rates, calculated on the basis of a number of frequent observations, if this effect of the crawling peg is to be properly reflected in a measure of the impact of the crawling peg on relative prices. The following section turns to the question of measuring the combined effect of both commercial and exchange policies on relative prices; the examination of the relative price effect of the crawling peg in this section suggests that the incentive provided by the crawling peg in a deterministic sense may be captured by the use of an appropriate average exchange rate.

5-6. Measuring the Relative Price Effects of Brazilian Commercial and Exchange Policies

In the preceding sections of this chapter we have examined the principal commercial and exchange policies pursued by Brazil after 1964 and their potential effects on the relative prices of exportables. As an increase in these prices provides at least in theory an explanation of the observed opening of the Brazilian economy to greater trade in the late 1960s, it remains to attempt to quantify these price changes so that this hypothesis may be compared with the uncertainty hypothesis advanced earlier.

Any attempt to express changes in the relative prices of Brazilian exportables over the last two decades in an econometrically usable form necessarily represents a series of compromises between theory and the data available. As the time series of relative prices used in the following chapter rest in part on such simplifying assumptions, it is worthwhile examining briefly the premises underlying the derivation of these series, as well as the results themselves.

The first such assumption is that Brazil may be considered a small country in world trade, at least with respect to the exportables considered in the following chapter. Although this assumption might be questioned if coffee and several other products were to be included among the exports studied, it appears valid for manufactures and for the primary products considered. World prices are consequently assumed to be given, with the price elasticity of demand for potential Brazilian exports infinite.

A related assumption is that potential Brazilian exportables are perfect substitutes for similar goods produced elsewhere. This assumption in effect unifies world and internal Brazilian prices for the same article, causing them to differ only to the extent that tariffs and transport costs act as a partial impediment to trade. This assumption may be challenged both on theoretical and empirical grounds. Many studies of import and export demand functions implicitly assume the contrary, by including as an argument in import demand or export supply functions the variable P_f/P_d, where the subscripts refer to the foreign and domestic prices.[11] Some Brazilian exporters, moreover, might argue that their products are not treated as perfect substitutes in world markets, having sometimes encountered considerable resistance as they are first marketed internationally.

Finally, it is assumed that from the point of view of the potential Brazilian exporter, the relevant export price is equal to the proceeds per unit in cruzeiros from an export after adjustments for taxes and subsidies, as well as any tax rebates earned as a result of the particular sale. Although hardly controversial, this assumption in effect says that the potential exporter is indifferent to whether an extra cruzeiro of net export earnings results from a devaluation, an increase in the world price of the good, a direct export subsidy, or the rebate of part of the cost of production. All of these influences may consequently be combined into a single relative price. As some export incentives required some administrative effort by the firm to collect the subsidies or rebates for which they were eligible, in contrast to the case of a cruzeiro price increase resulting from a world price increase for the good or from a devaluation, this assumption may be regarded as an approximation, but with the exception of the import drawback before 1964, the administrative costs of obtaining the incentives does not appear to have been a major factor.

Given these assumptions, we may define the cruzeiro price, cp, of export i as

$$cp_i = (1 + s_i)\ r\ p_i \tag{5.11}$$

where r is the real exchange rate, adjusted for both inflation in Brazil and its trading partners, p_i the world price of the ith product, and $1 + s_i$ an index of the increase in effective remuneration to the exporter due to commercial policies of the type discussed in Section 5-2, relative to a base period in which s_i is arbitrarily assumed to be zero. As r is defined as the real, rather than nominal exchange rate, p_i represents a constant (dollar) index of the price of good i.

In principle a time series for s_i and p_i would be necessary to determine cp_i; the actual procedure used in this study for some product groups represents a simplification of the above definition. Two major groups of exportables, manufactured goods and non-traditional primary products, are used in Chapter 6 to test the uncertainty and relative price hypotheses for the period 1957 through 1972.

In the first case, available international price series for specific categories of manufactured products do not correspond to the Brazilian industrial sector classification which has been used in this study. Although proxies for these series might be provided by sectoral wholesale price indices from the U.S. or other major Brazilian trading partners, such series for the U.S. for the 1957-1972 period are highly correlated with the general wholesale price index, which is one of the determinants of the real exchange rate, r. For this reason, the real cruzeiro price series for manufactured exports used in Chapter 6 assume that the effect of world price changes for manufactures is captured by movements in r, which is the nominal cruzeiro-dollar rate multiplied by the U.S. wholesale price index and deflated by the corresponding Brazilian index. In terms of 5.11, this is equivalent to assuming that p_i is equal to one over the whole period.

Indices of the effect of commercial policies on cruzeiro earnings for manufactured exports have been constructed by Tyler and used by Suplicy, Von Doellinger, and others. The principal limitation of these indices for our purposes is that they refer to the entire industrial and semi-industrialized products sector, rather than to specific industry groups, as definition 5.11 would require. To avoid this level of aggregation, a method similar to Tyler's was used, based on a cross-section study of the effects of Brazilian export incentives in 1971 made by Savasini et al.[12]

Savasini and his colleagues attempted to measure the effects of the six principal export incentives created after 1964, which were discussed in Section 5.2 and are listed with the month in which they went into effect in Table 5.1.

For each of the incentives listed below, the Savasini group estimated the net reduction in taxes or net subsidy paid per cruzeiro of exports by sector, using the Interministerial Price Council's (CIP) 1971 input-output table, and data supplied by the Finance Ministry and the

Central Bank's Foreign Trade Department (CACEX). Special problems arise in the estimation of the effect of the income tax credit, expressed in terms of net subsidy per cruzeiro of exports. The Savasini group's approach assumed that the effect of other income tax incentives for regional and sectoral development was known and constant across sectors, in addition to the implicit assumption that any tax shifting effects of the income tax were neutral among sectors. Fundamental to all of the Savasini estimates is the small-country assumption: world prices are given, so that a tax on an exportable must be borne completely by the producer.

TABLE 5.1

IMPLEMENTATION OF THE EXPORT INCENTIVES

Incentive	Date Effective
Drawbacks for Imports used in Exports	June 1964
IPI exemption	August 1965
ICM exemption	February 1967
Income tax credit	February 1967
IPI subsidy	July 1968
ICM subsidy	September 1971

The approach used here is similar to Tyler's in that it is assumed that each incentive's effect, given by the Savasini group's estimates, can be added to the existing index of total incentives in effect. Thus the index is 100 for the 1957-1963 period, during which there were no important commercial policy changes, with successive increases over the remaining years as incentives were added. The incentive for a given year can thus be calculated by summing the full effects of the incentives operating at the beginning of that year and adding incentives imposed during the year, pro-rated for the month they took effect. Under the small country assumption, an incentive which the Savasini group expressed as a percentage of a cruzeiro's worth of exports may be considered to go entirely to the producer, whose net effective price expressed as an index increases by this percentage.

The results of this method of estimating the index of incentives for manufactured exports are presented in Table 5.2 for the thirteen manufacturing sectors for which the uncertainty hypothesis was tested in Chapter 6. Although the results are largely self-explanatory, several points should be noted. First, the import drawback, which had been in legal existence since 1957 but only effectively implemented in 1964, had a relatively minor effect in most sectors even then. Second, the creation of both the ICM exemption and the income tax credit in early 1967 resulted in a fairly large increase in the index for most sectors between 1966 and 1968, with relatively smaller increases in the following years as the ICM and IPI subsidies went into effect. As the increase in the incentive level was contemporaneous with the adoption of the crawling peg in mid-1968, it raises a potential problem of multicollinearity in attempting to separate the effects of both an increase in relative prices and a decrease in exchange rate uncertainty on the structure of trade.

The second group of products examined in Chapter 6 are primary products, principally agricultural products. Although a discussion of the basis for their selection is deferred until that chapter, several

TABLE 5.2

INDICES OF EXPORT INCENTIVES FOR MANUFACTURES
(Index 1957 - 1963 = 1.00)

	1964	1965	1966	1967	1968	1969	1970	1971	1972	1973
Non-metallic mineral products	1.003	1.037	1.102	1.297	1.328	1.369	1.379	1.399	1.460	1.460
Metals	1.010	1.041	1.094	1.277	1.315	1.366	1.379	1.401	1.476	1.476
Machines	1.034	1.089	1.176	1.363	1.410	1.472	1.478	1.504	1.580	1.580
Electrical and communications equip.	1.040	1.095	1.178	1.296	1.336	1.388	1.401	1.424	1.492	1.492
Transportation Equipment	1.016	1.066	1.199	1.391	1.437	1.498	1.513	1.542	1.629	1.629
Paper products	1.001	1.035	1.100	1.243	1.283	1.337	1.350	1.377	1.457	1.457
Leather products	1.003	1.034	1.095	1.267	1.296	1.333	1.343	1.361	1.417	1.417
Textiles	1.024	1.071	1.151	1.343	1.389	1.450	1.465	1.493	1.576	1.576
Rubber products	1.010	1.074	1.193	1.377	1.433	1.507	1.525	1.559	1.661	1.661
Clothing and footwear	1.069	1.141	1.240	1.422	1.469	1.532	1.657	1.685	1.767	1.767
Food processing	1.001	1.028	1.058	1.242	1.256	1.274	1.310	1.319	1.346	1.346
Beverages	1.052	1.312	1.798	1.993	2.044	2.112	2.112	2.129	2.152	2.243
Tobacco	1.001	1.064	1.187	1.382	1.438	1.513	1.532	1.568	1.676	1.676

observations about the price series used for non-traditional primary products are relevant here.

First, as was noted in Section 5-2, the commercial policy incentives to greater export created after 1964 were virtually all for manufactured exports. As a result, even though a price index for primary products would in theory be determined by commercial policies, the real exchange rate, and world prices in constant dollars, as defined by equation 5.11, the commercial policy index remained constant throughout this period.[13]

Second, relevant world primary price indices in dollars are not available for all of the products considered over the 1957-1972 period. The alternative approach followed here is to use the unit prices of these exports as calculated from Brazilian trade statistics indicating the value of exports. Although the unit value approach has been criticized because of potential commodity composition changes, the products considered here are sufficiently uniform and narrowly defined that this is not likely to constitute a serious problem. Since the unit values in cruzeiros calculated from the quantity and value series for Brazilian primary products exports are expressed in current cruzeiros, the real price index for the product was determined by deflating the unit value series by the Brazilian wholesale price index. It should be noted that the real exchange rate, treated as a separate value in the case of the manufactured export price series, is implicit in the unit value if defined in cruzeiro terms.

FOOTNOTES FOR CHAPTER V

1. The theory of tariffs is treated in a number of texts and articles, including J. N. Bhagwati, Trade, Tariffs, and Growth, Cambridge, MIT Press, 1969; W. M. Corden, The Theory of Protection, London, Oxford U.P., 1970; and M. C. Kemp, The Pure Theory of International Trade and Investment, Englewood Cliffs, N.J., Prentice-Hall, 1969. Brazilian trade policies have been examined by J. Bergsman, Brazil: Industrialization and Trade Policies, London, Oxford U.P. (for OECD), 1970; C. Von Doellinger, H. B. de Castro Faria, R. N. Mendonça Ramos, and L. C. Cavalcanti, Transformação da Estrutura das Exportações Brasileiras, 1964-70, Rio de Janeiro, IPEA-INPES, 1973; W. G. Tyler, Manufactured Export Expansion and Industrialization in Brazil, Kiel, IWUK, 1976.

2. The multiple rate system is discussed by A. Kafka, "The Brazilian Exchange Auction System," Rev. Econ. and Statistics, Vol. 38, 1956, 308-322.

3. Tyler reports that prior to 1964, only 66 transactions were recorded under this provision, the majority for transactions of less than $25,000. Tyler, op. cit., 215.

4. This point is discussed by Tyler, op. cit., 216.

5. The ICM system has been examined by M. Guerard, "The Brazilian State Value-Added Tax," IMF Staff Papers, Vol. 20, 118-169, Washington, D.C., 1973.

6. J. Bergsman, "Foreign Trade Policy in Brazil," (mimeographed), Rio de Janeiro, USAID, 1971.

7. The consequences of relaxing this assumption have received considerable theoretical attention. In addition to Corden himself, op. cit., the problem has been examined by V. K. Ramaswami and T. N. Srinivasan, "Tariff Structure and Resource Allocation in the Presence of Factor Substitution," in Bhagwati, Jones, Mundell, and Vanek (eds.), Trade, Balance of Payments, and Growth, Amsterdam, North-Holland, 1971. In general, such investigations have concluded that in a rigorous sense, the substitution problem may invalidate the use of the effective protective concept as a guide to the structure of production and resource allocation.

8. Ramaswami and Srinivasan, op. cit.

9. These estimates of the domestic resource cost of foreign exchange appear in J. R. Mendonça de Barros, H. D. Lobato, M. A. Travolo, and M. H. G. P. Zockun, "Sistema fiscal e incentivos as exportações," Revista Brasileira de Economia, Rio, Vol. 29, Oct/Dec 1975, 3-24.

10. Although the argument becomes more tedious, our conclusions are unchanged if T/m is not an integer.

11. This procedure has been discussed by E. E. Leamer and R. M. Stern, Quantitative International Economics, Ch. 2, Boston, Allyn and Bacon, 1970.

12. J. A. A. Savasini, H. D. Lobato, M. A. Travolo, and M. H. G. P. Zockun, "O Sistema Brasileiro de Promoção às Exportações" (mimeographed), Inst. Pesquisas Economicas, Univ. São Paulo, 1974.

13. In the early 1970s several states, including Parana and São Paulo, reduced the ICM charged on a few agricultural products. Since 1974, increasing attention has been given to the possibility of extending the export incentives to agriculture.

CHAPTER VI

AN ECONOMETRIC TEST OF THE UNCERTAINTY HYPOTHESIS

We have argued in Chapters 2 and 3 that a decrease in demand uncertainty, like that resulting from Brazil's adoption of a crawling peg exchange policy in 1968, may be expected to increase production and sales in the sector in which uncertainty has decreased. In the Brazilian case, this would suggest that the crawling peg increased exports, independently of any relative price changes which occurred in the period. Chapters 4 and 5 have respectively examined the problems of measuring changes in uncertainty and in relative prices, the latter resulting both from exchange policy and from the extensive series of export incentives created after 1964. In the present chapter we turn to an econometric examination of the uncertainty hypothesis, using Brazilian data from the period from 1957 to 1973. Two major groups of exportable goods are examined, manufactures and primary products.

Although the central problem of measurement of uncertainty has been confronted in Chapter 4, a number of methodological issues remain before this variable can be used in a meaningful way in a test of the uncertainty hypothesis. Section 6-1 is a discussion of the choice of variables appropriate for a test of the hypothesis. It is followed by a consideration of possible functional forms for the relationship. Several remaining problems in estimation, among them lag estimation and potential autocorrelation, are discussed in Section 6-3. The results of our estimates for manufactured exports are presented in Section 6-4. They are followed by a similar set of estimates for primary products. The chapter concludes with a brief discussion of ways in which the econometric estimates might be interpreted.

6-1. The Choice of Variables for a Test of the Uncertainty Hypothesis

The theory of firm response to changes in demand uncertainty developed in Chapters 2 and 3 in its most rudimentary form states that a reduction in output price uncertainty as we have defined and measured it in Chapter 4 will increase the optimal level of output. When the model is extended to the firm facing more than one market, such as the domestic and international market, we concluded that a reduction in price uncertainty in one of these markets would increase both output and the share of output sold in the market in which uncertainty decreased. In the Brazilian context, this would imply that the crawling peg not only increased the output of exportables, but that the export coefficient, or the proportion of the sector's total output exported, also increased. This conclusion thus leaves some latitude for the choice of dependent variable in a test of the uncertainty hypothesis; we would predict that total exportable production, exports, and the export coefficient would all be inverse functions of the level of exchange rate uncertainty.

In this study the last of these three variables, the export coefficient, was used. This choice was motivated by a number of considerations. First, one of the principal concerns of this study is the impact of changes in uncertainty on the structure of an economy. In this sense, an increase in the relative importance of exports is of more interest than would be a change in their level or in the level of output of the whole sector. Second, and empirically more important, is the fact that the post-1968 period in Brazil was characterized by high rates of growth of both production and exports; even naive regressions of either sectoral output or sectoral exports on a time trend would explain a substantial proportion of the variance in either variable. Use of the export coefficient as a dependent variable is thus a more stringent test of the uncertainty hypothesis, since there is no a priori reason to assume that it would vary over time, even in a rapidly growing economy. Finally, it should be noted that investigations of export behavior, including some studies of Brazilian trade, sometimes postulate a relation between exports and total production of the exportable.[1] As total production, however, includes exports by identity, a problem of simultaneity arises, creating a bias in ordinary least squares estimates. Use of the export coefficient, rather than the level of exports, with total production consequently part of the dependent variable, avoids this problem.

The theory of price uncertainty developed in Chapters 2 and 3 points to several variables as potential determinants of the value of the export coefficient, in addition to the degree of uncertainty itself. As was shown in Section 2-3, the conventional positive response of output to an increase in its price under certainty continues to hold in the uncertainty case, in which we define the relevant price as the expectation of a random output price, thus justifying the inclusion of relative prices as one of the variables determining the export coefficient.

As was demonstrated in Section 3-2, the ability of a firm to stockpile its output will have an effect on the degree to which output responds to changes in uncertainty; the firm with sufficient storage capacity will ceteris paribus be less likely to reduce output in the presence of uncertainty, and in extreme cases might even increase it. This conclusion leaves open the question as to how this possibility should be treated in an export coefficient function. One approach would be to include an index of storage capacity by sector. The approach followed here, however, ignores this variable for two reasons. First, information on storage capacity by sector in Brazil during the 1957-1973 period is scanty and difficult to interpret in a meaningful way. Second, and perhaps more important, the degree to which a firm or whole sector may use inventories to avoid fluctuations in profits is more appropriately considered as a variable determining the degree of response of output to changes in uncertainty, rather than entering the export coefficient function directly. In this sense it is a variable determining a parameter of the coefficient of the uncertainty variable, as is the degree of risk aversion, and is not a separate independent variable.

We have to this point ignored potential effects of income changes on the export coefficient. Conventional microeconomic theory would suggest that both income in the importing countries and at home would affect the export coefficient, the former positively and the second negatively. The latter effect could be justified by the assumption underlying Section 2-5 that the firm may sell an exportable in either the domestic or the export market. Under the assumptions of the preceding chapter, domestic and foreign prices for the good differ only by tariffs and other forms of intervention, so that an increase in domestic incomes would have a direct negative effect on exports as they were diverted to the domestic market.

Several approaches to the problem of measuring these income effects were tried in this study. In principle one would require a world income series or alternatively, a measure of world expenditure or tradable goods, with Brazilian income or expenditure deducted, as well as another variable for Brazilian income. Data limitations might suggest a proxy, such as expenditures on imports by the U.S. and Brazil's other principal trading partners. As a proxy for the world aggregate price, the U.S. wholesale price index is already included in the relative price variable, requiring that world income or expenditure variables be expressed in real terms. In actuality, income and expenditure trends in real terms for Brazil's major trading partners in the 1957-1972 period appear to be reasonably well approximated by a simple time trend.

An alternative formulation focuses on Brazilian income in this period, which did not follow trends in the U.S. and other major industrial countries. Several authors, including Tyler and Von Doellinger, have noted that low growth of domestic demand in Brazil in the immediate post-1964 period, as government stabilization programs took effect, led a number of producers, particularly in the manufacturing sectors, to expand exports.[2]

The approach used in this study was to fit a semi-log time trend regression for Brazilian GNP, using the negative of residuals from this time trend as a proxy for the degree of excess capacity or slack in domestic demand. This formulation is similar to Tyler's, who found that the residuals from a time trend of industrial production were statistically significant when used as proxies for capacity utilization in estimates of export functions for manufactures.

Equation 6.1 and Table 6.1 below show the results, where the log of GNP was regressed on time:

$$\ln \text{GNP} = \underset{(5.7)}{-119.9} + \underset{(.0029)}{.0623\, t} \qquad (6.1)$$

$N = 17 \qquad R^2 = .969$

TABLE 6.1

RESIDUALS FROM A SEMILOG REGRESSION OF BRAZILIAN GNP ON TIME

Year	$\hat{e} = \ln Y - \ln \hat{Y}$	Year	$\hat{e} = \ln Y - \ln \hat{Y}$
1957	.0021	1966	-.0762
1958	.0135	1967	-.0931
1959	.0036	1968	-.0664
1960	.0345	1969	-.0442
1961	.0692	1970	-.0167
1962	.0564	1971	.0273
1963	.0085	1972	.0631
1964	-.0261	1973	.1074
1965	-.0628		

As is evident from the table, there was a marked slowing in the rate of growth of the Brazilian economy in 1964, as the new government's stabilization policy was implemented, with demand recovering only in the late sixties.

Several possible limitations of this approach should be noted. First, to the extent that Brazilian income and prices tend to move together, there is a potential problem of collinearity between this variable and the relative price term, one of whose components is the Brazilian wholesale price index. In actual practice, this problem did not appear important, since the other variables determining relative prices are not collinear with income. Second, it is implicitly assumed that both potential Brazilian GNP and world income are adequately described by the time trend, so that deviations from the trend are entirely attributable to fluctuations in actual Brazilian GNP. Although this assumption may be an acceptable approximation for the 1957-1972 period, it would not be after 1973, when world demand for Brazil's exportables was affected by the oil crisis and recession in the developed countries.

6-2. The Functional Form of the Export Coefficient Equation

The discussion of the preceding section led to the conclusion that the uncertainty hypothesis might be tested by attempting to explain changes in the export coefficient for a given product or sector (X/Q) as a function of the degree of exchange rate uncertainty, and a proxy for income or capacity utilization effects, or

$$(X/Q)_i = f\,(\underset{-}{U}, \underset{+}{P_i}, \underset{-}{Y}) \tag{6.2}$$

(The predicted signs of the coefficients of these determinants of the export coefficient are shown beneath each argument.)

Although the question of the specific functional form of a general function like 6.2 is often ignored, or at least subordinated to econometric convenience, some examination of alternative specific forms is in order at this point, in consideration of both the theory developed in earlier chapters and the way in which the variables in 6.2 have been defined and measured. Specific methodological problems arising once a functional form is chosen, including the problem of time lags, are deferred until the following section.

First, it should be noted that the dependent variable, the quantity of the ith sector's exports divided by total production in the sector, is a variable whose range is limited to the interval from zero to unity. As a result, straightforward application of least squares techniques may be inappropriate, since a number of these values may occur at the limits. This characteristic of the data suggests that the problem might be dealt with through a probit or Tobit limited dependent variable approach, estimating the probability that the export coefficient is either zero, one, or some intermediate value.[3]

In practice, the theoretical upper limit appears irrelevant to the data used in this study; the highest value attained by (X/Q) was .78 (for wool), and only in three of the remaining 21 sectors did the export coefficient exceed .20 (for beef, cashews, and soybeans). In manufacturing the highest export coefficient was .17 (leather products). The lower limit, however, is operative for several sectors early in the period. Even in this case, however, zero values of the dependent variable were infrequent. Of a total of 221 observations for the manufacturing sectors, only 12, or about five percent, were zero. In the primary products sectors, 11 of the 154 observations, or approximately seven percent, were zero. In most sectors the lower limit is inoperative; it appears more than once in manufacturing only in the electrical, paper, and rubber sectors, and in primary products more than once only for fish, corn, and soybeans. The estimation of time lags, moreover, requires that the first four years of observations (1957-1960) of the dependent variable be dropped from the sample. This requirement eliminates 8 of the 11 zero-valued observations of X/Q among the primary products and all 12 of these observations in the manufacturing sector. Thus despite the theoretical relevance of a limited dependent variable type of estimation technique to explain changes in a variable like the export coefficient, the use of an ordinary unconstrained least squares approach appears acceptable for this particular data set.

The way in which the independent variables in the export coefficient function have been defined also have implications for its specific form. The relative price, as defined in Chapter 5, is a positive variable with an expected positive effect on the export coefficient. The *ceteris paribus* relationship, given the limited range of the dependent variable, would consequently have a form like that shown in Figure 6.1.

This type of relationship might be approximated fairly closely a cubic or higher order polynomial, or by a form such as $Z/Q = e^{\alpha-\beta/p}$, which has the advantage of linearity in the reciprocal of price in log form. As noted above, however, the upper limit of one appears irrelevant to all of the cases examined in this study, suggesting that the function might be represented by a simpler form with no inflection point. As is evident from the diagram, even in this simplified case a linear function would in theory be inappropriate, as it would tend to underestimate X/Q for the highest and lowest values of p. To determine whether or not this problem was serious enough to warrant a non-linear specific form, several tests were performed. First, simple scatter plots of X/Q were created. In the majority of cases the plots did not show any easily discernible pattern, either linear or non-linear, although the omission of other independent variables could of course account for the absence of such a pattern even if it existed.

If we restrict non-linearity in the relationship between X/Q and P to the case in which $\partial^2(X/Q)/\partial P^2 > 0$, as is suggested by Figure 6.1, and assume that the function passes through the origin, then we may test for curvilinearity by regressing log (X/Q) on log P. Our hypothesis of approximate linearity is then equivalent to the assumption that the coefficient of log P is unity.

The definition and procedure for measuring the degree of uncertainty in Chapter 4 have similar implications for the form of the export coefficient function. By its definition, perfect certainty would be indicated by an index of zero with higher values representing increasing uncertainty. The predicted relation between uncertainty and the export coefficient, as we have shown in Chapter 3, would then have the form shown in Figure 6.2. Both variables are always non-negative, and if we assume that there is some level of uncertainty sufficient to eliminate all exports of a particular sector or product, then X/Q will asymptotically approach zero as U increases. Although this relationship might be crudely approximated by a linear function, it is clear that two superior alternatives would be

$$X/Q = \alpha + \beta\ (1/U) \tag{6.3}$$

or

$$X/Q = \alpha(U)^{-\beta} = \alpha(1/U)^{\beta} \tag{6.4}$$

It can be seen that 6.3 is linear in (1/U), while 6.4 is linear in its log.

In principle, the relation between X/Q and 1/U would have a form similar to that postulated for X/Q and P and shown in Figure 6.1, reflecting the restriction of X/Q to the interval between zero and one. Again restricting non-linearity in (1/U) to the case in which $\partial^2(X/Q)/\partial(1/U)^2 > 0$, as we did for price, curvilinearity can be tested by regressing log (X/Q) on log (1/U), with the hypothesis of linearity equivalent to the assumption of a coefficient of unity.

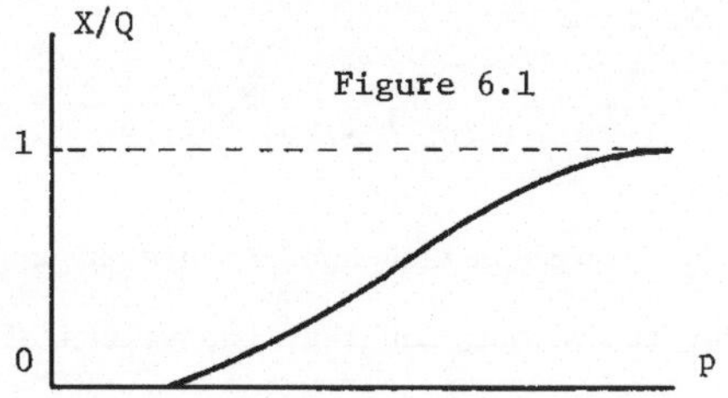

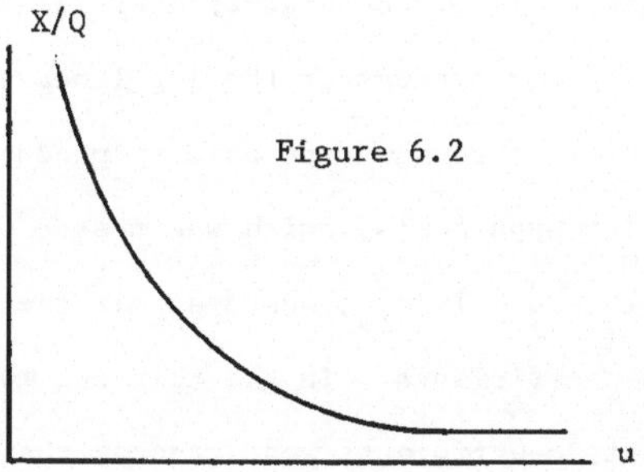

Figure 6.1 Hypothesized Relation between Relative Price and the Export Coefficient

Figure 6.2 Hypothesized Relation between Uncertainty and the Export Coefficient

To test the adequacy of the assumption of linearity in 1/U and in P, the relation between the export coefficient and its determinants was assumed to have the form

$$X/Q \quad = \quad \alpha(1/U)^{\beta_1} \cdot (P)^{\beta_2} \cdot (Y)^{\beta_3} \qquad (6.5)$$

where Y is the index of excess demand and any disturbance is assumed to be multiplicative. Under the assumption that the values of X/Q are sufficiently low so that they fall below the inflection point in either relationship, rejection of the linearity hypothesis requires that the estimates of the coefficients in 6.2 be significantly greater than unity.

Distributed lag regressions of the log-linear form of 6.5 for the thirteen manufacturing sectors and nine primary products in general failed to reject the linearity hypothesis, which was tested using the one-tailed t distribution of $(\sum_{j=1}^{N} b_{ij} - 1)/s_{\Sigma b}$, where $s_{\Sigma b}$ is the standard error of the sum of estimated coefficients. In the thirteen manufacturing sectors none of the uncertainty coefficients were greater than unity at the 90 percent level or higher; for the same sectors, only four of the price coefficients were greater than unity at the 90 percent level or higher.[4] Among the primary products studied, none of the uncertainty coefficients exceeded unity at the 90 percent level, and only one price coefficient, that for peanuts, was significantly greater than one. While these results can hardly be regarded as conclusive, they indicate that the available data do not appear to reject our hypothesis of linearity.

The remaining independent variable, as noted in the preceding section, may be interpreted as an index of excess demand, under the implicit assumption that both domestic supply and world demand are growing at a constant rate. This variable was also included in the log-linear regressions, with a constant added to make all values positive. By its definition, we would predict log Y to have a negative coefficient. In the thirteen manufacturing sectors the coefficient of log Y was less than zero at the 90 percent level in only five of the cases, and among the primary products, was significantly negative only in the case of wool. Given this generally weak relation between Y and X/Q the variable was dropped entirely from the primary product sample. In the case of manufacturing, it was assumed that the relationship could be approximated satisfactorily by expressing X/Q as a linear function of Y, though equation 6.5 would suggest the use of its reciprocal.

6-3. Methodological Problems in the Estimation of the Export Coefficient Function

The adoption of a specific functional form for the export function forces us to confront several problems of econometric methodology if the uncertainty hypothesis is to be successfully tested. In this section we consider the time pattern of response to changes in the determining variables and potential difficulties in significance test arising from autocorrelated disturbance terms and from multicollinearity.

Until now we have ignored the question of time lags in the response of exports to changes in uncertainty and relative prices. Although this is in part a consequence of the comparative statics approach of Chapters 2 and 3, the assumptions underlying the theory may provide some guide to the lag pattern. Firms in our model make output and export decisions based on their evaluation of a probability distribution of the uncertain output price. Although a number of models of expectation formation might be proposed, the implicit assumption underlying the model is that the subjective probability distribution upon which the firm bases its decisions is simply extrapolated from its recent experience. This formulation of the model would thus imply that the price and uncertainty levels of the "true" subjective distribution which actually determines the export coefficient may be constructed from some weighting of recent price and uncertainty levels. As the capacity or income variable is a measure of potential additional production which may be sold in the export market in periods of lower domestic demand, we assume that there is no time lag in its effect on the export coefficient. Together these assumptions imply a function which in linear form would be

$$(X/Q)_t = + \sum_{j=0}^{N} \beta_{1j}(1/H_k(b))_{t-j} + \sum_{j=0}^{M} \beta_{2j}P_{t-j} + {}_3Y_t + u_t \quad (6.6)$$

where the u_t is an element of the random vector of additive distrubances, u. We assume, moreover, that $E(u) = 0$ and $E(u'u) = \sigma^2\Omega$, the latter assumption recognizes the possibility of autocorrelation and other characteristics of the covariance matrix of disturbances which would violate the classical least squares assumptions.

The principal difficulty with this form is that the number of observations in the sample, at most 18, severely limits the number of parameters which may be estimated if any degrees of freedom are to be retained for tests of significance. For this reason the Almon lag technique of constraining the β_{ij} coefficients to lie on an nth degree polynomial was adopted. As this approach is discussed in detail in a number of sources,[5] we only note here some specific considerations in applying it to this particular case.

In the estimation of equations containing distributed lags it is quite common to experiment with different lag structures, deciding ex post on the basis of goodness of fit, significance tests, or other criteria which lag structure to use and report. While there may be cases in which this practice is defensible, it is clearly improper for our purposes, since ex post choice among different models applied to the same data set will produce spuriously high significance levels, rendering hypothesis tests meaningless. Ideally, one would like to have a new set of independent observations for each test of each model. In practice some compromises with the limitations imposed by a finite set of data are necessary.

The procedure followed in this study was to utilize those *a priori* restrictions which could reasonably be imposed to narrow model selection to several alternative lag structures. The thirteen industrial sectors comprising the industry data set were then indexed, and a set of random numbers was used to select one of the sectors, which turned out to be the electrical and communications equipment sector. From among the several potential lag structures decided upon using *a priori* restrictions, the structure was chosen which yielded the most significant regression, as determined by an F-test. This structure was then used for all the distributed lags estimated in this study. Judgments about the significance of coefficients of estimates in the electrical and communications equipment sector are therefore suspect; meaningful tests of the uncertainty hypothesis or other hypotheses should exclude this sector.

Although theory offers no definite set of *a priori* restrictions to apply in initial lag structure selection, our model suggests some choices. It has been assumed that potential exporters form their expectations about relative prices and the level of uncertainty attached to them on the basis of current information and recent past experience, with the more distant past having a diminishing importance in the formation of their expectations. The Almon lag weights were therefore constrained to decline to zero in the t-kth period, with the current period (t) allowed to have an immediate effect. It was also assumed *a priori* that only the experience of the current and at most four preceding years were relevant. This assumption may not always be appropriate, particularly in the more sophisticated and complex industrial sectors in which the planning and execution of projects may require an extended period. The shortness of the time series used, however, effectively limits our use of longer lags. Finally, it was assumed that the lag weights followed a relatively simple pattern, not characterized by many peaks. In terms of the Almon procedure, this is equivalent to using a fairly low degree polynomial.

On the basis of these restrictions, equation (6.6) was estimated with the electrical and communications equipment sector data for various lag structures based on combinations of either a second or third degree polynomial with non-zero weights on the lags back either 2, 3, or 4 years, constrained to be zero in the earliest year. In order to allow approximately the same opportunity for both lagged independent variables, price and the uncertainty level, to affect the dependent variable, identical lag structures for each independent variable were always used. Of the six alternatives initially chosen, the lag structure finally chosen constrained the weights to follow a quadratic, with non-zero weights in the current and three immediate proceeding periods.

As should be clear from this discussion, the lag structure of the estimated coefficients is more likely to reflect our choice of assumptions than it is any underlying characteristics of the data. Our central interest, however, is whether or not changes in uncertainty, as measured by the indices constructed in Chapter IV, have real economic effects. From this point of view, our conclusions are likely to be unaffected by the specific time structure of the response to uncertainty; it is not the effect of uncertainty in a single period which concerns us, but its total impact.

The second principal problem in estimation arises from our assumption of potential non-spherical forms of the covariance matrix of disturbances. Only one such form of non-spherical disturbances, first degree autocorrelation, was explicitly considered here. As significance tests of the uncertainty hypothesis are of more interest to us than the actual values of the estimates of the coefficient, positive autocorrelation poses a serious threat to the validity of conclusions drawn from ordinary least squares results.

The basic difficulty with the conventional test for autocorrelation, the Durbin-Watson statistic, in our case once again arises from the small number of observations and consequently limited number of degrees of freedom. Despite values of the d statistic ranging as low as one, none of these values permit unambiguous rejection of the null hypothesis of no positive autocorrelation at either the 5 or 1 percent levels.

From the point of view of significance testing of the uncertainty hypothesis, positive autocorrelation leads to an underestimate of the standard error of each coefficient and hence overestimation of its significance. The position adopted in this study was therefore to treat the data as guilty, as we are unable to prove it innocent, accepting the ordinary least squares estimates as valid if confirmed by an alternative procedure capable of dealing with potential autocorrelation of the disturbance term.

All of the equations were therefore re-estimated using the Cochrane-Orcutt iterative technique to obtain estimates of the coefficients and of ρ.[6] As is shown in the following sections, this approach did not alter the basic conclusions of this study, although the results by sector were occasionally altered by its use.

There are several drawbacks to this approach. First, the use of the technique entails the loss of a degree of freedom, as it requires the use of two of the original observations of each variable to create the series which is actually estimated. Although this might be no problem in a large sample, it may have some cost in terms of significance levels in a small one. Second, the estimate of the degree of serial autocorrelation, $\hat{\rho}$, produced by the technique is approximate; $\hat{\rho} > 0$ is not an infallible indication of positive serial correlation. Finally, the use of the technique when $\hat{\rho} \leq 0$, in addition to sacrificing a degree of freedom, might be regarded as superfluous, since in this case least squares estimates of the standard errors will be overestimated, increasing the likelihood of rejection of results that are in reality significant.

In Chapter 5 it was noted that several of the most important export incentives for manufactured goods were created in the late sixties, at the same time that the crawling peg was adopted. We would consequently expect that the time series for exchange rate uncertainty and for relative prices might be correlated, raising a problem of multicollinearity, since both are used to estimate the export coefficient. As a preliminary test to see how serious this problem might be, the simple correlation between the relative price variable for each manufacturing sector (P_i) and the inverse of the uncertainty index (1/U) was calculated. The results are shown in Table 6.2.

TABLE 6.2

CORRELATION BETWEEN P_i AND $1/H_3(b)$

Non-metallic minerals	.192	Leather products	.126
Metals	.207	Textiles	.325
Machinery	.329	Clothing	.495
Electrical equipment	.219	Food processing	.039
Transport equipment	.371	Beverages	.453
Paper products	.180	Tobacco	.408
Rubber products	.398		

As expected, the correlation between the price and (1/U) is positive in all the sectors. There is considerable variation, however, and in no case does it exceed .50. There are several reasons for this. First, export incentives began only after 1964, while the degree of exchange rate uncertainty varied considerably even before 1964. Second, the real exchange rate actually appreciated in the late 1960s, offsetting to some extent the effect of increases in export incentives. Finally, the level of uncertainty actually rose at the end of the period, while several further export incentives were created. As a result, the estimates of the effects of uncertainty presented in the following section do not appear seriously compromised by the possible presence of multicollinearity, despite some degree of correlation between the explanatory variables.

Although all of the equations estimated in this study were treated as independent and unrelated, several comments on this assumption are in order. The model of firm reaction to changes in uncertainty developed in Chapters 2 and 3 is a partial equilibrium one; the effects of changes in a firm's output on the demand and supply of factors used by other firms is ignored. Although a full general equilibrium treatment of the effects of a reduction in demand uncertainty in one sector is beyond the scope of this study, the possibility of such effects suggests that the individual equations may not be independent.

A simple example may provide some insight into this problem. Soybeans and rice, two of the exports in the primary products group discussed in Section 6-5, as cultivated in Brazil both use a similar type of land. Hence increases in the output of one might occur partially at the cost of reducing output of the other, implying that the export coefficients in each sector are jointly determined. It was shown in Chapter 2 that the effect of a reduction in exchange rate uncertainty would be to increase the total quantity of the exportable produced, with exports themselves increasing even more. Thus the export coefficient would rise, while the increase in one sector's output would reduce output in the other sector, raising the export coefficient *ceteris paribus*. Single equation least squares approaches would thus tend to bias upward the estimates of the regression coefficients of the uncertainty index, the independent variable common to both sectors. In principle, only simultaneous equation estimation procedures would be appropriate under this assumption of interdependence.

Finally, even if we ignore explicit interdependence among the dependent variables, the disturbances may not be interdependent. This might be due to a number of causes. Bureaucratic simplification of export procedures, which might be considered an omitted variable in our model, could affect a number of sectors simultaneously and in similar fashion. Other types of reductions in demand uncertainty, whose effects would be explained by our theoretical model but which are not captured by the actual econometric model used, could operate in a similar way. In this case our estimates are not biased, but single equation estimation methods may not be the most efficient approach. This formulation of the problem, in fact, turns it into an example of the "seemingly unrelated regression" model discussed by Zellner and others.[7] Estimation of the entire group of equations in this case would be assymptotically more efficient than an equation-by-equation approach.

6-4. Estimates of the Export Coefficient Function for the Manufacturing Sectors

We have seen in preceding sections how the uncertainty hypothesis might in principle be tested, as well as some of the econometric problems associated with the proposed model. We turn now to an application of the model to 13 Brazilian manufacturing sectors.

Although the data used, its sources and difficulties in its interpretation are discussed more fully in Appendix C, several comments on the choice of sectors used for the test are in order here. Brazilian industrial statistics are classified into 20 different sectors,[8] a division which has been used in the construction of the input-output tables on which our estimates of the export incentives are based, as well as in the organization of price and quantity information by sector. Complete quantity series were not available for the wood and wood products sector, furniture, and publishing and printing. In addition, the plastics, pharmaceutical, and cosmetics sectors have been included in the data for the chemical sector for part of the period, reducing the number of sectors to which the model may meaningfully be applied to 13.

As the actual distribution of the lag regression coefficients resulting from the Almon lag procedure is a question which may be addressed separately from the issue of their overall significance, we focus on the aggregate impact of the uncertainty and price variables. In this sense it is the sum of the coefficient on the lagged variables, together with the standard error of this sum, which is of interest here. Our maintained hypothesis is that $\sum_{i=0}^{N} \beta_{ij} > 0$, or that the total impact of a reduction in uncertainty on X/Q is positive, where the β_{1i} are the coefficients on $(1/U)_{t-i}$. The null hypothesis (that $\sum_{j=0}^{N} \beta_{ij} = 0$) may then be tested at the $100(1 - \alpha)$ percent significance level by dividing the sum of the coefficients by their standard error and rejecting the null hypothesis at the appropriate significance level if $\sum_{j=0}^{N} \beta_{ij} / s_{\Sigma b} = t$ $t_{df,(100-\alpha)}$, where $s_{\Sigma b}$ is the standard error, and the t statistic for df degrees of freedom at the $(100 - \alpha)$ percent level.

In Chapter IV it was shown that a series of indices of uncertainty can be derived, each one corresponding to a given degree stochastic dominance rule. Each higher level index adds a new central moment of the distribution, beginning with variance, which is the single argument of $H_3(b)$. The indices are thus correlated, and this effect is strengthened by the heavy weight which the lower moments, particularly variance, receive. In the real exchange rate data analyzed in Chapter IV, variance heavily dominates all four indices. In the econometric tests of the uncertainty hypothesis discussed in this chapter, all four of the $H_k(b)$ indices were used. Only the results of the estimates using $H_3(b)$ and $H_6(b)$ are reported here, since the other regressions results were almost identical, as is to be expected from the composition of $H_4(b)$ and $H_5(b)$, which represent intermediate measures between $H_3(b)$ and $H_6(b)$.

Table 6.3 presents the results of ordinary least squares estimates of the linear model of preceding sections, with $U = H_3(b)$. The coefficients, or sums of coefficients for the lagged variables, are reported on the first line, with the standard errors noted immediately below in parentheses. The calculated t-ratios are given on the third line, and when they may be used to test our hypotheses, the level at which the respective null hypothesis may be rejected is indicated beside the t-ratio. As we have no prediction as to the sign or magnitude of the constant term, only the t-ratios are reported. It was noted earlier that significance test for the electrical and communications equipment sector are of questionable value in the least squares estimates, since this data was used in the final selection of the lag structure of our estimated model. For this reason significance levels are omitted. The data used runs from 1960 through 1973 (14 observations), since 1957 - 1959 were used to provide the lagged values of uncertainty and price. With six parameters estimated, there are eight degrees of freedom. As the actual values of the $H_k(b)$ are small, on the order of .0001 in a few cases, the values of (1/U) are large in relation to the other variables. The indices were therefore scaled by multiplication by 1000, so that the actual coefficients reported in Table 6.3 and in subsequent tables should be divided by 1000 if the original index is used.

Examination of the second column of Table 6.3 shows strikingly the effect of uncertainty. In only one of the 12 tested cases did the sum of the coefficients fail to be significantly greater than zero at the 99 percent level. In contrast, the relative price coefficients are only significant at an 80 percent level or higher in 4 of the 12 cases, despite generally having the theoretically correct signs. The capacity utilization proxy variable appears significant, particularly in the heavier, durable goods sectors.

Table 6.4 repeats these estimates, the only difference being the use of the higher level index $H_6(b)$ rather than $H_3(b)$ as a measure of the

TABLE 6.3

ORDINARY LEAST SQUARES ESTIMATES OF THE EXPORT COEFFICIENT FUNCTION

$$(X/Q = b_o + \sum_{j=0}^{3} b_{1j}(1/H_3(b)) + \sum_{j=0}^{3} b_{2j}P + b_3Y)$$

b_o	$\sum_{j=0}^{3} b_{1j}$	$\sum_{j=0}^{3} b_{2j}$	b_3
Non-metallic mineral products			
.041	.099	-.012	-.064
(.016)	(.018)	(.006)	(.016)
2.50	5.55 > .995	-2.24 ---	-4.02 > .995
R^2 = .848	D.W. = 2.92	F = 8.92	
Metals			
-.006	.210	.007	-.223
(.061)	(.069)	(.021)	(.062)
-.109	3.04 > .990	.315 ---	-3.70 > .995
R^2 = .730	D.W. = 3.08	F = 4.33	
Machinery			
.011	.261	.002	-.287
(.053)	(.076)	(.018)	(.050)
.20	3.44 > .990	.10 ---	-5.73 > .995
R^2 = .870	D.W. = 1.53	F = 10.66	
Electrical and communications equipment			
-.008	.110	.004	-.047
(.016)	(.018)	(.005)	(.014)
.50	6.15	.67	-3.25
R^2 = .915	D.W. = 1.63		

TABLE 6.3--continued

b_0	$\sum_{j=0}^{3} b_{1j}$	$\sum_{j=0}^{3} b_{2j}$	b_3
Transportation equipment			
.003	.171	.001	-.035
(.022)	(.036)	(.007)	(.022)
.14	4.77 > .995	.08 ---	-1.60 > .90
R^2 = .916	D.W. = 2.89	F = 17.55	
Paper and paper products			
-.025	.195	.009	-.047
(.022)	(.024)	(.007)	(.023)
1.14	8.27 > .995	1.25 > .80	2.04 > .95
R^2 = .940	D.W. = 2.76	F = 24.91	
Rubber products			
-.072	-.054	.026	-.010
(.015)	(.025)	(.005)	(.014)
-4.80	-2.14 ---	5.10 > .995	-.69 ---
R^2 = .852	D.W. = 2.92	F = 9.23	
Leather and leather goods			
.215	.984	-.062	-.031
(.107)	(.109)	(.037)	(.110)
2.00	9.00 > .995	-1.70 ---	-3.41 > .99
R^2 = .921	D.W. = 2.36	F = 18.51	
Textiles			
.005	.109	.001	-.031
(.009)	(.013)	(.003)	(.009)
.53	8.23 > .995	.15 ---	3.49 > .99
R^2 = .964	D.W = 2.41	F = 42.55	

TABLE 6.3.--continued

	b_0	$\sum_{j=0}^{3} b_{1j}$	$\sum_{j=0}^{3} b_{2j}$	b_3
Clothing and footwear				
	-.028	.378	.009	.014
	(.010)	(.020)	(.003)	(.010)
	2.84	18.58 > .995	2.83 > .95	1.41 > .80
	R^2 = .998	D.W. = 2.15	F = 878.23	
Food processing				
	.061	.109	-.016	-.002
	(.014)	(.015)	(.005)	(.016)
	4.23	7.52 > .995	-3.32 ---	.13 ---
	R^2 = .916	D.W. = 2.64	F = 17.47	
Beverages				
	-.006	.110	.002	-.004
	(.001)	(.007)	(.001)	(.005)
	-4.37	16.49 > .995	4.95 > .995	.71 ---
	R^2 = .997	D.W. = 2.82	F = 530.56	
Tobacco products				
	-.005	.069	.002	.025
	(.009)	(.016)	(.003)	(.009)
	-.55	4.26 > .995	.70 ---	-2.68 > .95
	R^2 = .925	D.W. = 2.29	F = 19.84	

NOTE: The reported t-ratios may not equal the ratio of the reported sum of coefficients to their standard error, due to rounding of the three statistics. There are 8 degrees of freedom in each equation, based on observations from 1960 to 1973.

TABLE 6.4

ORDINARY LEAST SQUARES ESTIMATES OF THE EXPORT COEFFICIENT FUNCTION

$$(X/Q = b_0 + \sum_{j=0}^{3} b_{1j}(1/H_6(b)) + \sum_{j=0}^{3} b_{2j}P + b_3Y)$$

b_0	$\sum_{j=0}^{3} b_{1j}$		$\sum_{j=0}^{3} b_{2j}$		b_3	
Non-metallic mineral products						
.039	.025		-.012		-.065	
(.016)	(.004)		(.005)		(.015)	
2.47	5.64	> .995	2.21	---	-4.14	> .995
R^2 = .854	D.W. = 2.89		F = 9.38			
Metals						
.007	.054		.007		-.231	
(.064)	(.019)		(.022)		(.065)	
.12	2.90	> .95	.33	---	-3.57	> .95
R^2 = .706	D.W. = 3.00		F = 3.84			
Machinery						
.002	.065		.005		-.287	
(.056)	(.021)		(.019)		(.054)	
.04	3.14	> .99	.25	---	-5.34	> .995
R^2 = .849	D.W. = 1.47		F = 9.04			
Electrical and communications equipment						
-.009	.028		.004		-.047	
(.017)	(.005)		(.005)		(.015)	
-.56	5.58		.72		-2.97	
R^2 = .900	D.W. = 1.62					

TABLE 6.4-continued

	b_0	$\sum_{j=0}^{3} b_{1j}$		$\sum_{j=0}^{3} b_{2j}$		b_3	
Transportation equipment							
	-.001	.043		.002		-.035	
	(.022)	(.009)		(.007)		(.022)	
	.03	4.78	> .995	.26	---	-1.64	> .90
	R^2 = .916	D.W. = 2.97		F = 17.54			
Paper and paper products							
	-.023	.050		.009		-.046	
	(.018)	(.005)		(.006)		(.019)	
	-1.25	9.82	> .995	1.39	> .80	-2.39	> .95
	R^2 = .956	D.W = 2.73		F = 35.11			
Rubber products							
	-.071	-.013		.025		-.009	
	(.015)	(.006)		(.005)		(.015)	
	-4.73	-2.08	---	5.04	> .995	-.67	---
	R^2 = .847	D.W. = 2.827		F = 8.88			
Leather and leather goods							
	.218	.256		-.063		-.381	
	(.111)	(.029)		(.038)		(.113)	
	1.97	8.82	> .995	-1.66	---	-3.36	> .995
	R^2 = .915	D.W. 2.21		F = 17.23			
Textiles							
	.003	.028		.001		-.031	
	(.009)	(.003)		(.003)		(.008)	
	.39	8.73	> .995	.36	---	-3.70	> .995
	R^2 = .968	D.W = 2.03		F = 49.14			

TABLE 6.4.—continued

	b_0	$\sum_{j=0}^{3} b_{1j}$		$\sum_{j=0}^{3} b_{2j}$		b_3	
Clothing and footwear							
	-.037	.092		.012		.020	
	(.016)	(.008)		(.005)		(.016)	
	-2.34	10.89	> .995	2.37	> .95	1.23	> .80
	R^2 = .995	D.W. = 2.43		F = 317.46			
Food processing							
	.062	.029		-.017		-.003	
	(.015)	(.004)		(.005)		(.017)	
	4.12	7.32	> .995	-3.23	---	.18	---
	R^2 = .908	D.W. = 2.54		F = 15.86			
Beverages							
	-.007	-027		.003		-.000	
	(.002)	(.003)		(.001)		(.008)	
	-3.11	9.42	> .995	3.54	> .995	.004	---
	R^2 = .991	D.W. 2.82		F = 182.20			
Tobacco products							
	-.007	.017		.003		-.024	
	(.010)	(.004)		(.003)		(.010)	
	.70	3.91	> .995	.85	---	-2.47	> .95
	R^2 = .916	D.W. = 2.29		F = 17.50			

Note: The reported t-ratios may not equal the ratio of the reported sum of coefficients to their standard error, due to rounding of the three statistics. There are 8 degrees of freedom in each equation, based on observations from 1960 to 1973.

level of uncertainty. As is evident from the table, our basic results are little changed, with 11 of the 12 sectors again showing the uncertainty variable to be significantly positive.

It was argued in the preceding section that the presence of first order serial correlation of the distrubance terms may invalidate significance tests based on ordinary least squares. To avoid this potential problem, the equations were re-estimated using the Cochrane Orcutt iterative technique. The results, using both $H_3(b)$ and $H_6(b)$, are reported in Tables 6.5 and 6.6 respectively.

It is clear from the tables that our conclusions are scarcely altered by used of the Cochrane Orcutt procedure. If we use the estimate of ρ in the first order disturbance scheme $u_t = \rho u_{t-1} + \varepsilon_t$ as a rough indication of sectors for which ordinary least squares estimates might be misleading, this result is hardly surprising. Positive first order serial correlation appears to compromise the validity of earlier conclusions based on significance tests only in the machinery sector. Note that if the electrical and communications sector were also included, it too would no longer show a significant coefficient for the uncertainty term. In the other sectors the generally low and negative estimates of ρ suggest that serial correlation does not seriously compromise the validity of our hypothesis tests.

TABLE 6.5

COCHRANE-ORCUTT ITERATIVE TECHNIQUE ESTIMATES OF THE EXPORT COEFFICIENT FUNCTION

$$(X/Q = b_0 + \sum_{j=3}^{3} b_{1j}(1/H_3(b)) + \sum_{j=0}^{3} b_{2j}P + b_3Y)$$

b_0	$\sum_{j=0}^{3} b_{1j}$	$\sum_{j=0}^{3} b_{2j}$	b_3
Non-metallic mineral products			
-.047	.089	-.015	-.063
(.006)	(.007)	(.002)	(.006)
-7.68	12.61 > .995	-7.05 ---	-11.15 > .995
R^2 = .935	D.W. = 3.06	F = 20.11	ρ = -1.10
Metals			
.014	.205	-.001	-.217
(.037)	(.042)	(.013)	(.036)
.38	4.92 > .995	.03 ---	-5.97 > .995
R^2 = .796	D.W. = 2.61	F = 5.45	ρ = - .62
Machinery			
.056	.103	-.006	-.149
(.074)	(.109)	(.021)	(.099)
.76	.95 > .80	.26 ---	-1.50 > .90
R^2 = .884	D.W. = 2.62	F = 10.70	ρ = .83
Electrical and communications equipment			
.014	.030	.003	.001
(.018)	(.023)	(.004)	(.018)
.79	1.27 > .80	.81 ---	.08 ---
R^2 = .968	D.W. = 1.92	F = 42.60	ρ = .95

TABLE 6.5.-continued

b_0	$\sum_{j=0}^{3} b_{1j}$	$\sum_{j=0}^{3} b_{2j}$		b_3
Transportation equipment				
-.005	.174	.000		-.033
(.013)	(.019)	(.004)		(.011)
.41	9.10 > .995	.001	---	-3.05 > .99
R^2 = .955	D.W. = 2.76	F = 29.69		ρ = -.620
Paper and paper products				
-.023	.200	.009		-.045
(.016)	(.017)	.005		(.016)
-.147	11.90 > .995	1.63 > .90		-2.79 > .95
R^2 = .950	D.W. = 2.60	F = 26.44		ρ = -.525
Rubber products				
-.077	-.058	.027		-.009
(.011)	(.017)	.004		(.009)
-6.727	-3.30 ---	7.15 > .995		.98 > .80
R^2 = .878	D.W. = 2.26	F = 10.127		ρ = -.525
Leather and leather goods				
.240	.098	-.070		-.353
(.105)	(.010)	(.036)		(.106)
2.27	9.77 > .995	1.97	---	-3.32 >.99
R^2 = .922	D.W. = 2.31	F = 16.44		ρ = -.19
Textiles				
.011	.112	-.001		-.029
(.007)	(.009)	(.002)		(.006)
1.47	11.86 > .995	.56	---	-4.60 > .99
R^2 = .975	D.W. = 2.31	F = 54.80		ρ = -.29

TABLE 6.5.-continued

	b_0	$\sum_{j=0}^{3} b_{1j}$	$\sum_{j=0}^{3} b_{2j}$		b_3	
Clothing and footwear						
	.029	.373	.010		.013	
	(.010)	(.018)	(.003)		(.009)	
	2.98	19.82 > .995	2.97 > .95		1.46 > .90	
	R^2 = .998	D.W. = 2.05	F = 853.95		ρ = -.22	
Food processing						
	.064	.109	-.017		-.002	
	(.013)	(.012)	(.004)		.014	
	5.11	8.85 > .995	-3.85	---	-.11	---
	R^2 = .925	D.W = 2.11	F = 17.225		ρ = -.33	
Beverages						
	-.006	.110	.002		-.003	
	(.001)	(.005)	(.0033)		(.003)	
	5.81	23.08 > .995	6.36 > .95		-1.00 > .80	
	R^2 = .997	D.W = 2.75	F = 609.34		ρ = -.45	
Tobacco products						
	.003	.073	-.0007		-.027	
	(.006)	(.009)	(.0019)		(.005)	
	.56	8.20 > .995	-.36	---	-5.87 > .995	
	R^2 = .937	D.W = 2.10	F = 20.75		ρ = -1.0	

Note: The reported t-ratios may not equal the ratio of the reported sum of coefficients to their standard error, due to rounding of the three statistics. There are 7 degrees of freedom in each equation, based on observations from 1960 to 1973.

TABLE 6.6

COCHRANE ORCUTT ITERATIVE TECHNIQUE ESTIMATES OF THE EXPORT COEFFICIENT FUNCTION

$$(X/Q = b_0 + \sum_{j=0}^{3} b_{1j}(1/H_6(b)) + \sum_{j=0}^{3} b_{2j}P + b_3Y)$$

b_0	$\sum_{j=0}^{3} b_{1j}$		$\sum_{j=0}^{3} b_{2j}$		b_3	
Non-metallic mineral products						
.047	.024		-.015		-.064	
(.007)	(.002)		(.002)		(.006)	
6.83	12.27	> .995	-6.25	---	10.25	> .995
R^2 = .924	D.W. = 2.86		F = 17.13		ρ = -1.03	
Metals						
.013	.054		-.000		-.220	
(.041)	(.011)		(.014)		(.040)	
.32	4.67	> .995	.04	---	-5.49	> .995
R^2 = .764	D.W. = 2.52		F = 4.52		ρ = -.59	
Machinery						
.070	.020		-.008		-.139	
(.078)	(.028)		(.022)		(.101)	
.89	.70	---	-.36	---	-1.38	> .80
R^2 = .877	D.W = 2.78		F = 10.03		ρ = .86	
Electrical and communications equipment						
.016	.005		.003		.008	
(.019)	(.006)		(.005)		(.020)	
.85	.82	---	.71	---	.41	---
R^2 = .962	D.W. = 2.08		F = 35.31		ρ = .95	

TABLE 6.6--continued

	b_0	$\sum_{j=0}^{3} b_{1j}$	$\sum_{j=0}^{3} b_{2j}$	b_3
Transportation equipment				
	.003 (.013)	.044 (.005)	.009 (.045)	-.033 (.011)
	.22	8.83 > .995	.20 ---	-2.98 > .95
	R^2 = .954	D.W. = 2.68	F = 29.10	ρ = -.59
Paper and paper products				
	-.022 (.015)	.051 (.004)	.008 (.005)	-.045 (.015)
	-1.49	12.90 > .995	1.69 > .90	-2.92 > .95
	R^2 = .961	D.W. = 2.52	F = 34.85	ρ = -.41
Rubber products				
	-.075 (.012)	-.014 (.005)	.027 (.004)	-.009 (.010)
	-6.12	-2.96 ---	6.52 > .995	-.88 ---
	R^2 = .865	D.W. = 2.17	F = 8.99	ρ = -.46
Leather and leather products				
	.246 (.116)	.025 (.003)	-.072 (.039)	-.356 (.118)
	2.11	9.05 > .995	-1.83 ---	-3.00 > .99
	R^2 = .914	D.W. = 2.18	F = 14.96	ρ = -.11
Textiles				
	.010 (.008)	.028 (.003)	-.001 (.003)	.027 (.007)
	1.29	10.98 > .995	.41 ---	-3.88 > .995
	R^2 = .978	D.W. = 1.89	F = 61.24	ρ = -.09

TABLE 6.6.-continued

b_0	$\sum_{j=0}^{3} b_{1j}$	$\sum_{j=0}^{3} b_{2j}$	b_3
Clothing and footwear			
-.022 (.009)	.096 (.004)	.007 (.003)	.011 (.008)
-2.51	22.75 > .995	2.50 > .95	1.36 > .80
R^2 = .996	D.W. = 2.91	F = 381.25	ρ = -.12
Food processing			
.065 (.014)	.028 (.003)	-.018 (.005)	-.002 (.015)
4.74	8.31 > .995	-3.79 ---	-.15 ---
R^2 = .915	D.W. = 2.06	F = 15.11	ρ = -.29
Beverages			
.005 (.001)	.027 (.001)	.002 (.0004)	-.003 (.004)
4.44	20.98 > .995	4.89 > .995	.86 ---
R^2 = .995	D.W. = 2.94	F = 259.17	ρ = -1.05
Tobacco products			
-.001 (.008)	.018 (.003)	.001 (.003)	-.027 (.007)
-.14	5.65 > .995	.30 ---	-3.96 > .995
R^2 = .919	D.W. = 1.93	F = 15.78	ρ = -.57

Note: The reported t-ratios may not equal the ratio of the reported sum of coefficients to their standard error, due to rounding of the three statistics. There are 7 degrees of freedom in each equation, based on observations from 1960 to 1973.

6-5. Estimates of the Export Function for a Group of Primary Products

The data for manufactured exports tested in the preceding section strongly reject the null hypothesis of no relation between the level of exchange rate uncertainty and exports as a proportion of total production by sector. One might argue, however, that these results are in part due to inadequate specification of the price variable, which includes the export incentives created by the Brazilian government after 1964, and to collinearity between this variable and uncertainty. As the export incentives were directed almost entirely at manufactures, this potential criticism of the results of the preceding section may be addressed by testing the uncertainty hypothesis with exports which were not favored with incentives like those applied to manufactures.

In this section the results of such a test for a group of nine primary products are presented. The choice of products studied reflects several considerations, in addition to the obvious limitations imposed by the lack of adequate data. As was noted earlier, Brazil supplies a significant share of total world exports of several tropical commodities, among them traditional Brazilian exports like coffee, cocoa, and not surprisingly, Brazil nuts. In these markets the "small country" or perfect competition assumption implicit in the model is inappropriate. Even if this were not the case, the prevalence of international marketing agreements and other forms of government intervention in several of these markets suggest that the model would be inapplicable to them. These products were therefore eliminated *a priori* from the sample even though data is available.

For several other commodities, including sisal, black pepper, and vegetable gums, the reported quantity of exports in some years exceeded total production, indicating that exports were partially supplied from stocks. As was shown in Section 3.2, the possibility of storing output may weaken and possibly reverse the predicted negative relation between price uncertainty and the level of sales in the uncertain market; for this reason these products were also eliminated from the group (coffee would also have been eliminated here if it had not been earlier).

One difficulty remains among some of the products in the selected group. Domestic inflation and political pressures, especially in the early 1960's, occasionally induced the government to restrict exports of certain primary products considered "essential" to the domestic economy, either as foodstuffs or industrial inputs. To eliminate the effect of these actions on the data, observations for a product in a year in which such restrictions were in effect were discarded, as can be seen in the accompanying tables. Even so, the possibility of such policies is an additional source of uncertainty, which is recognized by our theoretical model, but not by our treatment of the data.

As was noted in Section 3, the excess demand variable proved to be insignificant in the primary products equations. This variable was therefore dropped from the equations in order to increase the limited number of degrees of freedom in the sample. Initial ordinary least squares estimates, using $H_3(b)$ as the index of uncertainty showed rather low values for the Durbin-Watson statistic, particularly for beef, fish, and seafood. It was therefore decided that the uncertainty hypothesis could not be tested in a meaningful way using the primary products data and ordinary least squares, and the Cochrane Orcutt technique was therefore used.

Table 6.7 shows the results of the Cochrane Orcutt technique estimates of the export coefficient function for the primary products. The uncertainty variable, $H_3(b)$, appears to have had a significant effect for all nine products studied except for cashews and rice, with the null hypothesis rejected at the 90 percent level or higher. Although the majority of price coefficients have the theoretically correct sign, none of them is significant at the 90 percent level, and only five are significant at the 80 percent level or higher.

TABLE 6.7

COCHRANE ORCUTT ITERATIVE TECHNIQUE ESTIMATES OF THE EXPORT FUNCTION FOR PRIMARY PRODUCTS

$$(X/Q = b_0 + \sum_{j=0}^{3} b_{1j}(1/H_3(b)) + \sum_{j=0}^{3} b_{2j}P)$$

	b_0	$\sum_{j=0}^{3} b_{1j}$		$\sum_{j=0}^{3} b_{2j}$	
Beef	1960 - 66, 1968 - 72	d.f. = 5			
	.276	.234		-.133	
	(.173)	(.123)		(.132)	
	1.59	1.90	> .90	-1.01	---
	R^2 = .850	D.W. = 2.29	F = 7.06	ρ = .64	
Fish	1960 - 72	d.f. = 7			
	.015	.016		.002	
	(.004)	(.003)		(.002)	
	3.76	4.59	> .995	1.04	> .80
	R^2 = .982	D.W. = 1.85	F = 85.59	ρ = .93	
Seafood	1960 - 72	d.f. = 7			
	-.071	.061		.023	
	(.100)	(.055)		(.018)	
	-.71	1.10	> .80	1.28	> .80
	R^2 = .840	D.W. = 1.04	F = 9.20	= .67	
Cashews	1960 - 73	d.f. = 8			
	-.005	.025		.073	
	(.173)	(.206)		(.097)	
	.03	.12	---	.75	---
	R^2 = .306	D.W. = 1.98	F = .88	ρ = .29	

TABLE 6.7.--continued

	b_0	$\sum_{j=0}^{3} b_{1j}$		$\sum_{j=0}^{3} b_{2j}$	
Wool	1960 -73		d.f. = 8		
	.455	.118		-.056	
	(.237)	(.023)		(.108)	
	1.92	4.99	> .995	-.52	---
	R^2 = .869	D.W. = 2.01	F = 9.26	ρ = -.55	
Rice	1960 - 71		d.f. = 6		
	-.030	-.240		.246	
	(.053)	(.189)		(.241)	
	-.57	-1.27	---	1.02	> .80
	R^2 = .250	D.W. = 2.14	F = .50	ρ = -.25	
Corn	1960 - 61, 1963 - 71		d.f. = 4		
	.024	.445		.048	
	(.024)	(.130)		(.241)	
	1.00	3.42	> .975	.20	---
	R^2 = .877	D.W. = 3.20	F = 7.11	ρ = -.71	
Peanuts	1960 - 73		d.f. = 8		
	-.042	.107		.147	
	(.060)	(.033)		(.134)	
	-.69	3.26	> .99	1.11	> .80
	R^2 = .773	D.W. = 1.95	F = 6.82	ρ = .30	
Soybeans	1960 - 62, 1964 - 72		d.f = 5		
	-.134	.555		1.43	
	(.317)	(.315)		(1.36)	
	-.42	1.77	> .90	1.05	> .80
	R^2 = .632	D.W. = 2.82	F = 2.15	ρ = -.56	

Note: The reported t-ratios may not equal the ratio of the reported sums of coefficients to their standard errors, due to rounding.

6-6. Some Possible Interpretations of the Estimates

It would be tempting to regard the regression results presented in the preceding sections as confirmation of the uncertainty hypothesis. Econometric estimates, however, never prove anything, but simply strengthen (or weaken) our degree of belief in the validity of our hypotheses.

A reasonable interpretation of the estimates, in particular the significance levels of the coefficients of the uncertainty variable, is that in this particular case, the data are not inconsistent with the theoretical predictions of Chapters II and III. This position is open to criticism for a number of reasons, based both on the data used and on the model selected.

First, the amount and quality of the data available to test our hypotheses is distressingly limited. With eight or fewer degrees of freedom, it is clear that our conclusions could easily be affected by the addition or omission of one or two observations. Some hint that this may be a problem is provided by comparing the coefficients estimated by ordinary least squares and by the Cochrane Orcutt technique. Despite approximately similar results in terms of significance levels, the estimates of the coefficients themselves sometimes vary substantially, due in part to the omission of one observation using the latter technique. Ideally, we could eliminate, or at least alleviate this problem with a longer time series. In our case, however, even if the data were available, the entirely different exchange regime and commercial policies prevailing in Brazil before 1957, and the changes in the world economy and heightened uncertainty resulting from the oil crisis in 1973 impose limits on the extent to which a longer time series would be meaningfully used.

Second, the tests of significance reported in the preceding sections are based on the assumption of normality in the distribution of the error terms. To the extent that fluctuations in the export coefficient about the predicted level are due to errors in observation or in the aggregation procedures implicit in the construction of the production and export quantity indices, normality may be a reasonable hypothesis. Having justified the use of stochastic dominance rules in part by the presumption of non-normality, however, it only fair to note its relevance to our hypothesis tests.

Third, we must confront the perennial problem of possible specification error. One might argue that the theoretically correct signs in the regressions for most sectors or products lend some support to the model adopted, but it is obviously possible that superior alternatives exist. One possible explanation of the movement in the export coefficient over the 1957 - 1973 period is that it simply represents a maturing process, as small, domestic-market-oriented firms grow and turn outward to the export market. As uncertainty generally fell substantially over the period taken as a whole, an apparent negative relation between the level of uncertainty and the export coefficient might simply be the result of this maturing process.

This alternative was examined by including time as well as the uncertainty level, relative prices, and the capacity proxy in least squares regressions for the thirteen manufacturing sectors. The results offer some support for this alternative explanation in some sectors. For the non-metallic minerals, machinery, electrical and communications equipment, and tobacco sectors, the coefficient on time was significantly positive at the 90 percent level or higher. In these four regressions the uncertainty coefficients retained the correct sign, but were not significant at the 90 percent level.

The maturity effect was not noticeable in any of the remaining nine sectors, however, and in the paper, rubber, and food processing sectors the coefficients were negative. The uncertainty coefficients were significantly positive, at the 90 percent level, in all nine sectors except rubber, and exceeded the 99 percent level in the paper, textiles, clothing, and beverages sectors. Although these results can hardly be regarded as conclusive, especially in view of the few degrees of freedom, they suggest that the uncertainty hypothesis is not simply a misspecification of a historical trend, and that the maturity effect, while important in a few cases, is less helpful in explaining the increase in the export orientation of the Brazilian economy than is the reduction in uncertainty.

If we do tentatively accept, or at least not reject, the uncertainty hypothesis, what can be said about the different ways in which uncertainty can be measured? Comparison of either Tables 6.3 and 6.4, or 6.5 and 6.6, show the different effects of measuring uncertainty by variance, which is equivalent to H_3(b), or by a combination of variance and the next three higher central moments of the distribution.

Despite the criticisms which have been made on theoretical grounds of variance as a measure of uncertainty, it is difficult to distinguish between the effects of using $H_3(b)$ or $H_6(b)$ in the analysis of the Brazilian data. As may be seen by referring to Chapter IV, the latter index is generally smaller in absolute terms than is the former, so that the coefficient estimates for $(1/H_6(b))$ are also smaller. Overall levels of significance remain approximately the same, however, and one must conclude that in this case, at least, variance is an acceptable measure of uncertainty.

One must be careful not to push this argument too far. The derivation of the $H_k(b)$ indices in Chapter IV shows why they will be dominated by variance. This parameter of the distribution of the real exchange rate changed markedly as a result of Brazil's adoption of the crawling peg in 1968. Had more subtle changes in the distributions occurred, for example the elimination of a few low extremes, without a substantial change in variance, there would be more noticeable differences between the two indices, with possibly substantially different results when used in econometric estimation. The situation is in some respects analogous to the choice between ordinary least squares and two stage least squares. In many cases, both methods will produce similar results, but if there is any theoretical reason to assume simultaneity, we would not be justified in using the former. If the answers given by the use of the two methods differ, moreover, the theoretical desirability of the higher level $H_k(b)$ index would argue for its use.

We conclude our examination of the regression results with a few speculative interpretations. The hypothesis of non-increasing absolute risk aversion has played a central role in the theoretical development of this study, as it has in much of the modern theory of economic behavior under uncertainty. One of its implications is that poorer individuals will be more affected by a mean preserving spread than those of greater wealth or income. If we are willing to extend this argument to firms of varying size, we would expect the impact of a reduction in uncertainty to be greater for small, "one-man" or family enterprises than it would be for a larger public or multinational enterprise.

If we compare the regressions for the different manufacturing sectors, it is apparent that there are marked differences in both the magnitudes and the significance of the coefficient for the uncertainty variable. Among the sectors apparently most affected by the change in uncertainty were the clothing and footwear, beverage, and textiles sectors, while the response to uncertainty appears considerable weaker or even non-existent in the rubber, electrical equipment, and machinery sectors. Reliable concentration indices or other measures of size compatible with the data were unavailable. Large enterprises, including a number of multinationals, are important in the latter sectors, while small enterprises appear to be more characteristic of the former. Such an interpretation of the differences in response is highly speculative, in addition to raising a number of theoretical difficulties. It would nevertheless be interesting to know what effect firm size or structure has on its responses to changes in the level of uncertainty.

Finally, there is a clear difference between the manufacturing and the primary product estimates, with the role of changes in uncertainty much less evident in the latter group. One explanation, in addition to the obvious one provided by the poorer quality of this data, is that uncertainty remained high for potential agricultural exporters after 1968. As noted earlier, government intervention in this market was (and is) a common occurence. From the point of view of the potential exporter, the continued threat of an export ban or other restriction may have far outweighed the reductions in real exchange rate uncertainty, the only type measured by our indices.

Comparison of the primary product and manufacturing data also suggests another interpretation. As was shown in Chapter III, the ability to store output may give even risk averse firms a reason to prefer greater price variability. Although an effort was made to eliminate sectors where this effect was clearly operative, it may also have occurred with some of the primary products considered, among them beef, cashews, and rice. While it is not our purpose to "explain away" non-significant econometric estimates, a proper examination of the uncertainty hypothesis in the primary product sectors would obviously require one to consider the inventory problem.

FOOTNOTES FOR CHAPTER VI

1. For a discussion of this approach, see E. E. Leamer and R. M. Stern, Quantitative International Economics, Boston, Allyn and Bacon, 1970, Ch. 2. A Brazilian study using total production as one of the determinants of exports is C. Von Doellinger et al., Transformação de Estrutura das Exportações Brasileiras 1964-1970.

   Rio, IPEA-INPES, Relatorio de Pesquisa 14, 1973.

2. See W. G. Tyler, Manufactured Export Expansion and Industrialization in Brazil, Kiel, Institut fur Weltwirtschaft an der Universitat Kiel, 1976, Ch. 8 and C. Von Doellinger et al., op cit.

3. Estimation methods with a limited dependent variable were developed by J. Tobin, "Estimation of Relationships for Limited Dependent Variables," Econometrica, Vol. 26, Jan. 1958, 24-36 and are discussed in A. Goldberger, Econometric Theory, New York, J. Wiley & Sons, 1964, and in S. M. Goldfeld and R. E. Quandt, Non-linear Methods in Econometrics, Amsterdam, North-Holland, 1972. A method appropriate to our export coefficient dependent variable is presented in R. N. Rosett and F. D. Nelson, Estimation of the Two-Limit Probit Regression Model," Econometrica, Vol. 43, Jan. 1975, 141-146.

4. These sectors were metals, rubber products, clothing, and tobacco products.

5. The method was proposed by S. Almon, "The Distributed Lag between Capital Appropriations and Expenditures," Econometrica, Jan. 1965, 178-196 and is discussed by J. Johnston, Econometric Methods (2nd ed.), N.Y., McGraw-Hill, 1972, Ch. 10. The computer program used to fit the Almon lag is the Time Series Processor (TSP) developed by R. E. Hall and associates.

6. This technique consists of obtaining a preliminary estimate, in the first order disturbance scheme $u_t = \rho u_{t-1} + \varepsilon_t$, using it to create a new matrix of regressors $Z_t = X_t - X_{t-1}$. The equations are then re-estimated using the Z_t to form a new estimate of ρ, repeating the process until the successive changes in are smaller than a specified limit. The method was proposed by D. Cochrane and G. H. Orcutt, "Application of Least-Squares Regressions to Relationships Containing Auto-correlated Error Terms," J. Am. Stat. Assoc., Vol. 44, 32-61, 1949. The TSP program permits the combination of this technique with the Almon lag scheme.

7. See A. Zellner, "An Efficient Method of Estimating Seemingly Unrelated Regressions and tests for Aggregation Bias," J. Am. Stat. Assoc., June 1962, 300-312, and J. Johnston, op. cit., Ch. 7.

8. Twenty-two sectors of mining and extractive industries and a "miscellaneous" sector are added, as is done in the input-output tables.

CHAPTER VII

CONCLUSION: SOME OBSERVATIONS ON PRICE UNCERTAINTY AND TRADE

This study might be described as a series of answers to a single question: does price uncertainty have real economic effects? One answer is given by the theory developed in the first part of our study, under the assumption that firms behave as if they were risk averse and are subject to a certain degree of short run inflexibility in setting their production and sales levels. A parallel answer is offered by the second part of our study, an empirical examination of the uncertainty-reducing effects of the Brazilian crawling in stimulating exports after 1968. Linking these two approaches to examining the effects of changes in price uncertainty is the development of a method for measuring the level of uncertainty in a way consistent with the expected utility hypothesis which underlies our model.

While it would perhaps be reassuring to have simple and categorical responses affirming that uncertainty has certain effects, neither good theory nor good econometrics always provides such answers. Although the simple multiplicative spreading of a distribution of random product prices does categorically decrease output, provided absolute risk aversion is non-increasing, under the more general characterization of a mean preserving spread proposed by Rothschild and Stiglitz, our results must be qualified. Nevertheless, there is a very strong presumption that a decrease in price variability will increase output, and the counterexample presented in Appendix

A appears almost pathological. A potentially more important theoretical qualification of our argument that a reduction in price uncertainty increases output comes when we relax the output and sales inflexibility assumption. If the firm may reserve output, then by selling the output only in periods of high prices it might benefit from greater price variability.

When our theoretical model is applied to an economy in which producers may sell in the domestic market or export, there is again a strong presumption that less uncertainty about the real remuneration from exporting, as would occur from a reduction in exchange rate uncertainty, will both increase production and shift sales to the export market.

The link between theory and empirical analysis is provided by the stochastic dominance-based approach to measuring the level of uncertainty developed in Chapter IV. Like the Rothschild-Stiglitz definition of increasing risk to which it is related, the method does not always provide simple and categorical answers, which is the price exacted for such a level of generality. Even if we know the actual distributions being compared, the criteria do not always permit a choice for all risk averters, and even further restricting the class of concave utility functions does not guarantee a complete ordering of distributions. To this we must add the fact that typically we are confronted with samples from the populations; even though we know that the $H_k(x)$ estimators developed in Chapter IV are consistent, little is known of their small sample properties.

Despite these difficulties, the ordering rules and the indices of uncertainty derived from them do appear to succeed in many cases; the analysis of the real cruzeiro-dollar exchange rate in the 1957 to 1974 period is a case in point.

Chapters V and VI represent an attempt to apply the theory to an actual case, the reduction in exchange rate uncertainty resulting from Brazil's adoption of the crawling peg in 1968. Following the theoretical argument of the first chapters, it is hardly surprising to conclude that exchange rate uncertainty matters; what is striking in the results presented in Chapter VI is how much it appears to matter. In general, we conclude that it was significantly more important than were changes in relative prices. Although this conclusion is to some extent anticipated by some of the arguments of Chapter 5, which show why relative price changes might not have their expected effects, it is still striking how little price changes seem to contribute to an explanation of changes in Brazil's exports in the last decade.

Both the methods and the conclusions of this study suggest a number of criticisms, as well as potential extensions. Our model of the firm facing price uncertainty is essentially a partial equilibrium one; yet we are using it to generate predictions for the economy as a whole. To the extent that the usual closure assumptions of general equilibrium theory, i.e. market clearing, full information and employment of factors, and unrestricted movement of factors among sectors, are not often satisfied, our approach may be more appropriate for a study like this. Nevertheless, it would be interesting to know how the theoretical conclusions might be modified if the model were developed in a general equilibrium context.

The specification of the firm's objective function is a second area in which our model could be extended and improved. As we have argued in Chapter III, it does not appear necessary to postulate the existence of firm utility functions; concave objective functions might arise in a number of ways without requiring us to aggregate individual preferences. Related to this question is whether or not we can reasonably postulate some type of firm analogue to individual non-increasing absolute risk aversion.

A third area for development of the theory presented here arises from the inventory effect, which tends to offset the pure risk aversion effect. Although a completely general model might be unwieldy, some further integration of these two effects would be a desirable extension of our model, despite our presumption that the inventory effect is not likely to dominate the risk aversion effect.

The stochastic dominance method of measuring uncertainty developed in Chapter IV raises a number of issues. To the extent that we use the indices of uncertainty to rank distributions which our qualitative, pairwise comparisons tell us are not rankable, we open ourselves to the same criticism that has been made of variance as a measure of uncertainty; i.e. that it gives possibly incorrect results. As the derivation of these indices showed, however, this possibility is substantially reduced by the use of higher level stochastic dominance indices. A second safequard against invalid rankings is provided by the prior application of the stochastic dominance rules themselves, which permit us to identify cases in which the cardinal measures are not always valid.

A more serious problem with our measure of uncertainty, or indeed with any measure based on past values of the variable of interest, is that we are forced to assume that the individual uses the recent past as a basis for forming a subjective probability distribution. It is obvious that this is only an approximation to the process of expectation formation, and is perhaps not even the most appropriate one. In the case of the Brazilian crawling peg, for example, the government announced how the new exchange regime would work; one could argue reasonably that the past experience of participants in the foreign exchange market was no longer relevant. From an econometric point of view, this might mean that the lag structure of our econometric estimates of the uncertainty coefficients was incorrectly specified,although we might justify the continued influence of the past with lags in information assimilation and inflexibilities in the response of firms to their managers' new subjective probabilities.

Perhaps the most interesting issue which our method of measuring uncertainty raises is the appropriateness of variance as a measure of risk. Although it would be presumptuous to believe the issue settled, both our theoretical measurements in Chapter IV and their application to the evaluation of the uncertainty hypothesis in Chapter VI offer some hope of reconciliation between the mean-variance school and its critics. The view that variance is an appropriate way of ordering distributions is clearly inconsistent with the expected utility hypothesis, for the simple reason that the decision maker may not treat deviations about the expectation symmetrically, as is assumed by the use of variance. Yet the derivation of the $H_k(b)$ indices, which are consistent with the expected utility hypothesis for all stochastic dominance orderable distributions, shows that any of these measures will be dominated by variance, and in the case of $H_3(b)$, perfectly correlated. The progressive addition of higher central moments as we impose higher degree rules narrows substantially the likelihood that we will choose the wrong distribution. The price we pay for this greater power to discriminate are restrictions on the form of the utility function, but as was argued in Chapter IV, these restrictions are both theoretically and intuitively more acceptable than is quadratic utility.

When used in empirical applications, it is clear that the $H_k(b)$ indices and variance are likely to give similar results, due to the high weight variance receives in these indices. Differences in the variances of two distributions would have to be small, or differences in higher central moments large, or both, for the stochastic dominance approach and the variance approach to give different answers. That this can happen is the argument of theorists who criticize the use of variance. An appropriate response by its defenders is that this is improbable. Our examination of the results of applying the method to the real cruzeiro-dollar rate provides a case in point. Despite their theoretical differences, either the use of variance, equivalent to $H_3(b)$, or the higher level $H_6(b)$ index appear to yield virtually similar results in evaluating the uncertainty hypothesis. Our method may be justified by the fact that agreement might not always be this close; if the answers differed then our arguments suggest that the less restrictive assumptions on which the stochastic dominance approach is based should give us greater confidence in its answers.

The derivation of the stochastic dominance rules and their corresponding indices rests in part on the hypothesis of non-increasing absolute risk aversion, as do many of the theoretical results in the preceding chapters. This hypothesis has had an extraordinary importance in the development of the modern theory of economic behavior under uncertainty. Despite its widespread use and general acceptance among economic theorists, one suspects that many of the implications of the hypothesis remain to be discovered. One question which our study leaves open is the relation between the hypothesis and the class of utility functions whose various order derivatives alternate in sign. As was mentioned in Chapter IV, members of this family which are not decreasingly risk averse for non-negative arguments of the utility function are difficult to find. It would be a useful theoretical contribution, placing our theory of the measurement of uncertainty or risk on even firmer ground, if this apparent connection could be better explained or clarified.

It would be tempting to regard the econometric results of our study as an argument that relative prices hardly matter. While the results do suggest that other changes in the distributions of prices may at times be more significant than changes in the expectation itself, we are not entitled to say much more than this. In addition to the technical econometric problems of specification, functional form, and other complications specific to our case discussed at length in Chapter VI, it should be remembered that empirical attempts to verify theoretical predictions based on changes in relative prices have often been disappointing. In empirical studies of trade this result was common enough to appear to justify a degree of "elasticity pessimism" about the efficacy of relative price changes in attaining balance of payments equilibrium.

Despite our attempts in Chapter V to capture movements in relative prices, our procedure is at best arbitrary and subject to a number of limitations, imposed primarily by the availability and quality of the data. On a more fundamental level, the apparently greater importance of the uncertainty variable in the Brazilian case is hardly cause for concluding that this type of result is common, or even likely. As we have seen in Chapter V, relative prices did not change greatly for much of the period. The change in the level of exchange rate uncertainty, however, was truly massive, judging from the results of Chapter IV. While this offers an interesting opportunity to see if uncertainty matters in explaining changes in production and trade, the data is not well suited to the task of judging the comparative importance of relative prices and the level of uncertainty. Conventional theory tells us the first variable is relevant; adding the dimension provided by uncertainty, theory tells us that it too matters. Which variable is most relevant is not necessarily even a meaningful question, since the answer will depend fundamentally on the case examined. The Brazilian case is instructive since it appears to ovide an example in which uncertainty does matter. Whether or not this result would be obtained in an examination of exchange rate uncertainty and the level of trade in other countries, however, is an open question. As we have argued in preceding chapters, the inventory effect, the existence of means of avoiding or shifting risks, decreasing absolute risk aversion, and the configuration of the data itself might lead us to different conclusions.

On an empirical level, our study has a number of interesting implications for a deeper understanding of changes in the Brazilian economy in the last two decades. A common view of recent Brazilian economic development is that changes in commercial policy instituted after 1964 are largely responsible for the increase in the importance of foreign trade to the economy. Our results suggest that this may not have been the only, or perhaps even the most important element in the movement towards a more open economy in the late sixties. The adoption of the crawling peg is simply one aspect of the whole policy of indexation or "monetary correction", which might be viewed fruitfully in terms of the effects it had in reducing uncertainties in a number of sectors of the economy. Although indexing is not usually analyzed in terms of its effects in an economy of risk averse individuals, it may be that its most important effects arise in ways analogous to those examined in the foreign sector in this study.

With the dramatic increase in Brazil's import costs after the oil price rises beginning in 1973, policy makers have devoted considerable attention to ways to increase Brazilian exports, and as a result have been concerned with an apparent slackening in the rate of growth of exports, particularly in sectors whose foreign sales expanded dramatically in the 1968 - 1972 period. Our model and estimated responses of the export coefficient to changes in uncertainty and prices shed some light on this problem. As was shown in Chapter IV, the level of exchange rate uncertainty was dramatically reduced after August 1968, but since then has not declined further. This suggests that part of the observed increase in exports after 1968 was simply part of the transition from a highly uncertain exchange rate climate to a more stable one. If so, we would expect the rate of growth of exports to level off, as actually seems to be the case in a number of sectors.

Finally, our study in a larger sense suggests that the whole topic of uncertainty and the effects it appears to have on economic structure deserve more attention both on a theoretical and a policy level. The question of appropriate exchange rate regimes, or proposed international agreements to stabilize the prices of primary products may be most meaningfully studied if we pay greater and more explicit attention to their impact on the level of uncertainty confronting the participants in trade. As this study has attempted to show, the simple assumption that people are risk averse may move the role of uncertainty to a central position in both international economic theory and policy.

APPENDIX A

OUTPUT RESPONSE TO CHANGES IN RISK; A COUNTER-EXAMPLE TO THE BATRA-ULLAH ASSERTION

Batra and Ullah have asserted that an increase in risk, which they identify as a mean-preserving spread like that introduced by Rothschild and Stiglitz, will umambiguously decrease output if absolute risk aversion is non-increasing.[1] Their demonstration uses a special type of mean-preserving spread introduced by Sandmo which consists of multiplying the original distribution of the random variable by some constant and then subtracting another constant from it so as to leave the mean of the distribution unchanged.

Under more general definitions of increases in risk satisfying the Rothschild-Stiglitz conditions the Batra-Ullah proposition does not necessarily hold. This appendix presents a counterexample.

Let the firm's attitude toward risk be characterized by the constant absolute risk aversion function $U(\pi) = A - e^{-\gamma\pi}$ where A and are positive constants. We assume that costs are given by the function $c(q) = c_o + c_1 q + c_2 q^2$; increasing marginal cost, as noted in Chapters 4 and 5, is not necessary for a solution under certainty, but permits comparison with the certainty case. We assume that the distribution of the random output price is initially

p	f(p)
0	.01
10	.95
100	.04

with E(p) = 13.5. We shall assume in this example that the degree of risk aversion, γ, equals 3 and that the parameters of the cost function are: $c_o = 1.0$, $c_1 = 2.0$, and $c_2 = .5$, implying that $c'(q) = 2.0 + q$.

The firm's problem is then to choose an output level, q, so as to maximize expected utility, yielding the first-order conditions

$$\int_a^b U'(\pi)\ (p - c')\ dF(p) = 0 \qquad \text{A-1}$$

or

$$\int_o^{100} \gamma e^{-\gamma[pq-c(q)]}\ (p - c')\ dF(p) = 0 \qquad \text{A-1'}$$

As $\gamma e^{\gamma c(q)} > 0$ is independent of p for a given q, we may simplify this expression, substituting in the parameters and probabilities to yield

$$.01\ \{-2.0 - q\} + .95\ \{e^{-3\cdot 10\cdot q}\ (8.0 - q)\} + .01\ \{e^{-3\cdot 100\cdot q}\ (98.0 - q)\} = 0$$

This equation may then be solved to yield the utility-maximizing output, which equals .194. We may then use this value of q to determine $\phi(p)$:

$$\phi(p) = U'(\pi(p,q)) + q(p - c')\ U''(\pi(p,q))$$

$$= 3e^{-3(.194p-1.407)} - .194(p - 2.194)\ 9e^{-3(.194p-1.407)}$$

$$= 3e^{-3(.194p-1.407)}\ [2.2769 - .582p]$$

The function $\phi(p)$ in this example is shown in Figure A-1, and as may be verified from the equations above, equals zero when p is 3.91, reaching a minimum of -2.45 with p equal to 5.15. At the mean (13.5), $\phi(p)$ is -.445 and thereafter rapidly approaches zero. The figure is not drawn to scale and omits an intermediate interval between 13.5 and 100.0.

Now let us assume that the original distribution of p, f(p), is replaced by a new distribution, g(p). Table A-1 shows this new distribution, together with the original frequency distribution, their respective cumulative distribution functions, the difference between these c.d.f.'s, and the sum to each p of this difference, multiplied by the length of the respective interval. As is clear from the table and the diagram, this type of change satisfies the RS integral conditions, leaving the mean of g(p) unchanged at 13.5. The difference between the integrals, G-F, is represented by the dashed line in Figure A-1.

TABLE A-1

p	f(p)	g(p)	F(p)	G(p)	(G - F)	$\int(G - F)\,dp$
0.0	.01	.01	.01	.01	0.0	0.0
5.0	-	.50	.01	.51	.5	2.5
10.0	.95	.45	.96	.96	.0	2.5
100.0	.04	-	1.00	.96	-.04	0.0
162.5	-	.04	1.00	1.00	.0	.0

The new first order conditions after this mean-preserving spread has occurred require that

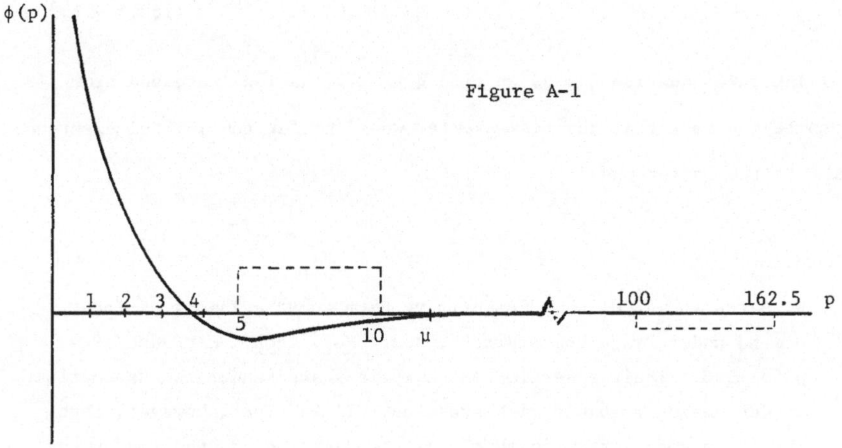

Figure A-1

An Output Increasing Mean Preserving Spread

$$\int_0^{162.5} U'(\pi(\hat{q},p))\ (p - c'(\hat{q}))dG(p) = 0$$

or, after the usual cancellations,

$$.01\ \{-2.0 - \hat{q}\} + .5\{e^{-3\cdot 5\hat{q}}\ (8.0 - \hat{q})\}$$
$$+ .45\ \{e^{-3\cdot 10\hat{q}}(98.0 - \hat{q})\} + .04\ \{e^{-3\cdot 162\cdot 5\hat{q}}(160.5 - \hat{q})\} = 0$$

Solving this equation for $\hat{q}$, we find $\hat{q} = .275$, having increased from .194, despite the fact that any risk averter would prefer the initial distribution to the latter one.

Footnote:

1. R. Batra and A. Ullah, "Competitive Firm and the Theory of Input Demand under Price Uncertainty", Jour. Pol. Econ., May/June 1974, p 537-548. Their assertion actually is stated under the assumption of decreasing absolute risk aversion. It is clear, however, that they mean non-increasing absolute risk aversion, as their argument would apply to this case as well.

APPENDIX B

LISTING OF THE FORTRAN IV PROGRAM USED TO COMPUTE THE STOCHASTIC DOMINANCE MATRICES AND INDICES

```
      COMMON     NE(20), X1(20,150), Z1(20,150), XM(20),
     1 ADJM(4,20), HB(4,20), ISTD(4,20,20)
      DIMENSION  X(300),  Z(300)
      CALL CLEAR
      CALL READV(M,IM,MB)
      DO 15  I = 1,M
      N =  NE(I)
      DO 2   J = 1,N
      X(J)   =   X1(I,J)
    2 CONTINUE
      IF  (IM - 1)  3, 3, 4
    3 CALL EVEN(N, X, XM(I), Z)
      GO TO 5
    4 CALL EVENG(N, X, XM(I), Z)
    5 IF (N-1)  15, 15, 6
    6 CALL ORDER(N,Z)
      DO 10    J = 1,N
      Z1(I,J) =  Z(J)
      Z(J)    =  0.0
   10 CONTINUE
   15 CONTINUE
      CALL MAXB(M, MB, Z1MAX)
      CALL MOMENT(M)
   25 CONTINUE
      DO 40  I = 1,M
      DO 40  J = I,M
      IF (I - J)    30,35,40
   30 CALL CMPR1(I,J)
      ISTD(1,J,I) = -ISTD(1,I,J)
      ISTD(2,J,I) = -ISTD(2,I,J)
      GO TO 40
   35 ISTD(1,I,J) = 10
   40 CONTINUE
      ZMX = Z1MAX
      CALL CMPR2(M, MB,ZMX)
      CALL OUT(M,MB, Z1MAX)
      RETURN
      END
```

```
      SUBROUTINE CLEAR
C CLEARS COMMON ARRAYS
      COMMON    NE(20), X1(20,150), Z1(20,150), XM(20),
     1 ADJM(4,20), HB(4,20), ISTD(4,20,20)
      DO 110  I = 1,20
      NE(I)     =   0
      XM(I)     = 0.0
      DO 106  K = 1,4
      DO 105  J = 1,20
  105 ISTD(K,I,J) =0.0
      ADJM(K,I) = 0.0
  106 HB(K,I)   = 0.0
      DO 108  J = 1, 150
      X1(I,J)   = 0.0
      Z1(I,J) = 0.0
  108 CONTINUE
  110 CONTINUE
      RETURN
      END


      SUBROUTINE   READV(M, IM,MB)
C READS M VECTORS OF NE ELEMENTS, STORES AS X1 MAX M = 15  MAX NE = 150
C PARAMETER  IM=1 ARITHMETIC MEAN, IM=2 GEOMETRIC MEAN
      COMMON    NE(20), X1(20,150), Z1(20,150), XM(20),
     1 ADJM(4,20), HB(4,20), ISTD(4,20,20)
  115 FORMAT (2I2, I1, 20I3)
  120 FORMAT  (  11 ( 65X, F10.5,  / ),  65X, F10.5)
      READ (5, 115)  M,MB,IM,(NE(I), I= 1,20)
      DO 125  I = 1,M
      NT = NE(I)
      READ(5,120,END=125)    (X1(I,J), J = 1,NT)
  125 CONTINUE
      RETURN
      END


      SUBROUTINE EVEN (N,X,XM,Z)
C FINDS MEAN XM OF N*1 VECTOR X   RETURNS VECTOR Z,  Z(I) = X(I) - XM
      DIMENSION  X(300),  Z(300)
      XSUM = 0.0
      DO 220  I = 1,N
  220 XSUM = XSUM + X(I)
      XM   = XSUM/N
      DO 225  I = 1,N
      Z(I) = X(I) - XM
  225 CONTINUE
      RETURN
      END
```

```
      SUBRCUTINE ORDER (N,X)
C REARRANGES N*1 VECTOR IN ASCENDING ORDER
      DIMENSION X(300)
      N1 = N-1
      DO 210  I = 1,N1
      T1 = X(I)
      J1 = I+1
      DO 205  J = J1,N
      IF (X(J) - T1)  200, 205, 205
  200 X(I) = X(J)
      X(J) = T1
      T1   = X(I)
  205 CONTINUE
  210 CCNTINUE
      RETURN
      END


      SUBROUTINE MAXB(M, MB, BMAX1)
C FINDS MAX ELEMENT IN ALL DATA AND STANDARDIZES Z1 SO THAT B = 1.0
      COMMON    NE(20), X1(20,150), Z1(20,150), XM(20),
     1 ADJM(4,20), HB(4,20), ISTD(4,20,20)
      BMAX1 = Z1(1,1)
      DO 1110  I = 1,M
      N = NE(I)
      DO 1110 J = 1,N
      IF (Z1(I,J) - BMAX1)   1110, 1110, 1105
 1105 BMAX1 = Z1(I,J)
 1110 CONTINUE
      IF (MB)    1130, 1130, 1115
 1115 DO 1120  I = 1,M
      N  = NE(I)
      DO 1120  J = 1,N
      Z1(I,J) = Z1(I,J)/BMAX1
 1120 CONTINUE
 1130 CONTINUE
      RETURN
      END
```

```
      SUBROUTINE MOMENT(M)
C   CALCULATES 2 - 5 ADJUSTED SAMPLE MOMENTS ABOUT SAMPLE MEAN
      REAL N2, N3, N4, CM2SQ, CM2M3, N,NP2, NP3, NP4
      DOUBLE PRECISION RM(4,20), RMS(4), M2SQ, M2M3
      COMMON    NE(20), X1(20,150), Z1(20,150), XM(20),
     1 ADJM(4,20), HB(4,20), ISTD(4,20,20)
C CALCULATES UNADJUSTED CENTRAL MOMENTS
      DO 140  I = 1,M
      DO 130  K = 1,4
      RMS(K)  = 0.0
  130 CONTINUE
      N = NE(I)
      NJ = NE(I)
      DO 132  J = 1,NJ
      ZA = Z1(I,J) * Z1(I,J)
      RMS(1) = RMS(1) + ZA
      ZB = Z1(I,J) * ZA
      RMS(2) = RMS(2) + ZB
      ZC = Z1(I,J) * ZB
      RMS(3) = RMS(3) + ZC
      ZD = Z1(I,J) * ZC
      RMS(4) = RMS(4) + ZD
  132 CONTINUE
      DO 134  K =  1,4
      RM(K,I) = RMS(K)/N
  134 CONTINUE
C ADJUSTS MOMENTS FOR SMALL SAMPLE BIAS
      N2  =  N*N
      N3  =  N2*N
      N4  =  N3*N
C SECOND CENTRAL MOMENT (VARIANCE)
      ADJM(1,I)  =  RM(1,I)*(N/(N-1))
C THIRD MOMENT
      NP2  =  (N-2)*(N-1)
      ADJM(2,I)  =  RM(2,I)*(N2/NP2)
C FOURTH MOMENT
      NP3  = N3 - (4*N2) + (6*N) - 3
      M2SQ = RM(1,I)*RM(1,I)
      CM2SQ = (3*(2*N - 3))/(N*(N-1))
      ADJM(3,I) = (N3/NP3)*(RM(3,I)-CM2SQ*M2SQ)
C FIFTH MOMENT
      NP4 = N4 - (5*N3) + (10*N2) - (10*N) + 4
      M2M3  =  RM(2,I) * RM(1,I)
      CM2M3 = (10*(N2 - N + 4))/(N*((N-1)*(N-2)))
      ADJM(4,I) = (N4/NP4)* (RM(4,I)- CM2M3* M2M3)
  140 CONTINUE
      RETURN
      END
```

```
      SUBROUTINE CMPR1(K1,K2)
C COMPARES CUMULATIVE DISTRIBUTIONS OF Z1(K1) AND Z1(K2).  IF K1 PREF TO
C K2 BY SSD, ISTD(1,K1,K2) = 1, IF K2 PREF TO K1, ISTD(1,K1,K2) = -1.
C IF NO RANKING POSSIBLE ISTD(1,K1,K2) = 0. ISTD(1,K1,K2)=-ISTD(1,K2,K1)
C TESTS FOR  TSD AND ENTERS  1, -1, OR 0 IN ISTD(2,K1,K2)
      COMMON     NE(20), X1(20,150), Z1(20,150), XM(20),
     1 ADJM(4,20), HB(4,20), ISTD(4,20,20)
      COMMON     ZT(300),F(2,300),H2(300),H2S(300),H3(300),ZS(300),
     1  H3SMXN(300), H3S(300)
C COMBINES VECTORS Z1(K1) AND Z1(K2) TC FORM ORDERED ZT  (NT*1)
      N  =  0
      NT = NE(K1)
      DO 310    I = 1,NT
      N  =   N+1
      ZT(N) = Z1(K1,I)
  310 CONTINUE
      NT = NE(K2)
      DO 320    I = 1,NT
      N  =   N+1
      ZT(N) = Z1(K2,I)
  320 CONTINUE
      CALL ORDER(N,ZT)
C REDUCES ZT TO ZS BY ELIMINATING DUPLICATE VALUES
      L =  1
      DO 330    J =  2,N
      ZS(L)  =   ZT(J-1)
      IF (ZT(J) - ZT(J-1))  325, 330, 325
  325 L = L + 1
  330 CONTINUE
      ZS(L)  =   ZT(N)
C COMPUTES CUMULATIVE DISTRIBUTIONS FOR K1 AND K2
      K = K1
      KI  =  1
  332 I = 1
      F (KI,1)  =    0.0
      FN  =  NE(K)
      IF (Z1(K,1) - ZS(1))  335, 335, 340
  335 I = I + 1
  340 CONTINUE
      DO 360   J = 2,L
      FI   =   I - 1
      F (KI,J)  =    FI/FN
      IF  (Z1(K,I) - ZS(J))  345, 350, 360
  345 IF (I - NE(K))  347, 360, 360
  347 I =   I + 1
      FI   = I - 1
      F (KI,J)   =    FI/FN
      GO TO 360
  350 I   =   I + 1
  360 CONTINUE
```

```
  390 IF  (K - K1)  400, 395,  400
  395 K   = K2
      KI  =  2
      GO TO 332
  400 IDN = 0
C FINDS DIFFERENCES IN AREAS UNDER CUMULATIVE DISTRIBUTIONS.  SUM (H2S)
C TO ZT(I) IS SSD INTEGRAL.  COUNTS OCCURENCES OF H2S +,0,- FOR SSD TEST
      IDN  = 0
      IDZ  = 1
      IDP  = 0
      H2(1)= 0.0
      H2S(1) = 0.0
      DO 450  J = 2,L
      H2(J) = (F(1,J) - F(2,J)) * (ZS(J) - ZS(J-1))
      H2S(J)=  H2S(J-1) + H2(J)
      IF (L -J)  410,  405,  410
  405 H2S(J)  =  0.0
  410 IF (H2S(J))   420, 430, 440
  420 IDN = IDN + 1
      GO TO 450
  430 IDZ = IDZ + 1
      GO TO 450
  440 IDP = IDP + 1
  450 CONTINUE
      IT1 = IDN + IDZ
      IT2 = IDP + IDZ
      IF  (L - IT1)   470, 480, 460
  460 IF  (L - IT2)   470, 490, 470
  470 ISTD(1,K1,K2) = 0
      GO TO 500
  480 ISTD(1,K1,K2) = 1
      ISTD(2,K1,K2) = 1
      ISTD(3,K1,K2) = 1
      ISTD(4,K1,K2) = 1
      GO TO 590
  490 ISTD(1,K1,K2) =-1
      ISTD(2,K1,K2) =-1
      ISTD(3,K1,K2) =-1
      ISTD(4,K1,K2) =-1
      GO TO 590
C TESTS FOR TSD IFF SSD TEST FAILED
  500 H3(1) = 0.0
      H3S(J) = 0.0
      H3SMXN(1) =  0.0
      MXN = 1
C CALCULATES TSD INTEGRAL TO EACH OBSERVATION ON A,B
      DO  540  J = 2,L
      H3(J) = (.5*(H2S(J)+H2S(J-1)))*(ZS(J)-ZS(J-1))
      H3S(J) = H3S(J-1) + H3(J)
```

```
C TESTS FOR H3S MAX OR MIN VIA H2S = 0
      IF ( H2S(  J))    504, 508, 506
  504 IF ( H2S(J-1))    540, 540, 510
  506 IF ( H2S(J-1))    510, 540, 540
  508 MXN  =   MXN + 1
      H3SMXN(MXN)  = H3S(J)
      GO TO 540
C INTERPOLATES FROM ZS(J-1) TO ZS(J) TO FIND H3S MAX OR MIN
  510 MXN  =   MXN + 1
      H3SMXN(MXN) = H3S(J) - (((H2S(J)/(H2S(J)-H2S(J-1)))*
     1   H2S(J)* .5) * (ZS(J) - ZS(J-1)))
  540 CONTINUE
C TESTS VECTOR OF H3S MAX/MIN FOR SIGN CHANGE=TSD FAILURE
C SINCE SSD FAILED HAVE AT LEAST ONE INTERIOR H2S=0, HENCE
C MXN .GE. 3 SINCE H2(1) = H2(L) = 0
      IDN  = 0
      IDZ  = 1
      IDP  = 0
      DO 560 M = 2, MXN
      IF  ( H3SMXN(M))    550, 552, 554
  550 IDN  = IDN + 1
      GO TO 560
  552 IDZ  = IDZ + 1
      GO TO 560
  554 IDP  = IDP + 1
  560 CONTINUE
      IT1 =  IDN + IDZ
      IT2 =  IDP + IDZ
      IF (MXN - IT1)  575, 580, 570
  570 IF (MXN - IT2)  575, 585, 575
  575 ISTD(2,K1,K2) = 0
      CALL SD4(L,K1,K2)
      GO TO 590
  580 ISTD(2,K1,K2) = 1
      ISTD(3,K1,K2) = 1
      ISTD(4,K1,K2) = 1
      GO TO 590
  585 ISTD(2,K1,K2) =-1
      ISTD(3,K1,K2) =-1
      ISTD(4,K1,K2) =-1
  590 CONTINUE
      RETURN
      END
```

```
      SUBROUTINE CMPR2(M, MB, BMAX)
C COMPUTES H(K) INTEGRAL VALUES AT B=MAX(Z), K= 3,6
      COMMON    NE(20), X1(20,150), Z1(20,150), XM(20),
     1 ADJM(4,20), HB(4,20), ISTD(4,20,20)
      IF (MB)  748, 748, 746
  746 BMAX = 1.0
  748 DO 750  I = 1,M
      HB(1,I)  =  ADJM(1,I)/2.0
      HB(2,I)  =  (BMAX*ADJM(1,I))/2.0 - ADJM(2,I)/6.0
      HB(3,I)  = ((BMAX**2.0)*ADJM(1,I))/4.0 - (BMAX*ADJM(2,I))
     1 /6.0  + ADJM(3,I)/24.0
      HB(4,I)  = ((BMAX**3.0)*ADJM(1,I))/12.0 - ((BMAX**2.0)
     1 *ADJM(2,I))/12.0 + (BMAX*ADJM(3,I))/24.0 - ADJM(4,I)/120.0
  750 CONTINUE
      RETURN
      END


      SUBROUTINE OUT(M,MB, Z1MAX)
C PRINTS ORIGINAL SERIES, TRANSFORMED SERIES, MEAN, H-INTEGRALS,
C AND STOCHASTIC DOMINANCE MATRICES
      COMMON    NE(20), X1(20,150), Z1(20,150), XM(20),
     1 ADJM(4,20), HB(4,20), ISTD(4,20,20)
      DIMENSION  A(20),    S(8), NS(20)
  800 FORMAT (1H1,///,50X,28HSTOCHASTIC DOMINANCE PROGRAM,//,62X,4HDATA,
     1 ///)
  805 FORMAT(1H0,/,5X,30HOBSERVATIONS NOT STANDARDIZED.,
     1 10H MAXIMUM =, 2X, F10.5)
  806 FORMAT(1H0,/,5X,26HOBSERVATIONS STANDARDIZED.,
     1 10H MAXIMUM =, 2X, F10.5)
  810 FORMAT (1H0,/,10X,I2,15X,I2, 8X, F10.6, 5X, 4(F13.6))
  830 FORMAT (1H0,/, 5X,34HVALUES OF TRANSFORMED DISTRIBUTION,//,
     1 14(5X, 10F10.5, / ), 5X, 10F10.5)
  820 FORMAT (1H0,/, 5X,31HVALUES OF ORIGINAL DISTRIBUTION,//,  14(5X,
     1  10F10.5, /), 5X, 10F10.5)
  840 FORMAT (1H0,/)
  843 FORMAT (1H1, //)
  845 FORMAT (1H0, //, 5X, 35HEND OF STOCHASTIC DOMINANCE PROGRAM)
  850 FORMAT(1H0,///,5X, 12HDISTRIBUTION, 5X, 12HOBSERVATIONS,
     1  9X, 4HMEAN, 12X,   5HH3(B), 8X, 5HH4(B), 8X, 5HH5(B),
     2 8X, 5HH6(B))
  855 FORMAT (1H0, /, 5X, 24HADJUSTED CENTRAL MOMENTS,/,
     1 11X,6HSECOND, 9X, 5HTHIRD,10X, 6HFOURTH, 9X, 5HFIFTH,
     2 //, 5X, 4F15.10)
  860 FORMAT (1H1,//,50X,29HSTOCHASTIC DOMINANCE MATRICES,//,45X,41H + =
     1 ROW DISTRIBUTION PREFERRED TO COLUMN,/, 45X,38H - = COL DISTRIBUT
     2ION PREFERRED TO ROW,/, 45X,23H 0 = RANKING IMPOSSIBLE)
  870 FORMAT (1H0,15X,  20I4)
  875 FORMAT (1H0,10X, I2, 4X, 20A4)
  876 FORMAT (1H0, /, 10X, 8HDEGREE =, I2, //)
      DATA  S(1),  S(2), S(3), S(4), S(5)/
     1  4H   + , 4H   - , 4H  0 , 4H   * , 4H     /
```

```
      DATA  NS(1),  NS(2), NS(3), NS(4), NS(5), NS(6), NS(7), NS(8),
     1  NS(9), NS(10), NS(11), NS(12), NS(13), NS(14), NS(15)
     2 ,  NS(16), NS(17), NS(18), NS(19), NS(20)/
     3   4H  1 , 4H  2 , 4H  3 , 4H  4 , 4H  5 , 4H  6 , 4H  7 ,
     4   4H  8 , 4H  9 , 4H 10 , 4H 11 , 4H 12 , 4H 13 , 4H 14 ,
     5   4H 15 , 4H 16 , 4H 17 , 4H 18 , 4H 19 , 4H 20 /
C PRINTS STATISTICS AND DATA
      WRITE (6, 800)
      IF (MB)  878, 877, 878
  877 WRITE(6, 805)  Z1MAX
      GO TO 879
  878 WRITE(6, 806)  Z1MAX
  879 DO 880  I = 1, M
      NT =  NE(I)
      WRITE (6, 840)
      WRITE (6, 850)
      WRITE (6, 810) I, NT, XM(I), (HB(K,I), K = 1,4)
      WRITE (6, 855)  (ADJM(K,I),K=1,4)
      WRITE (6, 820) (X1(I,J),  J = 1,NT)
      WRITE (6, 830) (Z1(I,J),  J = 1,NT)
  880 CONTINUE
C PRINTS STOCHASTIC DOMINANCE MATRICES
      DO 882  I = 1,20
  882 A(I) = S(5)
      K = 1
      WRITE (6, 860)
  885 KD = K + 1
      WRITE (6, 876)   KD
      DO 890  I = 1,M
  890 A(I) = NS(I)
      WRITE (6, 870)  (I,  I=1,M)
      DO 1060  L = 1,M
C PREPARES ROW OF K-DEGREE MATRIX
      DO  900  I = 1,M
  900 A(I) =  S(5)
      DO 1030  I = 1,M
      IF (L-I)          930, 1020, 980
  930 IF (ISTD(K,L,I)) 950,  960, 970
  950 A(I)  = S(2)
      GO TO 1030
  960 A(I) =  S(3)
      GO TO 1030
  970 A(I) = S(1)
      GO TO 1030
  980 A(I) = S(5)
      GO TO 1030
 1020 A(I) = S(4)
 1030 CONTINUE
      WRITE(6, 875) L, (A(I), I =1,20)
 1060 CONTINUE
```

```
      IF (K - 4)   1070, 1080, 1080
1070  K = K + 1
      WRITE (6,843)
      GO TO 885
1080  WRITE (6, 845)
      RETURN
      END
```

NOTE: The main program includes a call for the optional subroutine EVENG, which is not listed. This subroutine was used to apply the stochastic dominance rules to distributions centered on the geometric mean. The CMPR1 subroutine includes a call for the subroutine SD4, which is not listed. SD4 was used to apply a fourth degree stochastic dominance rule.

APPENDIX C

DATA USED IN THE EXPORT COEFFICIENT REGRESSIONS

The sources, methods of preparation, and resulting time series data used in the regressions in Chapter 6 are presented in this appendix. As the uncertainty index and the index of incentives for manufactured exports have been explained and reported in Chapters 4 and 5 respectively, they are not discussed here. Section 1 treats the exchange rate, Section 2 the data for manufactures, and Section 3 the primary product data.

C-1. The Exchange Rate

The exchange rate data was used both in the computation of the uncertainty index discussed in Chapter 4 and in the price variable for manufactured exports. Data from 1957 to 1972 are monthly quotes of the cruzeiro dollar export (free or "livre") rate, which are given in Conjuntura Economica, Volume 26, November 1972, page 34, as part of a group of historical time series. The reported monthly rates are averages of the daily closing rates; from 1957 to August 1968 this was the free or "parallel" rate, and after 1968 the buying rate of the Banco do Brasil. For the 1972-1974 period the buying rate was taken from various issues of the Boletim do Banco Central do Brasil.

As was explained in Chapter 4, Section 5, the nominal rate was used to calculate a real, or price adjusted monthly rate for use in computing the stochastic dominance uncertainty index. This same real rate was used in the manufactured export regressions of Chapter 6. The real rate was defined as

$$R_t = \frac{\text{Nominal Rate}_t \times \text{US Wholesale Price Index}_t}{\text{Brazilian Wholesale Price Index}_t}$$

The US index is the WPI for all commodities as reported in various issues of the Survey of Current Business. The Brazilian index is the General Wholesale Price Index for all commodities (series 16 in the Conjuntura Economica). Table C.1 below shows these series and the calculated monthly real rate.

C-2. Manufactured Export Data

The dependent variable of Chapter 6 is the export coefficient, or ratio of the quantity of exports to the quantity of production, for each of 13 different categories of manufactures. Due to the relatively high level of aggregation involved, indices must be used rather than direct measures of either quantity.

Production indices for the 1957-1964 period prepared by the Instituto Brasileiro de Economia of the Fundação Getúlio Vargas were published in Conjuntura Economica, Volume 25, No. 9 (September 1971), with a base of 1949 = 100. A gap for one series, clothing and footwear between 1959 and 1961 was filled using estimates from Conjuntura e Desenvolvimento, various issues, and the Censo Industrial for 1960. For the 1965-72 period the indices used were prepared by W. Suzigan et al. and published in Crescimento Industrial no Brasil (IPEA Relatorio de Pesquisa No. 26, p. 114), with a base of 1966 = 100. Coverage of the IBE-FGV series extended into this period, permitting the conversion of the two series into a single one. This data was checked with base 1969 = 100 series published

TABLE C.1

MONTHLY NOMINAL AND REAL CRUZEIRO-DOLLAR RATES

Month		Nominal Rate	Brazilian WPI	US WPI	Real Cr$/$ Rate	Ann. Avg.
1957	1	0.0657	3.47	92.7	1.755	
	2	0.0665	3.46	92.8	1.784	
	3	0.0665	3.44	92.7	1.792	
	4	0.0700	3.38	93.0	1.926	
	5	0.0742	3.37	92.9	2.046	
	6	0.0720	3.37	93.2	1.991	
	7	0.0745	3.40	93.8	2.055	2.110
	8	0.0795	3.39	94.0	2.204	
	9	0.0830	3.37	93.7	2.308	
	10	0.0873	3.36	93.5	2.429	
	11	0.0915	3.38	93.7	2.537	
	12	0.0910	3.44	94.1	2.489	
1958	1	0.0980	3.49	94.3	2.648	
	2	0.0995	3.49	94.4	2.691	
	3	0.1090	3.51	95.0	2.950	
	4	0.1240	3.57	94.7	3.289	
	5	0.1250	3.64	94.8	3.256	
	6	0.1340	3.66	94.6	3.464	
	7	0.1350	3.740	94.6	3.415	3.250
	8	0.1680	3.86	94.5	4.113	
	9	0.1580	3.98	94.5	3.752	
	10	0.1470	4.140	94.4	3.352	
	11	0.1400	4.35	94.6	3.045	
	12	0.1410	4.40	94.6	3.032	
1959	1	0.147	4.57	94.8	3.049	
	2	0.142	4.84	94.8	2.781	
	3	0.141	4.86	94.9	2.753	
	4	0.139	4.95	95.2	2.673	
	5	0.133	5.01	95.2	2.527	
	6	0.150	5.07	95.0	2.811	
	7	0.155	5.19	94.8	2.831	2.865
	8	0.156	5.46	94.5	2.700	
	9	0.167	5.61	95.0	2.828	
	10	0.186	5.72	94.5	3.073	
	11	0.198	5.90	94.3	3.165	
	12	0.203	6.00	94.3	3.191	

TABLE C.1--Continued

Month		Nominal Rate	Brazilian WPI	US WPI	Real Cr$/$ Rate	Ann. Avg.
1960	1	0.186	6.11	94.7	2.883	
	2	0.186	6.35	94.7	2.774	
	3	0.192	6.43	95.2	2.843	
	4	0.189	6.48	95.2	2.777	
	5	0.186	6.48	95.0	2.727	
	6	0.188	6.54	94.8	2.725	2.637
	7	0.186	6.69	95.0	2.641	
	8	0.187	6.97	94.6	2.538	
	9	0.192	7.26	94.6	2.502	
	10	0.192	7.61	94.9	2.394	
	11	0.195	7.78	94.9	2.379	
	12	0.206	7.94	94.8	2.460	
1961	1	0.230	8.10	95.2	2.703	
	2	0.221	8.09	95.2	2.601	
	3	0.277	8.26	95.2	3.193	
	4	0.283	8.67	94.7	3.091	
	5	0.265	8.81	94.3	2.837	
	6	0.262	8.97	93.8	2.740	2.875
	7	0.261	9.12	94.2	2.696	
	8	0.298	9.67	94.3	2.906	
	9	0.297	10.10	94.3	2.773	
	10	0.345	11.10	94.3	2.931	
	11	0.358	11.50	94.3	2.936	
	12	0.390	11.90	94.6	3.100	
1962	1	0.367	12.7	95.0	2.745	
	2	0.378	12.9	94.9	2.781	
	3	0.358	13.0	94.9	2.613	
	4	0.353	13.1	94.6	2.549	
	5	0.398	13.6	94.4	2.763	
	6	0.435	14.0	94.3	2.930	3.328
	7	0.493	14.7	94.6	3.173	
	8	0.650	15.0	94.7	4.104	
	9	0.675	15.4	95.4	4.182	
	10	0.642	15.9	94.8	3.828	
	11	0.732	17.1	94.9	4.062	
	12	0.795	17.9	94.6	4.202	

TABLE C.1--Continued

Month		Nominal Rate	Brazilian WPI	US WPI	Real Cr$/$ Rate	Ann. Avg.
1963	1	0.760	19.6	94.7	3.672	
	2	0.685	20.8	94.4	3.109	
	3	0.640	22.1	94.2	2.728	
	4	0.710	22.2	94.0	3.006	
	5	0.750	23.1	94.3	3.062	
	6	0.794	24.6	94.5	3.050	
	7	0.850	25.2	94.8	3.198	3.145
	8	1.210	26.2	94.6	4.369	
	9	1.090	27.8	94.5	3.705	
	10	1.210	29.6	94.7	3.871	
	11	1.135	30.6	94.9	3.520	
	12	1.189	32.6	94.5	3.447	
1964	1	1.380	36.5	95.2	3.599	
	2	1.405	38.9	94.7	3.420	
	3	1.880	41.8	94.6	4.255	
	4	1.220	43.5	94.5	2.650	
	5	1.285	44.4	94.3	2.729	
	6	1.291	46.3	94.3	2.629	
	7	1.385	49.3	94.6	2.658	3.035
	8	1.665	51.0	94.5	3.085	
	9	1.771	53.0	94.9	3.171	
	10	1.676	55.6	95.0	2.864	
	11	1.645	60.0	94.9	2.602	
	12	1.830	63.0	94.9	2.757	
1965	1	1.840	66.0	95.2	2.654	
	2	1.885	67.1	95.4	2.680	
	3	1.883	69.8	95.5	2.576	
	4	1.870	70.7	95.9	2.537	
	5	1.865	71.5	96.2	2.509	
	6	1.860	72.3	96.9	2.493	
	7	1.860	74.2	97.0	2.432	2.532
	8	1.865	75.3	97.0	2.403	
	9	1.865	76.8	97.1	2.358	
	10	1.865	78.0	97.2	2.324	
	11	2.215	79.2	97.5	2.727	
	12	2.220	80.0	98.1	2.695	

TABLE C.1--Continued

Month		Nominal Rate	Brazilian WPI	US WPI	Real Cr$/$ Rate	Ann. Avg.
1966	1	2.219	87.8	98.6	2.492	
	2	2.220	89.5	99.3	2.463	
	3	2.220	90.8	99.3	2.428	
	4	2.215	95.1	99.4	2.315	
	5	2.210	97.8	99.5	2.248	
	6	2.210	99.5	99.6	2.212	2.208
	7	2.210	103.0	100.3	2.152	
	8	2.210	105.0	100.7	2.120	
	9	2.210	107.0	100.7	2.080	
	10	2.210	110.0	100.1	2.011	
	11	2.210	111.0	99.8	1.987	
	12	2.210	111.0	99.8	1.987	
1967	1	2.210	116.0	100.1	1.907	
	2	2.715	118.0	99.9	2.299	
	3	2.715	120.0	99.6	2.253	
	4	2.720	122.0	99.2	2.212	
	5	2.720	122.0	99.7	2.223	
	6	2.715	123.0	100.2	2.212	2.266
	7	2.725	128.0	100.3	2.135	
	8	3.250	129.0	100.0	2.519	
	9	3.150	130.0	100.1	2.426	
	10	3.120	133.0	100.1	2.348	
	11	3.130	135.0	100.1	2.321	
	12	3.150	136.0	100.8	2.335	
1968	1	2.470	141.0	101.1	2.488	
	2	3.440	145.0	101.9	2.418	
	3	3.370	148.0	102.1	2.325	
	4	3.520	150.0	102.1	2.396	
	5	3.720	152.0	102.4	2.506	
	6	3.710	155.0	102.5	2.453	2.349
	7	3.580	157.0	102.8	2.344	
	8	3.280	159.0	102.5	2.115	
	9	3.661	163.0	102.9	2.311	
	10	3.675	167.0	102.9	2.264	
	11	3.707	170.0	103.3	2.253	
	12	3.793	170.0	103.6	2.311	

TABLE C.1--Continued

Month		Nominal Rate	Brazilian WPI	US WPI	Real Cr$/$ Rate	Ann. Avg.
1969	1	3.805	173.0	104.3	2.294	
	2	3.900	175.0	104.7	2.333	
	3	3.941	175.0	105.3	2.371	
	4	2.975	177.0	105.5	2.369	
	5	4.006	178.0	106.3	2.392	
	6	4.025	183.0	106.7	2.347	
	7	4.066	186.0	106.8	2.335	2.301
	8	4.082	191.0	106.9	2.285	
	9	4.125	198.0	107.1	2.231	
	10	4.180	204.0	107.4	2.201	
	11	4.229	207.0	108.1	2.209	
	12	4.291	207.0	108.5	2.249	
1970	1	4.325	212.0	109.3	2.230	
	2	4.373	215.0	109.7	2.231	
	3	4.390	218.0	109.9	2.213	
	4	4.460	218.0	109.9	2.213	
	5	4.490	221.0	110.1	2.237	
	6	4.530	226.0	110.3	2.211	
	7	4.580	230.0	110.9	2.208	2.199
	8	4.630	235.0	110.5	2.172	
	9	4.650	240.0	111.0	2.151	
	10	4.690	244.0	111.0	2.134	
	11	4.800	245.0	110.9	2.173	
	12	4.860	247.0	111.0	2.184	
1971	1	4.920	251.0	111.8	2.192	
	2	4.970	255.0	112.8	2.199	
	3	5.03	261.0	113.0	2.178	
	4	5.08	265.0	113.3	2.172	
	5	5.155	270.0	113.8	2.173	
	6	5.220	278.0	114.3	2.146	
	7	5.250	278.0	114.3	2.146	2.170
	8	5.355	283.0	114.9	2.174	
	9	5.430	287.0	114.5	2.166	
	10	5.470	290.0	114.4	2.158	
	11	5.561	294.0	114.5	2.166	
	12	5.600	297.0	115.4	2.176	

TABLE C.1--<u>Continued</u>

Month		Nominal Rate	Brazilian WPI	US WPI	Real Cr$/$ Rate	Ann. Avg.
1972	1	5.619	303.0	116.3	2.157	
	2	5.750	309.0	117.3	2.183	
	3	5.781	314.0	117.4	2.161	
	4	5.810	317.0	117.5	2.154	
	5	2.864	318.0	118.2	2.180	
	6	5.880	322.0	118.8	2.169	
	7	5.909	329.0	119.7	2.150	2.150
	8	5.930	335.0	199.9	2.122	
	9	5.980	338.0	120.2	2.127	
	10	6.024	342.0	120.0	2.114	
	11	6.081	346.0	120.7	2.121	
	12	6.157	349.0	122.9	2.168	
1973	1	6.180	356.0	124.5	2.161	
	2	6.080	361.0	126.9	2.137	
	3	5.995	366.0	129.7	2.125	
	4	6.010	269.0	130.7	2.129	
	5	6.06	373.0	133.5	2.169	
	6	6.060	377.0	136.7	2.197	
	7	6.080	383.0	134.9	2.142	2.166
	8	6.090	387.0	142.7	2.245	
	9	6.101	391.0	140.2	2.188	
	10	6.120	397.0	139.5	2.151	
	11	6.120	402.0	141.8	2.159	
	12	6.153	408.0	145.3	2.191	
1974	1	6.180	418.0	150.4	2.224	
	2	6.348	430.0	152.7	2.254	
	3	6.415	450.0	154.5	2.203	
	4	6.465	476.0	152.7	2.074	
	5	6.515	495.0	155.0	2.040	
	6	6.567	503.0	155.7	2.033	
	7	6.775	505.0	161.7	2.169	2.194
	8	6.775	509.0	167.4	2.228	
	9	6.912	517.0	167.2	2.235	
	10	7.090	526.0	170.2	2.294	
	11	7.090	533.0	171.9	2.287	
	12	7.280	547.0	171.5	2.283	

in APEC, A Economia Brasileira e Suas Perspectivas, 1974. The Anuario Estatistico and the "Sondagems Economicas" section periodically published in Conjuntura Economica were used to supplement and check this data. The complete series was then converted to a 1969 = 100 base.

Export quantity indices with a base 1970 = 100 corresponding to the Brazilian industrial classification for metals, machinery, electrical equipment, transportation equipment, textiles, and food products were published in various issues of Conjuntura Economica and provided the source for this data from 1959 to 1973. For the remaining sectors, non-metallic mineral products, paper, leather, clothing and footwear, beverages, and tobacco, quantity series published in various years of the Anuario Estatistico were used. This was also the source for all sectors for 1957 and 1958. The resulting series were all converted to a base 1969 = 100.

The export coefficients series used in the regressions were then calculated for the 13 manufacturing sectors as follows. Export coefficients expressed in cruzeiro value terms in 1969, based on data in the 1971 Anuario Estatistico, published in Von Doellinger et al., Transformação da Estrutura das Exportações Brasileiras 1964-1970 (IPEA Relatório de Pesquisa 14), Table 4.4, were multiplied by the 1969 = 100 base export quantity indices and divided by the 1969 = 100 base production quantity indices to create the 13 series of export coefficients used in the estimates of Chapter 6. Table C.2 below shows these three variables by sector for the 13 sectors between 1957 and 1973. The 1969 export coefficients defined in value terms for the 13 sectors appear on the 1969 line of the table.

TABLE C.2

Sector & Year	Production (1969=100)	Exports (1969=100)	Export Coefficient
Non-metallic mineral products			
1957	54.8	17.8	.0033
1958	56.0	14.7	.0026
1959	57.4	16.8	.0030
1960	65.8	19.3	.0030
1961	70.2	15.4	.0022
1962	73.0	16.8	.0023
1963	72.9	19.8	.0027
1964	77.2	15.9	.0021
1965	69.8	35.5	.0051
1966	76.0	42.9	.0057
1967	83.7	133.2	.0161
1968	94.3	122.7	.0131
1969	100.0	100.0	.010.
1970	125.4	125.3	.0101
1971	130.3	209.6	.0163
1972	147.7	190.7	.0130
1973	171.9	224.9	.0132
Metals			
1957	28.1	9.2	.0093
1958	33.7	2.2	.0018
1959	39.8	.4	.0003
1960	44.3	1.8	.0012
1961	48.4	4.1	.0024
1962	58.2	1.9	.0009
1963	60.2	46.0	.0218
1964	63.9	21.8	.0097
1965	61.4	58.2	.0270
1966	75.6	42.2	.0159
1967	75.3	118.0	.0447
1968	93.5	85.5	.0260
1969	100.0	100.0	.0285
1970	105.9	181.8	.0489
1971	121.9	105.5	.0247
1972	136.0	181.8	.0381
1973	144.6	189.1	.0373

TABLE C.2--Continued

Sector & Year	Production (1969=100)	Exports (1969=100)	Export Coefficient
Machinery			
1957	36.7	.6	.0008
1958	39.7	.8	.0009
1959	44.9	2.4	.0025
1960	57.2	2.7	.0021
1961	71.0	3.8	.0024
1962	78.7	10.9	.0063
1963	80.7	17.0	.0097
1964	81.8	25.0	.0140
1965	72.0	46.6	.0297
1966	73.2	77.0	.0482
1967	73.3	77.0	.0482
1968	90.3	77.5	.0394
1969	100.0	100.0	.0459
1970	116.5	132.1	.0520
1971	149.9	134.7	.0413
1972	185.7	183.6	.0454
1973	264.5	220.6	.0383
Electrical and communications equipment			
1957	14.5	0.0	.0000
1958	24.2	0.0	.0000
1959	27.4	0.1	.0000
1960	34.9	0.3	.0001
1961	43.4	0.9	.0002
1962	48.0	1.8	.0003
1963	46.2	7.3	.0014
1964	50.5	16.8	.0030
1965	55.9	34.4	.0063
1966	70.0	49.2	.0063
1967	76.7	55.9	.0065
1968	94.8	64.7	.0061
1969	100.0	100.0	.0089
1970	116.3	160.3	.0123
1971	136.8	217.9	.0142
1972	164.0	275.6	.0150
1973	191.7	469.6	.0218

TABLE C.2--Continued

Sector & Year	Production (1969=100)	Exports (1969=100)	Export Coefficient
Transportation equipment			
1957	15.8	8.7	.0038
1958	23.1	12.9	.0039
1959	31.3	11.9	.0026
1960	40.2	2.5	.0004
1961	41.3	32.7	.0055
1962	51.7	29.2	.0039
1963	46.1	10.7	.0016
1964	47.7	41.6	.0060
1965	47.4	66.0	.0096
1966	58.7	131.7	.0155
1967	58.8	45.7	.0054
1968	74.3	64.5	.0059
1969	100.0	100.0	.0069
1970	116.3	253.8	.0151
1971	136.8	286.8	.0145
1972	164.0	776.6	.0327
1973	209.0	926.4	.0306
Paper and paper products			
1957	41.9	0.0	.0000
1958	40.1	0.0	.0000
1959	50.8	0.0	.0000
1960	54.7	0.0	.0000
1961	57.9	0.4	.0001
1962	64.6	1.9	.0002
1963	69.6	8.6	.0009
1964	74.2	36.5	.0036
1965	72.5	137.2	.0138
1966	79.5	86.3	.0079
1967	92.1	39.4	.0031
1968	96.6	43.1	.0033
1969	100.0	100.0	.0073
1970	117.3	103.4	.0064
1971	125.2	125.3	.0073
1972	132.8	526.8	.0290
1973	146.2	822.9	.0411

TABLE C.2--Continued

Sector & Year	Production (1969=100)	Exports (1969=100)	Export Coefficient
Rubber products			
1957	29.8	.7	.0001
1958	33.7	.2	.0000
1959	40.4	.1	.0000
1960	49.4	.4	.0000
1961	51.8	1.2	.0001
1962	60.1	20.9	.0011
1963	60.7	29.1	.0015
1964	64.7	320.9	.0153
1965	60.9	249.2	.0127
1966	77.3	131.6	.0053
1967	85.6	56.1	.0020
1968	94.4	43.9	.0014
1969	100.0	100.0	.0031
1970	122.0	409.8	.0104
1971	140.4	430.3	.0095
1972	161.7	295.1	.0057
1973	181.7	483.6	.0083
Leather and leather goods			
1957	70.4	6.1	.0083
1958	77.6	2.6	.0033
1959	76.5	13.4	.0168
1960	71.6	17.9	.0240
1961	72.9	15.3	.0202
1962	72.4	12.4	.0165
1963	67.2	3.2	.0046
1964	73.9	10.1	.0132
1965	88.3	61.0	.0666
1966	83.3	82.5	.0953
1967	88.8	70.6	.0765
1968	100.1	54.6	.0525
1969	100.0	100.0	.0959
1970	104.4	89.8	.0828
1971	103.9	103.1	.0955
1972	110.5	190.3	.1658
1973	103.9	164.7	.1526

TABLE C.2--Continued

Sector & Year	Production (1969=100)	Exports (1969=100)	Export Coefficient
Textiles			
1957	67.4	17.4	.0026
1958	79.4	46.5	.0059
1959	85.2	28.3	.0033
1960	91.8	33.1	.0036
1961	98.6	60.2	.0061
1962	102.8	63.3	.0062
1963	100.1	64.8	.0065
1964	104.4	66.0	.0065
1965	87.6	71.5	.0082
1966	83.4	82.6	.0099
1967	74.6	73.3	.0098
1968	89.0	81.8	.0092
1969	100.0	100.0	.0100
1970	100.1	112.1	.0112
1971	113.9	122.2	.0107
1972	114.5	229.8	.0201
1973	126.9	354.3	.0279
Clothing and footwear			
1957	50.2	2.2	.0002
1958	61.2	2.7	.0002
1959	65.4	5.4	.0004
1960	68.7	6.6	.0005
1961	72.8	8.6	.0006
1962	75.1	27.9	.0026
1963	75.7	10.2	.0007
1964	84.9	17.0	.0010
1965	82.7	19.4	.0012
1966	84.0	14.7	.0009
1967	84.6	28.8	.0017
1968	96.1	30.4	.0016
1969	100.0	100.0	.0051
1970	118.0	313.5	.0135
1971	129.1	802.5	.0317
1972	133.8	1470.2	.0560
1973	136.3	2511.0	.0940

TABLE C.2--Continued

Sector & Year	Production (1969=100)	Exports (1969=100)	Export Coefficient
Food products			
1957	53.6	36.5	.0137
1958	58.7	52.1	.0179
1959	64.4	64.6	.0203
1960	68.0	53.2	.0158
1961	72.8	60.9	.0169
1962	76.8	37.8	.0099
1963	76.2	39.3	.0104
1964	77.3	24.0	.0063
1965	73.6	54.9	.0151
1966	77.2	61.0	.0160
1967	82.8	65.8	.0161
1968	87.9	81.1	.0186
1969	100.0	100.0	.0202
1970	109.8	109.2	.0201
1971	112.4	128.8	.0232
1972	.27.4	204.1	.0324
1973	141.4	204.1	.0292
Beverages			
1957	63.6	0.0	.0000
1958	69.2	2.0	.0001
1959	69.2	3.5	.0001
1960	68.6	7.3	.0003
1961	79.7	5.8	.0002
1962	77.6	1.6	.0001
1963	79.3	7.6	.0002
1964	70.8	42.0	.0015
1965	81.1	19.0	.0006
1966	90.8	37.5	.0010
1967	85.4	79.1	.0023
1968	91.7	87.0	.0024
1969	100.0	100.0	.0025
1970	109.6	162.3	.0037
1971	119.3	308.4	.0065
1972	124.7	641.2	.0129
1973	138.6	1763.0	.0318

TABLE C.2--Continued

Sector & Year	Production (1969=100)	Exports (1969=100)	Export Coefficient
Tobacco products			
1957	56.4	.7	.0001
1958	60.5	.5	.0000
1959	62.0	1.0	.0001
1960	63.8	1.0	.0001
1961	70.9	6.3	.0005
1962	77.8	6.9	.0005
1963	78.1	5.6	.0004
1964	77.2	28.1	.0020
1965	73.5	16.9	.0013
1966	84.0	61.7	.0041
1967	90.3	72.4	.0045
1968	95.9	60.6	.0035
1969	100.0	100.0	.0056
1970	106.3	115.1	.0061
1971	111.4	198.2	.0100
1972	118.1	216.1	.0102
1973	117.2	322.7	.0154

3. The Primary Product Data

In contrast to the manufactured product groups discussed above, each of the nine primary products examined in this study are sufficiently homogeneous to permit the direct use of export and production quantity data in the calculation of the export coefficient, thus avoiding the use of indices.

The independent variables in the primary product regressions are relative prices and the exchange rate uncertainty index. As the latter has been presented and discussed in detail in Chapter 4, only the relative price data is discussed here. The relative price of a primary product, as defined in Chapter 5, Section 6, was simply assumed to be the unit price of the export in current cruzeiros, deflated by the Brazilian wholesale price index for all commodities (the annual average of column 3 in Table C.1). Note that changes in the relative cruzeiro price of a product sold in world markets due to changes in the exchange rate are implicit in this definition.

The principal source for most of the primary product data was Carlos Von Doellinger et al., Transformação da Estrutura das Exportações Brasileiras: 1964-70, Appendix IX, for production and export quantity data and the cruzeiro unit price data from 1957 through 1970. Where possible, the series were extended to 1973 using more recently published data from the Anuario Estatistico, the primary source used by Von Doellinger et al. Table C.3 below presents this data by primary product; the units are expressed in metric tons. The unit price shown in column 4 of the table is expressed in thousands of cruzeiros per ton. In years in which there were no exports, the unit price shown is the domestic unit price multiplied by the average of the ratios of export unit prices to domestic unit prices in the preceding and succeeding years.

TABLE C.3

Product & Year	Production	Exports	Export Coefficient	Unit Price
Beef				
1957	157 352	0	.0000	.0078
1958	180 349	9	.0001	.0142
1959	211 116	0	.0000	.0684
1960	217 550	2	.0000	.1226
1961	233 903	0	.0000	.1419
1962	329 508	0	.0000	.1611
1963	264 581	5	.0000	.1804
1964	283 927	80	.0003	.2087
1965	357 569	558	.0016	.6381
1966	368 367	1 358	.0036	.7674
1967	267 688	1 663	.0045	1.2106
1968	414 529	358	.0037	.7674
1969	418 541	1 663	.0045	1.2106
1970	449 322	4 215	.0094	2.4254
1971	499 281	4 388	.0088	3.2621
1972	509 504	8 030	.0158	3.0310
Shellfish				
1957	23 796	346	.0145	.0655
1958	23 326	433	.0186	.1890
1959	24 741	616	.0239	.1707
1960	30 639	1 196	.0390	.2736
1961	38 625	1 741	.0451	.4472
1962	48 711	2 070	.0425	.7230
1963	44 711	1 778	.0399	1.0422
1964	43 316	1 578	.0364	1.8976
1965	57 155	1 880	.0329	4.3870
1966	57 587	1 608	.0279	6.2906
1967	55 564	1 702	.0306	6.8016
1968	70 814	3 340	.0472	9.0886
1969	70 400	5 721	.0813	12.5922
1970	64 044	5 883	.0919	12.6918
1971	76 693	6 960	.0908	18.1892
1972	87 263	9 371	.1074	21.5914

TABLE C.3--Continued

Product & Year	Production	Exports	Export Coefficient	Unit Price
Fish				
1957	157 352	0	.0000	.0078
1958	180 349	9	.0001	.0142
1959	211 116	0	.0000	.0684
1960	217 550	2	.0000	.1226
1961	233 903	0	.0000	.1419
1962	329 508	0	.0000	.1611
1963	364 581	5	.0000	.1804
1964	283 927	80	.0003	.3087
1965	357 569	558	.0016	.6381
1966	368 367	1 350	.0037	.7674
1967	367 688	1 663	.0045	1.2106
1968	414 529	2 741	.0066	1.3885
1969	418 541	3 361	.0087	1.8196
1970	449 322	4 215	.0094	2.4254
1971	499 281	4 388	.0088	3.2621
1972	509 504	8 030	.0158	3.0310
Cashews				
1957	3 300	42	.0127	.0915
1958	2 302	36	.0156	.1175
1959	5 571	82	.0147	.1227
1960	5 506	672	.1221	.1022
1961	9 670	380	.0393	.1140
1962	11 987	610	.0509	.1741
1963	13 621	1 070	.0786	.2120
1964	9 644	1 110	.1151	.9090
1965	13 789	714	.0518	1.8825
1966	13 677	1 790	.1309	2.1197
1967	24 181	1 491	.0617	2.3646
1968	23 683	3 342	.1411	3.278
1969	23 443	5 092	.2172	3.697
1970	20 309	6 523	.3212	4.997
1971	28 602	4 286	.1499	6.174
1972	32 769	7 170	.2188	7.303
1973	36 936	5 998	.1624	10.012

TABLE C.3--Continued

Product & Year	Production	Exports	Export Coefficient	Unit Price
Wool				
1957	28 289	4 654	.1645	.1143
1958	31 626	1 459	.0461	.1081
1959	30 351	8 852	.2917	.1457
1960	22 686	1 059	.0467	.1869
1961	24 570	407	.0166	.1587
1962	25 547	135	.0053	.1771
1963	26 515	3 304	.1246	.5228
1964	28 107	18 452	.6565	1.4796
1965	29 075	14 334	.4930	1.9264
1966	27 942	21 787	.7797	2.5526
1967	28 324	20 914	.7384	2.3722
1968	30 682	19 413	.6327	2.5325
1969	30 481	22 640	.7428	3.7576
1970	31 713	18 314	.5775	4.2876
1971	32 550	19 963	.6133	3.2709
1972	33 395	14 376	.4305	4.5374
1973	34 234	17 792	.5197	13.1398
Rice				
1957	4 072 051	329	.0001	.0066
1958	3 829 276	51 552	.0135	.0144
1959	4 101 447	9 815	.0024	.0148
1960	4 794 810	434	.0001	.0120
1961	5 392 477	150 762	.0280	.0226
1962	5 556 834	43 678	.0079	.0323
1963	5 740 065	0	.0001	.0550
1964	6 344 931	12 425	.0020	.0943
1965	7 579 649	236 788	.0312	.1857
1966	5 801 814	289 252	.0499	.2525
1967	6 791 990	31 882	.0047	.4048
1968	6 652 508	158 176	.0238	.4536
1969	6 394 285	70 178	.0110	.4344
1970	7 535 083	95 050	.0126	.3368
1971	6 593 000	148 829	.0226	.3978

TABLE C.3--Continued

Product & Year	Production	Exports	Export Coefficient	Unit Price
Corn				
1957	7 763 439	0	.0000	.0036
1958	7 370 101	0	.0000	.0038
1959	7 786 739	0	.0000	.0589
1960	8 671 952	9 927	.0011	.0075
1961	9 036 237	4 449	.0005	.0082
1962	9 587 285	6	.0000	.0200
1963	10 478 267	699 206	.0667	.0248
1964	9 408 043	62 315	.0066	.0282
1965	12 119 211	559 675	.0462	.0912
1966	11 371 455	627 063	.0551	.1109
1967	12 824 500	430 443	.0336	.1374
1968	12 813 638	1 237 966	.0966	.1507
1969	12 693 435	658 543	.0519	.2016
1970	14 216 00	1 470 620	.1035	.2555
1971	14 300 000	1 279 696	.0906	.3063
Peanuts				
1957	191 621	121	.0006	.0136
1958	308 268	2 050	.0067	.0099
1959	357 403	654	.0018	.0145
1960	408 410	0	.0000	.0396
1961	581 194	4 626	.0000	.0526
1962	647 811	21 912	.0338	.0662
1963	603 840	14 871	.0246	.0828
1964	469 671	103	.0002	.1109
1965	742 686	18 436	.0248	.4047
1966	894 902	13 727	.0153	.5430
1967	750 741	15 639	.0208	.5790
1968	753 905	10 043	.0133	.6885
1969	753 863	30 841	.0409	.8796
1970	928 073	53 473	.0576	1.0387
1971	944 700	35 666	.0378	1.2937
1972	879 240	55 923	.0636	1.4426

TABLE C.3--Continued

Product & Year	Production	Exports	Export Coefficient	Unit Price
Soybeans				
1957	121 501	17 399	.1432	.0055
1958	130 893	33 914	.2591	.0100
1959	151 574	42 070	.2776	.0116
1960	205 744	0	.0000	.0186
1961	271 755	73 267	.2696	.0249
1962	342 745	96 771	.2823	.0298
1963	322 915	33 449	.1036	.0544
1964	304 897	0	.0000	.1315
1965	523 176	75 286	.1439	.1781
1966	594 975	121 241	.2038	.2361
1967	715 606	304 543	.4256	.2562
1968	654 476	65 859	.1006	.2888
1969	1 056 607	310 147	.2935	.3765
1970	1 508 540	289 623	.1920	.4290
1971	2 218 000	213 426	.0962	.6043
1972	3 223 000	1 037 273	.3218	.7286

REFERENCES

Books and Articles

Allen, R. G. D. Mathematical Analysis for Economists. London: MacMillan, 1938.

Almon, S. "The Distributed Lag between Capital Appropriations and Expenditures." Econometrica, Jan. 1965, pp. 178-196.

Apostol, T. Mathematical Analysis. Reading, Mass.: Addison Wesley, 1957.

Arrow, K. Aspects of a Theory of Risk Bearing. Helsinki, 1965.

Batra, R. N. Pure Theory of International Trade under Uncertainty. New York: Halstead Press, 1975.

Batra, R. N., and Ullah, A. "Competitive Firm and the Theory of Input Demand under Price Uncertainty." Jour. Pol. Econ., May/June 1974.

Bergsman, J. Brazil: Industrialization and Trade Policies. London: Oxford University Press, 1970.

Bergsman, J. "Foreign Trade Policy in Brazil." Rio de Janeiro, USAID, 1971. (Mimeographed.)

Berle, A., and Means, G. The Modern Corporation and Private Profits. New York: MacMillan, 1933.

Bhagwati, J. N. Trade, Tariffs, and Growth. Cambridge: MIT Press, 1969.

Bhagwati, J. N.; Jones, R.; Mundell, R.; and Vanek, J., eds. Trade, Balance of Payments, and Growth. Amsterdam, North-Holland, 1971.

Cochrane, D., and Orcutt, G. H. "Application of Least Squares Regressions to Relationships Containing Auto-correlated Error Terms." Jour. Amer. Statistical Assoc. 44 (1949): 32-61.

Coes, D. "Firm Output and Changes in Uncertainty." Amer. Econ. Rev., March, 1977.

Corden, W. M. The Theory of Protection. London: Oxford University Press: 1970.

Fraser, D. A. Non-Parametric Methods in Statistics. New York: J. Wiley and Sons, 1957.

Goldberger, A. Econometric Theory. New York: J. Wiley and Sons, 1964.

Guerard, M. "The Brazilian State Value-Added Tax." IMF Staff Papers, Vol. 20, pp. 118-169.

Hadar, J., and Russell, W. "Rules for Ordering Uncertain Prospects." Amer. Econ. Rev., March 1969.

Hanoch, G., and Levy, H., "The Efficiency Analysis of Choice Involving Risk." Rev. Econ. Studies, Vol. 36, July 1969.

Hicks, J. "The Theory of Monopoly." Econometrica, Vol. 3, Jan. 1935, pp. 1-10.

Johnston, J. Econometric Methods. 2nd ed. New York: McGraw-Hill, 1972.

Kafka, A. "The Brazilian Exchange Auction System." Rev. Econ. and Statistics, Vol. 38, 1956, pp. 308-322.

Kemp, M. The Pure Theory of International Trade and Investment. Englewood Cliffs, N.J.: Prentice-Hall, 1969.

Leamer, E., and Stern, R. Quantitative International Economics. Boston: Allyn and Bacon, 1970.

Leland, H. E. "Theory of the Firm facing Uncertain Demand." Amer. Econ. Rev. June 1972, pp. 278-291.

McCall, J. "Competitive Production for Constant Risk Utility Functions." Rev. Econ. Studies. Oct. 1967, pp. 417-420.

Mendonça de Barros, J.; Lobato, M.; Travolo, M.; and Zockun, M. "Sistema Fiscal e Incentivos as Exportações." Revista Brasileira de Economia. Rio de Janeiro, Vol. 29, Oct./Dec. 1975, pp. 3-24.

Mills, E. "Uncertainty and Price Theory." Quart Jour Econ. Feb. 1959, pp. 116-129.

Perry, G. Unemployment, Money Wage Rates, and Inflation. Cambridge: MIT Press, 1966.

Pratt, J. "Risk Aversion in the Small and the Large." Econometrica, Vol. 32, 1964, pp. 127-136.

Quandt, R., and Goldfeld, S. Non-linear Methods in Econometrics. Amsterdam, North-Holland, 1972.

Quirk, J., and Saposnik, R. "Admissibility and Measurable Utility Functions." Rev. Econ. Studies, Vol. 29, 1962, pp. 140-146.

Richter, M. "Cardinal Utility, Portfolio Selection and Taxation." Rev. Econ. Studies, Vol. 27, June 1960, pp. 152-166.

Rosett, R., and Nelson, R. "Estimation of the Two Limit Probit Regression Model." Econometrica, Vol. 43, Jan. 1975.

Rothschild, M., and Stiglitz, J. "Increasing Risk I: A Definition." Jour. Econ. Theory, Vol. 2, Sept. 1970.

Rothschild, M., and Stiglitz, J. "Increasing Risk II: Its Economic Consequences." Jour. Econ. Theory, Vol. 3, Jan. 1971.

Savasini, J.; Lobato, H.; Travolo, M.; and Zockun, M. "O Sistema Brasileiro de Promoção as Exportações." Instituto de Pesquisas Economicas, Universidade de São Paulo, 1974. (Mimeographed.)

Sandmo, A. "On the Theory of the Competitive Firm under Price Uncertainty." Amer. Econ. Rev. March 1971, pp. 65-73.

Scitovsky, T. "A Note on Profit Maximization and its Implications." Rev. Econ. Studies, Vol. 11, Winter 1943, pp. 57-60.

Suplicy, E. The Effects of Minidevaluations on the Brazilian Economy. Unpublished Ph.D. dissertation, Michigan State University, 1973.

Suzigan, W. Crescimento Industrial no Brasil. (Relatorio de Pesquisa No. 26) IPEA, Rio de Janeiro, 1974.

Tobin, J. "Estimation of Relationships for Limited Dependent Variables." Econometrica, Vol. 26, Jan. 1958, pp. 24-36.

Tyler, W. Manufactured Export Expansion and Industrialization in Brazil. Kiel, Institut fur Weltwirtschaft an der Universitat Kiel, 1976.

Von Doellinger, C.; Castro Faria, H.; Ramos, R.; and Cavalcanti, L. Transformação da Estrutura das Exportações Brasileiras: 1964/1970. (Relatorio de Pesquisa No. 14) IPEA, Rio de Janeiro, 1973.

Von Neumann, J., and Morgenstern, O. Theory of Games and Economic Behavior. 2nd ed. Princeton, N.J.: Princeton University Press, 1947.

Whitmore, G. "Third Degree Stochastic Dominance." Amer. Econ. Rev. June 1970.

Williamson, O. "Managerial Discretion and Business Behavior." Amer. Econ. Rev. Dec. 1963, 1032-1057.

Zabel, E. "A Dynamic Model of the Competitive Firm." International Econ. Rev., Vol. 8, June 1967.

Zabel, E. "Risk and the Competitive Firm." Jour. Econ. Theory, Vol. 3, Sept. 1971, pp. 109-133

Zellner, A. "An Efficient Method of Estimating Seemingly Unrelated Regressions and test for Aggregation Bias" Jour. Amer. Stat. Assoc. June 1962, pp. 300-312

Government and Institutional Publications

APEC. A Economia Brasileira e suas Perspectivas. São Paulo, 1974

Fundação Getúlio Vargas. Conjuntura Economica. Various issues.

Instituto Brasileiro de Geografia e Estatistica (IBGE), Anuário Estatístico. Various years.

IBGE. Censo Industrial 1960

International Monetary Fund, International Financial Statistics. Various issues.

U.S. Dept. of Commerce. Survey of Current Business. Various issues.

Author Index

Author Index

Subject Index

Subject Index

Subject Index